GLOBAL PALESTINE

JOHN COLLINS

GLOBAL PALESTINE

Columbia University Press
New York

Columbia University Press
Publishers Since 1893
New York
cup.columbia.edu

Library of Congress Cataloging-in-Publication Data

Global Palestine / John Collins.
    p. cm.
  ISBN 978-0-231-70310-9 (cloth: alk. paper)
  ISBN 978-0-231-80074-7 (e-book)
  1. Arab-Israeli conflict—1993—Peace. 2. West Bank—Politics and
government—21st century. 3. Gaza Strip—Politics and government—
21st century. 4. Israel—Politics and government—21st century. 5. Palestinian
Arabs—Political activity. 6. Jews—Colonization—West Bank. 7. Israelis—
Colonization—West Bank.

DS119.76.G596 2011
956.95'3044—dc23

2011029521

∞

Columbia University Press books are printed on permanent and durable acid-free
paper. This book is printed on paper with recycled content.
Printed in India

c 10 9 8 7 6 5 4 3 2 1

CONTENTS

LIST OF IMAGES

Between pages 78 and 79

PREFACE

Having focused my research and writing on Palestine for nearly two decades, I began this book with a desire to step outside the circle of often tired political frameworks within which Palestine has generally been imprisoned. Like so many who have devoted significant political energy to the struggle for Palestinian rights, I also needed a way to deal with the sense of despair that inevitably surfaces when the situation only seems to go from bad (say, Ariel Sharon's 2002 assault on the West Bank) to worse (say, Ehud Olmert's 2008 assault on Gaza). And like so many scholars who have grounded themselves in one of the most researched places on earth in an attempt to fill in the smallest pieces of the Israel/Palestine puzzle—my first book was an ethnographic study of the first Palestinian *intifada* seen through the recollections of young West Bank refugees—I was looking for new ways of thinking about the entire situation.

My professional location in one of the first Global Studies departments in the United States has pushed me to articulate this new project in terms of the reciprocal relationship between the specific settler colonial dynamic taking place on the ground in Israel/Palestine, and a series of broader global processes. Put in the simplest terms, the book's core idea is that the same forces operating to produce Palestine's troubling realities are also operating globally in ways that have implications for all of us, and that examining Palestine's recent past and present in this light can yield new insights about Palestine itself while also revealing important clues about global processes that too often remain hidden, camouflaged, and poorly understood.

I hope this idea of a "Global Palestine"—a Palestine that is globalized and a globe that is becoming Palestinized—will appeal not only to a variety of academic readers, but also to activists and concerned citizens who are interested in leveraging knowledge for social change. Indeed, one of the book's primary motivations is to give readers a chance to connect with Palestine in a new way. If recent decades have shown us anything, it is that there are significant interpretive and political limitations associated with the seductive narratives of nationalism, with the binary logic that splits the world into hierarchically-ordered halves (us/them, East/West, Orient/Occident, developed/developing, terrorism/legitimate state violence, etc.), and with the stale language of *realpolitik* and "national interests." All of these have served to lock Palestine into restrictive patterns of familiarity and unfamiliarity that reflect and reinforce prevailing global hierarchies. As an alternative to this unhelpful dynamic, I have tried to write this book in a way that will enable everyone to see something of themselves not only in Palestine's local story, but also in the larger story of its global significance.

The book's orientation also reflects the fact that I have always been, at heart, an interdisciplinary (I sometimes prefer the term anti-disciplinary) researcher who seeks to probe the boundaries of conventional wisdom and provoke critical thought on contemporary politics, while also contributing to the never-ending struggle for social justice. Writing and speaking about Palestine out of the latter motivation, of course, can itself be act of rebellion given that the forces aligned in support of Israel's settler colonial project have traditionally been quite successful at policing the borders of acceptable discourse. Yet even among those of us whose work is grounded in a sense of solidarity with the Palestinian people, there is always a need for fresh perspectives and critical questions. I am hardly the only one pushing in this direction; on the contrary, I see this book as a humble contribution to what is already an exciting and inspiring new wave of Palestine-focused writing and activism, much of which is referenced in the pages that follow.

Readers of the book will notice that in addition to drawing on scholarship from a number of disciplinary and interdisciplinary academic fields, many of my key arguments draw on the work of relatively unconventional thinkers, three of whom I would like to highlight here. Walter Benjamin, the German-Jewish philosopher and literary critic, remains a haunting and provocative figure some seventy years after his tragic death on the Franco-Spanish border. John Trudell, a former leader of the American Indian Movement (AIM), continues to build a formidable legacy through political activism, on film, in interviews and lectures, and in his distinctive spoken-word recordings. French theorist Paul Virilio, an architect by training, pioneered the study of "dromology" (the logic of speed) and its application to everything from war and technology to cinema and urban planning. It is most accurate to say that I view each of them, in their own way, as a poetic and prophetic figure. Whether marked by starkness and directness (Trudell), epigrammatic eloquence (Benjamin), or a combination of playfulness, hyperbole, and opacity (Virilio), all of their words possess an explosive, subversive quality that deserves to be heard on its own terms. When paraphrasing their ideas, I have done my best not to drain the power from them.

These influences also signal the use of an approach that embraces the practice of theoretical, methodological and thematic diversity for the simple reason that the deep structures of global politics have as little respect for disciplinary borders as they do for national ones. As a result, rather than situating my work primarily in relation to narrow bodies of literature within political science or any other field, I have proceeded analytically wherever the critical examination of these processes might lead. Each chapter in the book follows its own specific analytical trajectory and can certainly be read on its own; needless to say, however, none of these global processes exist in isolation from the others. For this reason, the themes addressed in the individual chapters bleed into one another. The effect of this, I hope, is that the book's core argument is a cumulative one, adding both depth and detail from chapter to chapter.

Many of the ideas presented in the book were test-driven not only in the usual scholarly venues (conferences, articles, public lectures, book chapters), but also in the classroom. I owe a great debt of gratitude to the intellectually curious and empathetic undergraduates who threw caution to the wind and took my Global Palestine seminar or otherwise offered critical feedback, particularly Sal Cania, Mallory Craig-Kuhn, Paige Evans, Brian Lind, Kelly O'Ryan, Chris Prener, Shazia Shahnaz, Tom Simunovic, Alexander Tedeschi, and Sean Watkins. Numerous friends, family members, and colleagues provided similar input and all manner of moral, editorial, and logistical support along the way, including Marina Boudreau, Kenneth Church, Andy Clarno, Donald Collins, Edith Collins, Michael Dwyer, R. Danielle Egan, Howard Eissenstat, Traci Fordham-Hernandez, Mercedes Guirado Garrido, Michael Greenwald, Barbara Harlow, Daniel Hernandez, Eric Hooglund, Laleh Khalili, Laurie King, Saree Makdisi, Erin McCarthy, Dale Miguel, Andrea Nouryeh, Christopher Nouryeh, Celia Nyamweru, Ronnie Olesker, Paloma Roman Marugan, Shane Rogers, Khaldoun Samman, Joyce Sheridan, Stephan Stetter, Eve Stoddard, Cathy Tedford, Andrea Teti, Chris Toensing, Ganesh Trichur, Morten Valbjorn, Jessica Winegar, Patrick Wolfe, and anonymous readers for *Globalizations, Social Text, Studies in Social Justice,* and Columbia University Press. Rula Halawani, Diego López Calvin, and Chris Prener graciously agreed to contribute their wonderful photographs to the book. St. Lawrence University provided financial support, opportunities for presenting my work, and leave time, all of which were crucial in helping me complete the project.

The most decisive sources of support for the project, however, have always been three: Tarak Barkawi, Ross Glover, and Marina Llorente. While none of them bear any responsibility for the book's shortcomings, it is no exaggeration to say that without them I easily could have abandoned the project in despair at any number of key moments. For their consistent encouragement, their incisive commentary, and their willingness to tell me what I needed to hear as many times as necessary, I am deeply and eternally grateful.

1

APPROACHING GLOBAL PALESTINE

The global importance of Palestine seems to be increasing in inverse proportion to the amount of territory controlled by Palestinians. This is evident within the global justice movement, where the growing centrality of Palestine ("we are all Palestinians") indicates that the conditions affecting Palestinians, particularly those living under Israeli domination, are recognized and are becoming increasingly generalizable. It is also present in the decision by governments to enact structures of warfare, counterinsurgency, forced displacement, surveillance and rhetorical violence that call to mind the tactics that have been used against Palestinians for decades. We see it also in the considerable ripple effects that are generated when acts of Israeli state violence (for instance, Israel's 2008 "Operation Cast Lead" assault on Gaza or its 2010 attack on the international flotilla seeking to break its blockade of Gaza) are rapidly disseminated through the circuits of mainstream, independent and social media. In short, the remarkable global profile of Palestine tells us a great deal about the politics of globalization in general, from the impact of "time-space compression" to the complex dynamics of deterritorialization and reterritorialization, from the troubling realities of permanent war to the changing face of international solidarity activism.

1

This book begins from the premise that understanding why and how Palestine matters globally requires situating the "local" struggle over Palestine in relation to a series of global processes that continue to shape the conditions within which all of us live our lives. The central argument here is that far from simply being shaped by global and globalizing processes, Palestine has been and continues to be an often prophetic index of and shaper of these processes, a kind of monadic unit that contains important clues to a series of much broader realities. The book's title serves as a shorthand descriptor of the two basic sides of this complex relationship: the globalization of Palestine and the Palestinization of the globe.

In what sense is Palestine prophetic? While it might be tempting to activate the notion of prophecy in a religious sense when writing about the "Holy Land," what I have in mind is something more secular and historical. The kinds of liberal, often patronizing narratives associated with Euro-American colonization have typically insisted on positioning colonized territories as "behind" their colonial masters.[1] Such a rhetorical move does more than simply deny the fact that we all inhabit the same world, a world that is constituted for everyone by imperial relations. It also hides the crucial fact that colonized territories have long served as laboratories for new forms of violence and social control and should thus be viewed, in an important sense, as ahead of their time. Unfortunately, when it comes to learning from those territories, we have done a much more diligent job of sending archaeologists to dig in the ground underneath them for traces of the distant past than we have of excavating the present for traces of the future.

Palestine, of course, has long served as the site of intensive (and often polemical) archaeological work that itself tends to be buried under layers of nationalist, settler colonial, and anticolonial politics. Yet it is also an ideal location for engaging in the excavation of the present. Palestine is located at the intersection of two sets of global processes that symbolize not only the profundity of the structural injustices that are being confronted today, but also the resilience and creativity with which many people are confronting those injustices. First, as the primary targets of an ongoing settler colonial project (Zionism), Palestinians have been test subjects for, and in some cases active agents helping to cat-alyze, an emerging world of pervasive securitization and violent accel-eration, a world order symbolized by the "Global War on Terrorism" (GWOT)—a war in which anyone can be a target. At the same time, they also continue to be important actors in and symbols of the ongo-ing struggle for global justice, a struggle in which the defense of life and locality plays an increasingly prominent role.

Palestine's Global Turn

In recent years, an important and welcome shift in the scholarly lit-erature on Palestine has occurred. For decades that literature was dom-inated by an implicit exceptionalism rooted in the exceptionalist claims of the Zionist movement, claims that have often produced corre-sponding claims of exceptional victimization on the part of Palestin-ians. As a result, comparative studies were rare, and important theoretical advances in the study of global politics had a hard time finding their way into discussions of Palestine. When seeking to ana-lyze Palestine in a way that stretched beyond its geographic bound-aries, scholars tended to do so in the context of discussing regional (e.g., pan-Arab) dynamics or else in the relatively narrow context of national liberation struggles focused on the taking of state power.

The literature was similarly over-determined by the binary, zero-sum logic through which the dominant Israeli and Palestinian polit-ical positions (typically described as distinct "sides") tend to be articulated. On the Palestinian side, the long domination of Palestin-ian politics by the Palestine Liberation Organization (PLO)—a rel-atively traditional national liberation movement influenced by its counterparts in Algeria and elsewhere—left many scholars implicitly or explicitly employing nationalist approaches rooted in the post-WWII wave of decolonization. On the Israeli side many of the nation-alist myths associated with Zionism and the founding of the Israeli state held a privileged place, squeezing out voices that sought to fos-ter non-nationalist or post-nationalist conversations.

Thankfully, these patterns have come under sustained contestation during the past two decades, opening the door for the kind of global approach employed in this book. A key development in Israel was the emergence of a group of historians and sociologists who took advantage of newly-declassified documents to challenge many of the narratives, categories and assumptions that had long provided reliable ideological support to Israel's ethno-national project.[2] This shift in the literature played a key role in what amounts to a profound legitimacy crisis for the Zionist project, a crisis that continues to unfold with increasing urgency today in debates in Israel over the nature of Zionism itself as well as the related issues of immigration, multiculturalism, security, national identity and the politics of inclusion and exclusion.[3]

Hand in hand with this important shift, an increasing number of scholars have been pushing back against inherited frameworks of all sorts. As a result, work on Palestine is increasingly characterized by references to transnational processes such as militarization, racialization, capital accumulation, "states of exception," biopolitics and a range of power/knowledge structures. The opening up of the literature to these broader debates is, in its own way, part of the globalization/Palestinization phenomenon referred to above. As Palestine became arguably the most visible focus of global solidarity beginning in the late 1990s, the old exceptionalist frameworks became even more untenable; what was happening in Palestine could no longer be contained within them.

The truth, however, is that the Palestinian struggle has always been a global one. More than a simple location on a map, Palestine is an excellent example of what Arjun Appadurai calls a "process geography." For Appadurai, such geographies are best understood as "precipitates of various kinds of action, interaction, and motion" rather than as "relatively immobile aggregates of traits."[4] They are closely related to the "imagined worlds" (an extension of Benedict Anderson's "imagined communities") created by the movement of people across the boundaries of nation-states, continents and regions.[5] There is little doubt that the worldwide Palestinian diaspora, beginning with the *Nakba* (the dispossession of 1947–48), has created just such an imagined world.

The Palestinian refugee camps in Lebanon and elsewhere in the region are the most (literally) concrete locations where this world is actualized.[6] By their very nature, the camps are spaces where violently deterritorialized pieces of Palestine are precariously brought together to await a return that never seems to come. The long odyssey of the *fedayeen* (Palestinian guerrilla fighters) from the late 1960s to the early 1990s—stopping variously in Jordan, Lebanon, Tunisia and elsewhere—contributes another narrative thread to this transnational Palestinian tapestry. Like the members of any globalized community, Palestinians who live in exile carry with them memories and markers of the homeland. Keys to family homes, land ownership documents, photographs, identity papers, oral histories, experiences of traumatic border crossings—all of these are components of the global Palestinian experience. Moreover, as their community remains focused on its anticipated territorial reconstitution, Palestinians on the "outside" have always found ways of maintaining direct connection with those on the "inside," whether through radio broadcasts or the poignant calling walls and "shouting fences" at the borders that separate them from one another. More recently, internet technology has enabled a sharp increase in the possibilities for creating new linkages.

The "process geography" of Palestine is also visible in other ways. Perhaps most obviously, on the level of geopolitics as it is traditionally understood, this struggle has long been enabled and shaped by a range of outside powers. It is no exaggeration to say that Israel owes its existence to British and US imperialism. For decades the various attempts to resolve the violence set in motion by Israel's creation have been shadowed by a host of international actors including successive US administrations, European diplomats, the Vatican, the Arab states and so forth, to say nothing of the pressure exerted by Jews in the diaspora and Palestinian refugees who have continued to demand their right of return. Even though Israeli strategies of domination have long had a sort of relative local autonomy, in the sense of "creating facts" regardless of what the international community might think, all of these strategies—the land confiscation, the settlement colonies, the assassinations and the perpetual counterinsurgency—have relied on money, machines and manpower from outside Israel. In comparison to this relationship, the material support that Palestinians have received through the years, including the infamous cash payments given to the families of suicide bombers, pales into relative insignificance.

The global flow of the technologies of violence constitutes another related aspect of Palestine's globality. Public discussion of this issue tends to occlude more than it reveals. Extensive attention is given, for example, to the tunnels that Palestinians have created under the Gaza-Egypt border for purposes of bringing weapons and other supplies into that incarcerated territory. Meanwhile the infinitely more lethal pipeline of weapons that stretches back and forth between Tel Aviv and many other international capitals (especially Washington) continues humming along, cloaked in a protective coating of state legitimacy. For this reason Palestinians and their external supporters are at great pains to make visible the role of firms such as Caterpillar (which builds the infamous D-9 bulldozers used to destroy Palestinian homes) in enabling Israeli state violence. With all of the work that has been done on commodity chains within the global economy, it is perhaps time to focus on the chains that link Zionism, American taxpayers and those defense industry moguls whom Bob Dylan scathingly labeled the "Masters of War" in his 1963 song by that name.

Palestine also continues to be globalized through the workings of media worldwide. As Edward Said argues, the media are much more than a network of transmitters, satellites, computers and the like; they are, in his words, "a very efficient *mode of articulation* knitting the world together."[7] In the case of Palestinians, to be in the media can be both a blessing and a curse. On the one hand, it has often meant being subject to a global regime of compulsory discursive hyper-visibility that makes Palestinians seen and (to a lesser extent) heard—but only in forms that are constructed and tightly controlled by others. Within such a regime, one's identity is routinely transmogrified into a question, a source of fear, a call to arms, a nagging "problem" that will not go away. It means constantly having to defend oneself against broadbrush and often racist charges of "terrorism" even as one is defending oneself against the theft of one's land.

On the other hand, media visibility has also functioned as a way for Palestinians to ensure that their struggle remains in the world's consciousness. The similar double-edged visibility that is typical of a globalized media environment helps ensure that the Palestinian struggle, even when it is rendered problematically, remains accessible to a range of sympathetic audiences around the globe. The age of globalization, after all, is the age of linkages. Just as globalization is not new—only the generalized consciousness of it is new—so too are linkages not new As will be discussed in greater detail in Chapter 5, there are many people—particularly members of subaltern groups—who have long been making linkages between their own experiences and those of Palestinians.

In recent years Palestine, a common (if often empty) theme in the speeches of Arab nationalists for decades, has also become central to the complex rhetorical frameworks associated with "globalized Islam" and the many critiques launched by Islamist groups against US imperialism.[8] As Faisal Devji demonstrates in his analysis of jihadist discourse, prominent Islamists such as Osama bin Laden often invoke the Palestinian struggle even as they emphasize the overriding importance of the larger (global) jihad.[9] This discourse, in turn, exists in complex articulation with the concerns of ordinary Arabs and Muslims who gain access to images of Palestinian suffering through the reach of global satellite media.[10]

As part of the same dynamic, the period following the September 11 attacks saw a sharp "Israelization" of US national security discourse as the categories, metaphors and justifications long employed in official Israeli discourse came to frame public debate in the US even more pervasively than they had in the past.[11] Having already been ideologically constructed for over three decades as key purveyors of "terrorism" (see Chapter 3), Palestinians found that 9/11 and the US response only intensified the impact of this discourse. In documents such as the 2002 US "National Security Strategy," the notion of "terror(ism)," rather than simply one plank among many in the national security platform, became the central concept undergirding a borderless US war, and empowered other states to channel Israeli and US actions for their own purposes.

Meanwhile, the growth of transnational activist networks working alongside Palestinians on the ground in the West Bank and Gaza represents a determined global riposte, at the level of civil society, to the post-9/11 consolidation of the US-Israeli state alliance.[12] Whether in the form of the "Free Gaza" blockade-breaking campaign, the International Solidarity Movement (with which Rachel Corrie was affiliated), or a host of other efforts involving Palestinian, Israeli and international civilians, the new solidarity activism is built upon a recognition that the injustices taking place in Palestine are important not only in and of themselves, but also in terms of their global implications. The movement's tactics—bringing volunteers from around the world and making extensive use of new communication and information technologies—represent the union of a local struggle with a networked sensibility rooted in the realities of twenty-first-century globalization.

Palestine, much like the 1994 Zapatista rebellion in Chiapas, Mexico, has also emerged as a focus of attention for activists connected with the broader global justice movement that has targeted a whole range of hierarchical, undemocratic and predatory structures associated with global capitalism and US imperialism. The most recent US Social Forum, for example, held in Detroit in June 2010, featured an entire program devoted to Palestine including a "People's Movement Assembly," multiple workshops, cultural events and a solidarity mural. From the ubiquity of the *kufiya* (the traditional black and white Palestinian headscarf) to the seemingly endless diffusion of the term "intifada," one wonders with Gargi Bhattacharyya whether what is really occurring is "a lot of talk about Palestine without much attention to the situation of Palestinians."[13] At the same time there is no question that the ability of diverse groups to articulate linkages between their own experiences and concerns and those of Palestinians has helped combat Israeli efforts to render the political will of the Palestinian people invisible.

Palestine's Settler Colonial Turn

In another important development that has shaped this book profoundly, scholars from a variety of disciplinary perspectives have begun to explore Israel/Palestine through the specific lens of settler colonialism in an effort to combat both Zionist and Israeli exceptionalism and the common yet mistaken belief that Israel/Palestine is the site of a Balkan-style ethnic conflict marked by visceral hatreds that reach back into the mists of time. This settler colonial turn has contributed to a welcome process of gradually pulling the conversation away from its traditional nationalist moorings and opening new lines of comparative and world-historical inquiry.

This shift has also coincided with changes in the political realm, where the ever-disappointing peace process and the gradual eclipse of the two-state solution have sparked a resurgence of interest in the idea of a single, secular and democratic state in Israel/Palestine. Advocates of the "one-state solution"[14] argue that the failure of Zionism to eliminate the vast majority of Palestine's indigenous population, combined with Israel's sustained colonization efforts throughout historic Palestine, has created a fundamentally unjust yet decidedly single state situation that has much in common with apartheid South Africa or the Jim Crow-era US South. Rather than seeking the kind of territorial partition often advocated and practiced to solve the contradictions produced by colonialism, the challenge, as will be explored in greater detail in Chapter 6, is to embrace Israel/Palestine's multicultural reality while overturning its hierarchical, "ethnocratic" and "politicidal" elements in favor of creating a truly democratic polity.[15]

Both the settler colonial turn and the one-state solution call the foundational mythologies of Zionism into question. Given this connection, it is not surprising that these critical interventions have produced strong opposition from those who seek to defend the basic legitimacy of Israel's current structure and self-definition as a "Jewish state." One of the most common objections leveled by these critics is that because no two historical cases are identical, the comparisons explored within the settler colonial framework (e.g., between Israel and South Africa) are inherently illegitimate. Lurking beneath this objection to comparisons is an exceptionalist argument: the claim that Israel is fundamentally different and therefore cannot be analyzed critically except on its own (self-defined) terms. Such exceptionalism, however, is actually integral to the ideological armature of settler colonialism; one finds a similar logic at work, for example, in the discourses historically associated with Afrikaner identity in South Africa. In short, the critics' exceptionalist objection ultimately serves to validate the settler colonial framework they seek to discredit.

Moreover, the claim that comparative analysis is designed to prove absolute sameness is an anti-intellectual claim that misunderstands the purpose of the analytical enterprise. Gabriel Piterberg makes the point clearly and concisely:

The comparative studies of settler nations undercut the claim to uniqueness not because they find all settler nations identical; in fact many of these comparisons result in understanding historical specificity as much as similarity. What they do, however, is to offer a language that, like the popular joke about the giraffe, identifies a white settler trajectory when it sees one and renders it reminiscent of other trajectories.[16]

What this means is that the interventions provided by scholars of settler colonialism are deeply political and could not be otherwise. The point of the intervention is not to claim a privileged place from which to engage in detached, "objective" analysis. Neither, however, is it to engage in purely polemical argumentation unaccompanied by the fair treatment of evidence. The point is to bring all the relevant tools of critical, engaged scholarship to bear on the subject at hand in order to pursue two related objectives: to understand the complex set of structures and processes, particularly those associated with settler colonial projects, that have combined to produce the intolerable reality evident today; and to think creatively about how this understanding might enable individuals to transform that reality.

Commitments and Angles of Vision

The decision to place Palestine at the center of this form of global analysis is an ethical choice rooted in the belief that one's understanding of the world depends both on one's social location and on the angle of vision one chooses to adopt. The most dominant angle of vision in the study of global politics is the one that implicitly or explicitly adopts the point of view of elites and the structures they create: states, international institutions, corporations and armies, to name a few of the most important. Such a perspective, regardless of who is articulating it, may be described as stereotypically white, male, "Western" (that is, associated with the long historical projection of Western European political, economic and cultural power across the globe), and middle to upper-class. From this dominant perspective, the story of globalization and global politics is largely a story of how the intentional actions of elite actors come to filter down into the lives of everyone else; hence the large and influential literature examining the impact of globalization on places and communities that are effectively constructed in this literature as existing outside of the processes that are impacting them. Such a view is shared not only by those who celebrate global neo-liberalism ("a rising tide lifts all boats"), but also by many of those who see globalization more critically as a destructive, even suicidal process of domination produced by the actions of the United States and the international financial institutions (IFIs) it has historically dominated.

The vast majority of the world's population, however, shares neither the social location nor the angle of vision of the globalized elite. It is my contention that anyone who wishes to understand the many competing meanings of globalization must make a deliberate effort to think outside the dominant categories. At the risk of oversimplification, I have found it useful to organize my own thinking around a counter-hegemonic sentiment that is powerfully encapsulated in the words of the German-Jewish philosopher Walter Benjamin. Shortly before his tragic death in the Spanish border town of Portbou in 1940, Benjamin crystallized decades of his work on the politics of violence, representation and redemption into what are arguably two of the most important sentences of the twentieth century:

The tradition of the oppressed teaches us that the "state of emergency" in which we live is not the exception but the rule. We must attain to a conception of history that is in keeping with this insight.[17]

These lines challenge us to alter our angle of vision in a fundamental way. They call on us to loosen our faith in the narrative of progress and listen deeply to the voices of those whose experiences cast doubt on that narrative. We have barely begun to answer this challenge.

These oft-quoted lines from Benjamin's "Theses on the Philosophy of History" inspired the subtitle of my earlier book on *intifada* memories.[18] In that book, I sought to explore the permanence of Palestine's particular state of emergency through a close examination of the personal narratives of young Palestinians from Balata Refugee Camp, at a time when disappointment with the failures of the Oslo peace process was beginning to set in. The present book is a further attempt to come to grips with the implications of Benjamin's challenge, this time by stepping back strategically from the ethnographic ground in order to bring a broader set of questions, connections and possibilities into the light.

What, then, are the implications of the "tradition of the oppressed" for the way global politics is understood? Consider the kinds of narratives that are typically produced by the elite, institution-centered view of history—narratives of invasions, battles with fixed beginnings and endings, treaties, international agreements and political transitions, all stretching forward into what is generally assumed to be a brighter future. From an elite perspective, such narratives make perfect sense; they embody the belief that the existing social arrangements, while imperfect, are nonetheless relatively desirable and under control.

Yet as Benjamin famously asserted: "There is no document of civilization which is not at the same time a document of barbarism." A good example that has drawn attention from critics of mainstream media representations of Israel/Palestine is the language of "relative calm" (as in, "the Palestinian attacks followed three months of relative calm"). In Middle East-speak, "relative calm" usually means, in effect, a period in which no citizens of the dominant nation-state (Israel) are being attacked.[19] The fact that these periods often include the deaths of many Palestinians illustrates the extent to which the discourse is framed by a dominant angle of vision associated with the Israeli state and its supporters in Washington.[20] But even in a period where no Palestinians are being killed, the situation is hardly calm—if viewed from the perspective of those with the least access to state and other institutional power. Colonization, economic exploitation, ecological destruction, the gradual militarization of everyday life—all of these proceed amidst the calm.

Benjamin's invocation of the "tradition of the oppressed" is meant to highlight the fact that there are other, dramatically different narratives circulating in the world, narratives that can open provocative new modes of understanding—if only this were taken seriously. This book is an attempt to construct one among many possible frameworks through which to understand how global politics might look if viewed in terms of the "tradition of the oppressed." It prioritizes an angle of vision associated with those who have been victimized by the deepest and most far-reaching form of colonization: settler colonialism.

What might globalization look like if viewed from this perspective? A clue can be found in one of John Trudell's concise observations, made in a 2005 documentary: "We have never really seen the war go away." The idea of permanent war, a radical and alien idea for those who have been schooled to see war as a periodic interruption of an otherwise peaceful reality, makes perfect sense to those whose main role in the story of European expansion has been that of an obstacle to be overcome or eliminated. Trudell's maxim is an on-the-ground translation of what Achille Mbembe describes as one of the cardinal principles of colonization:

A fact remains, though: in modern philosophical thought and European political practice and imaginary, the colony represents the site where sovereignty consists fundamentally in the exercise of a power outside the law (*ab legibus solutus*) and where "peace" is more likely to take on the face of a "war without end."[21]

When the discourse of "homeland security" emerged after 9/11 as a master term governing a broad range of US policies affecting subaltern groups, one humorous response came in the form of a t-shirt depicting homeland security as the original project of indigenous self-defense against settler colonialism. This is the sort of thing I have in mind when I talk about shifting one's angle of vision toward the "tradition of the oppressed."

Aside from the political implications of such a shift, there are solid analytical reasons to prioritize this alternative angle of vision. Globalization is, at least partly, a function of the efforts of Western and Westernized elites to extend particular social arrangements across the world.

The flip side of this process, however, is that those who have been displaced, exploited, enslaved and murdered in the name of "progress" are in a position to offer a compelling and incisive counter-narrative, one that critiques the actions of the elites who often appear to be driving globalization. This is what qualitative researchers in the social sciences call "studying up"—seeking to understand radically hierarchical social systems by exploring how they look from below.

Equally important, globalization involves more than the conscious choices of ruling elites. There are important globalizing processes that stretch beyond the control of any state, corporation, military or other powerful institution. Consequently, if these processes and their global significance are to be understood, one must look beyond the frameworks constructed by the individuals associated with these institutions, individuals whose privileged social location often tends to leave them blinded by the illusion of their own control. Giving analytical prominence to the "tradition of the oppressed" allows us to capitalize on the insights derived from the cumulative experience of those for whom all of the diverse processes associated with globalization—those that are more clearly under institutional control and those that are less so—are part of a long, ongoing story of struggle and resistance.

In a more abstract sense, the facts of globalization, especially the time-space compression that creates "global immanence,"[22] ensure that the basic elements of the system can be viewed from any single point. As any number of recent events from the 9/11 attacks to the global financial crisis to the 2010 interventions of WikiLeaks and its "hacktivist" supporters demonstrate, a system built upon networks also leaves itself vulnerable to attack from virtually anywhere.[23] Anthropologist George Marcus had these realities in mind when he argued in 1995 that in the context of globalization, ethnography needed to be both "in" and "of" the world-system. One possibility is to engage in multi-sited ethnography by following a particular analytical object (e.g., a commodity, image or group of people) as it travels through the circuits of the system. Another possibility is to focus on one specific place, but with an eye to illuminating how the entire system is, in effect, contained within that place.[24] The "monadic" approach to Global Palestine employed in this book, which views Palestine both as a concrete "local" place and as a thoroughly globalized space, both immersed in and shaping of emergent global realities, is very much in keeping with this impulse.

Throughout the book significant weight is placed on a series of global and globalizing processes, most notably colonization, militarization, securitization and acceleration. The influence of these processes on social life across all scales, from the most local to the truly planetary, cannot be overstated. They are, in many ways, among the most important "deep structures" of global politics, even though they are rarely acknowledged as such. Taken together, these deep structures point us toward two closely-connected understandings of globalization. Both acknowledge the importance of powerful institutions, as well as the perspectives to which they give rise, while also insisting on the need to rein in their obsession with their own agency. Both are also closely connected with Benjamin's "tradition of the oppressed."

The first is best described as a process of global colonization that has produced a world marked by both radical integration and radical hierarchy. From this perspective, the year 1492 looms large and may be viewed not only as the symbolic beginning of European expansion and imperialism but also as the beginning of globalization itself.[25] Yet as postcolonial theorist Ella Shohat emphasizes, 1492 also occupies a central place in the story of how Europe (in this case, imperial Spain) came to apply tools of racialized, institutionalized intolerance against Jews and Muslims in a way that foreshadowed the genocidal structures of "New World" colonization.[26] Bringing "the two 1492s" together, as Shohat does, enables us to see today's Palestinians and Israeli Jews not as many nationalists might wish to see them—as absolutely distinct groups representing opposite sides of an unbridgeable cultural divide—but rather as close cousins whose shared story reveals a great deal about the Eurocentric structures of global colonization.

The second understanding of globalization is more abstract and refers to the extension of the logic of permanent war across the globe in a way that complicates those narratives that focus almost exclusively on capital accumulation as the motor driving global history. Permanent or "pure" war, a process illuminated most provocatively in the work of Paul Virilio,[27] refers to what he calls the "infinite preparation" for war via the militarization of science, technology and economy. One of the important implications of this revolutionary transformation is that it produces an ongoing struggle between runaway techno-logistical acceleration on the one hand, and the human impulse toward rootedness and ecological defense on the other. Permanent war, in other words, is a kind of social auto-immune disorder in which the tools of human productivity and invention rebound on their makers, not only threatening to destroy the conditions of life but also provoking new forms of resistance and solidarity.

Virilio's critical work on "dromology" (the logic and study of speed and acceleration) is famously elliptical and full of neologisms: as one of his primary interpreters and interlocutors, James Der Derian, once commented: "In a typical Virilio sentence…the concepts can spew out like the detritus of a *Mir* supply ship."[28] Nonetheless, Virilio helps to reorient the angle of vision in provocative ways, pushing new questions about the relationships among technology, war, and broader processes of social militarization to the fore. His references to Palestine, while few in number, are inevitably valuable and suggestive in terms of illuminating Palestine's prophetic global significance.

Organization of the Book

Chapter 2 explores Palestine's particular location within the long-term historical structures of colonization in general and settler colonialism in particular. Like many other settler colonial situations, and notwithstanding the hegemonic discourses associated with the "peace process," the dispossession of the Palestinians effected by the Zionist project is a problem that was never intended to be "solved." If we recognize the depth and staying power of the settler colonial structures in Palestine, we can begin to understand how the broader phenomenon of settler colonialism itself has played a central role in cementing the deep structures of globalization. In addition to situating Palestine within this general trajectory, the chapter discusses how the experience of Palestinian refugees—the first-order victims of Zionist settler colonialism—in the years after 1948 is emblematic of the global politics of containment and the gradual shift from the era of "total war" to the unacknowledged era of "total peace."

Chapter 3 addresses the process of securitization, focusing on how the politics of Israeli/Palestinian violence during the "long 1960s" (a period extending roughly from the late 1940s to the mid-1970s) illustrates the central role of settler colonial projects in pushing forward what amounts to an ongoing global process of social militarization whose full outlines are only becoming visible now. Key in this process was the emergence of militant resistance movements opposing settler colonialism in many places (the US, Israel, Australia and South Africa, to name several of the most prominent examples) and the particular decision of some Palestinian groups to employ spectacular political violence in pursuit of their aims. Settler states responded by waging increasingly aggressive and repressive campaigns against these groups both inside and outside their own borders while leading the construction and circulation of a new discourse of anti-terrorism. In this way settler colonialism unwittingly partnered with those it had originally displaced to help lay the foundation for today's world of borderless wars and generalized obsession with security—terrorism being the generalized threat serving to justify these developments.

Chapter 4 focuses on the process of acceleration that is illuminated most notably in Virilio's work. The settler colonization of Palestine, I argue, has turned that territory into a laboratory of "dromocratic" violence in two related senses. First, the Israeli state's project of maintaining its domination over the Palestinian people continues to be fueled by its use of technologies of violent acceleration that have recently made Israel a world leader in the emerging global homeland security economy. On the local level, the application of these technologies in the context of Israel's colonial project has produced radical forms of confinement for Palestinians. On the global level, the circulation of the same technologies (for example, via the use of Israeli drones for purposes of surveillance and assassination) is producing new patterns of violence, exclusion and social control. Second, the dromopolitics of Palestine—particularly the phenomenon of suicide bombing as an accelerated response to Israeli state violence—also illustrate how acceleration can spin beyond the control of powerful political actors, to the point where acceleration itself becomes a colonizing power.

Chapter 5 addresses Palestinian efforts to defend their lives and their land within the shrinking conditions of possibility produced by the realities of settler colonization and violent acceleration. For Palestinians, occupation—defined here as the process of continuing to inhabit the land in the face of settler colonial incursions—continues to be a key part of the strategy of resisting the deep structures of Israeli domination. It is in this arena that the indigenous nature of the Palestinian struggle comes most clearly into focus and reveals the ongoing, transnational nature of the struggle against settler colonialism. A similar logic, however, also informs the actions of other groups such as the squatters who occupy public spaces in major cities in opposition to processes of privatization, gentrification and dislocation. The centrality of what I term "habitational resistance" to life in Palestine today not only helps explain why so many international volunteers have gone to Palestine in recent years to stand and work in solidarity with those living under Israeli domination, but also reveals a great deal about the changing contours of place-based struggles for justice across the globe.

The book concludes in Chapter 6 with some reflections on how thinking about the decolonization of Palestine might help to conceptualize the decolonization of Global Palestine. There is no question that Palestine is hard-wired—never without controversy, of course—into the circuits of the struggle for global justice. At a time when the deep structures of globalization threaten to render politics itself a thing of the past, this struggle seeks to defend and breathe new life into the process of participatory, democratic politics. At a time when the actions of powerful settler states such as the US and Israel threaten to render international law useless, this struggle insists on the need to move past the politics of exceptionalism. And at a time of permanent war and immanent social militarization, this struggle aims to imagine and actualize productive and liberating ways of using the tradition of nonviolent "popular defense" in order to exit from the suicidal dynamic that combines war, ecological destruction and the predatory search for endless capital accumulation. Palestine remains both the site of a struggle to decolonize itself and a key node in the globally networked struggle to decolonize a world whose current structures of inequality and injustice have been shaped by the global politics of settler colonialism.

2

COLONIZATION

None of this is new for the natives. But if the non-natives could remember, none of it's new for them either.

John Trudell

Israel/Palestine. Everyone knows it is one of the world's perpetual "hotspots," a place of seemingly unending violence, enmity and hopelessness. Over the years, this deadly dance has come to be known, almost universally, as "the Israeli-Palestinian conflict." Most journalists, scholars, government officials and other observers who speak and write about the situation tend to use this phrase reflexively—and why not? Isn't it an accurate label? No. Although it may appear to be a common-sense way to describe the situation, the phrase "Israeli-Palestinian conflict" is inaccurate and misleading. What is happening in Israel/Palestine is not a "conflict."

Does this mean that there is no violence happening? Does it mean that there are not two (or more) parties engaging in violence? Of course not. Using the term "conflict" in this case, however, encourages the belief that the relationship between Israel and the Palestinians is, in some basic way, a relationship between two sides that share equal responsibility for the situation. This assumption is false, on one level, because there is a great imbalance in the relative ability of each side to inflict violence: Israel is by far the stronger party. But it is fundamentally false because it obscures the fact that Israel/Palestine is the site of an ongoing project of settler colonialism.

This settler colonial project has put into place a set of political, economic and social structures that form the basis of the current relationship between Israeli Jews and Palestinians, including the violent aspects of that relationship. These structures are, to quote the editors of an important comparative volume on settler colonialism, "the persistent defining characteristic, even the condition of possibility," of a settler state such as Israel.[1] Take the issue of land: much as the wealth of the dominant class in the US is built upon the original conquest of indigenous land and the exploitation of African slave labor, the prosperity enjoyed by Israel's dominant class cannot be separated from the settler colonial land expropriation that began in the period immediately following the 1948 war.[2] The same holds true for the issue of demographics, where the removal of much of Palestine's Arab population during and after the war provided the basis for a new social reality that extends to the present day.

Rather than a conflict, what is happening in Israel/Palestine is Zionism. Identifying Zionism as the core of the issue, however, can lead to the mistaken impression that Zionism is either uniquely special (as some of its supporters claim) or uniquely objectionable (as some of its critics claim). The reality is that Zionism is far more ordinary and far less exceptional than either of these groups would care to admit. As a settler colonial project, it is embedded in a set of deep structures that continue to be constitutive of the world today.

The focus of the present chapter, then, is on how an understanding of colonization as a general process can enhance one's understanding of Palestine; and, equally important, what a close look at the settler colonization of Palestine can teach us about global colonization. Palestine essentially reveals that colonization, rather than a fading relic of a past era, is the stuff of contemporary reality. Similarly, it reveals the central role that settler colonial projects, in particular, have played in cementing some of global colonization's most important and far-reaching structures. Finally, Palestine illustrates in microcosm how colonization itself remains contingent upon a range of factors that shape its specific modalities, directions and objects of exploitation. All of this provides crucial context for the discussion of decolonization offered in this book's conclusion.

Talking About Colonization

The symmetrical language of a conflict between two sides is incompatible with the realities of colonization in general and settler colonialism in particular. Take the example of South Africa. Throughout the decades-long struggle for majority rule in that country, there undoubtedly were many who preferred to view the violence there as a kind of zero-sum game between two opposing sides: "whites" vs. "blacks." Yet the violence was a direct function of the colonial structures put into place, quite openly, by the South African state, structures that positioned all South Africans in a complex set of social relationships organized according to a logic of strict, racialized hierarchy. This logic was integral to the settler project, once again forming the "condition of possibility" for the settler state's existence. What was happening was not a "conflict"—what was happening was apartheid.

South Africa's black population did not enter into a violent relationship with the white settlers willingly; they did so because they needed to defend themselves against a political project that was increasingly bent on subjugating, displacing and killing them. By any reasonable calculation—unless, of course, one subscribes to the nihilistic belief that "might makes right"—the settlers bear the bulk of the moral responsibility for initiating a system of structural violence that has even outlived, in many ways, the era of formal apartheid.[3]

A similar argument could be made in relation to the United States and Australia, two locations where the white settler population carried out colossal and murderous land-grabs, provoking understandable resistance from those who were being removed from their land and homes, stripped of key aspects of their culture and killed in large numbers. The violent structures put in place by settler colonialism in these "new world" territories continue to shape social reality today, as even a brief look at basic socioeconomic indicators for native and non-native populations reveals.[4] To refer to this dynamic, whether historically or currently, as a "conflict" would not only be inaccurate, but it would also be an insult to the indigenous people who, along with millions of enslaved Africans brought to North America against their will, were the primary victims of settler colonialism in these two territories.

An analysis of these comparative cases helps to reorient one's understanding of Israel/Palestine's recent history of violence.[5] How did the Palestinians become involved in this so-called conflict with Zionism and, later, the state of Israel? The answer, quite simply, is that they became involved because they were already living on the land when the settlers arrived. Consequently, any discussion of Israel/Palestine that does not acknowledge the settler colonial nature of the situation is an exercise in denial that is likely to lead to a fundamental misunderstanding of what has already happened, what is happening now, and what needs to happen in order to bring about a real decolonization.

Equally important, using Palestine as an entry point into the larger issue of settler colonialism helps us reorient our understanding of colonization itself and its profound, often hidden global significance. Just as settler colonialism has often operated by exnominating itself— no state in the world identifies itself as a settler state—colonization in general is also buried beneath a host of institutions, categories and assumptions that tend to dominate public discourse. When war and peace is referred to here, for example, colonization is present but unacknowledged, its absence defining the limits of the discourse. Similarly, when people debate the merits of globalization, or humanitarian assistance, or state security policy, or genetically modified foods, colonization is present. Even when the promises and successes brought by new technologies are celebrated, colonization is present as well.

One of the reasons that colonization is able to maintain its relative invisibility in this way is that the structures and processes associated with it cannot be solely reduced to a simple politics of control. Powerful political actors have leveraged colonization for their own purposes and continue to do so. As the body of literature on colonialism amply demonstrates, there is much to be gained through the analysis of how colonial ventures are shaped by the interests, designs and policy choices of their metropolitan sponsors and other key actors. From a state-centered and actor-centered perspective, colonization comes and goes along with the rise and fall of hegemons and their self-interested strategies. From a world-historical perspective, however, colonization remains. Bigger than any specific example, it possesses a kind of relative independence that lies beyond the purview of conventional explanatory frameworks.

As I argued in Chapter 1, the world of radical integration and radical hierarchy associated with globalization may be understood, from one perspective at least, as the product of a process of global colonization through which human societies have collectively sought to inhabit, extract resources from and profit from all corners of the earth. One way to see the limitations of a state-centered approach to this phenomenon is to ask the question: how could global colonization be stopped or reversed? The answer would lie not with the actions of any particular actor (although this would undoubtedly help); rather, it would require a revolutionary paradigm shift in relationships among human beings, and the relationship between human beings and the land.

Beyond an examination of single examples of colonization, then, even beyond the comparative study of colonial experience, how do we begin to take account of colonization itself? Where does settler colonialism fit into this larger picture? A good starting point is to recognize that a truly global understanding of these issues requires operating outside the structures provided by disciplinary thinking. Referring to four of the most influential intellectual figures of the past two centuries, one scholar advocates employing a mixture of Karl Marx (capitalism), Frantz Fanon (violence), Edward Said (culture) and Michel Foucault (governmentality)—a formidable array of theories, concepts, and frameworks, to which I would add Paul Virilio (acceleration).[6] One significant advantage of such a rich analytical toolbox is that it pushes us to consider both the actor-centered explanations traditionally favored by social scientists as well as the more abstract (but no less important) explanations found in the work of scholars operating in the margins of, in between, or completely outside academic disciplines as they have been historically constituted.

The Deep Structures of Colonization

Understanding the constitutive place of colonization in Global Palestine challenges us to grasp the nature of colonization as a permanent structural reality, while also recognizing how the nature of colonization can and does change in response to changing conditions of possibility. This discussion of global colonization will be framed with reference to three overlapping modes that have effectively collided in the settler colonization of Palestine in a way that sheds a great deal of light on the compressed, accelerated and hierarchical nature of globalization. The first two of these modes form the analytical core of the present chapter. Exocolonization may be understood as an extensive and outwardly-directed vector operating within the realm of geopolitics (the politics of territorial control). The second, endocolonization, represents an intensive and inwardly-directed turn of the colonial impulse. In Chapter 4 a third mode, dromocolonization, will be introduced to designate how techno-logic acceleration, while still being used by particular actors for purposes of colonization, is itself colonizing humanity in a way that brings the realm of chronopolitics (the politics of temporal control) to the fore.

As with any heuristic device, this framing comes with its limitations. There is a danger, for example, that the first two modes might be interpreted as positing an absolute separation between "external" and "internal" colonization. Here it is important to emphasize (as will be discussed in greater detail in Chapter 3) that the division of the world into "internal" and "external" realms of sovereignty, territory, security, etc. is a primary mechanism through which power operates. Settler colonial projects, grounded in the peripatetic logic of the frontier, are experts at this kind of operation; the state of Israel, which has never declared its own borders and accepts no geo-political limits on its own search for "security," is an excellent example. The analytical purpose of using the terms exocolonization and endocolonization when referring to a specific colonial project, therefore, is not to insist uncritically that they refer to ideal types of colonization that take place "outside" and "inside" the state, respectively. The purpose is to make a careful distinction between two modes (think of them as analogous to major and minor modes in a musical score) that are often two faces—simultaneous, sequential, or both—of the same process.

At the same time, there is a real sense in which all three modes can be mapped onto a gradual shift in the nature of colonization, a shift that both colors the historical trajectory of a place such as Palestine and reveals the outlines of a fundamentally global process that has acquired considerable momentum over time. The emergence of the second mode, for example, illustrates how extensive colonization eventually reaches its limits and gives way to more intensive and all-encompassing forms of exploitation, surveillance and social control. Yet global colonization is also a story of how the relationship between human beings and the technologies they create has gradually been inverted, with far-reaching consequences for the practice of politics and the nature of humanity. The third mode, dromocolonization, thus reveals how what may once have been simple tools in the arsenal of the colonizer, can later become—both in and of themselves—colonizing forces.

The mode of exocolonization refers to a process of geo-political expansion that rushes literally to the ends of the earth—the "blank spaces" on the map famously described in Joseph Conrad's childhood recollections and later by Marlow, his narrator in *Heart of Darkness*—with the primary goal of incorporating and exploiting territory, labor, resources and other factors necessary for the stockpiling and generation of wealth. As Marlow says matter-of-factly: "It was just robbery with violence, aggravated murder on a grand scale, and men going at it blind…not a pretty thing when you look into it too much." The various types of colonialism found in the highly taxonomic literature on the topic—settler, exploitation, metropole, maritime, dependent, administrative and so forth—can be bewildering,[7] but all of them have played their role in the global operation of this exocolonial mode. The story of this process is organically related to the story of how the modern world system emerged through the intertwining of the histories of capitalism and imperialism, the emergence of the modern interstate system, and the rise of particular technologies of violence, communication and transport.

It would be a mistake, however, to assume that a mode of colonization most commonly associated with the age of imperialism, industry and "discovery" has passed firmly into history; on the contrary, evidence of the "colonial present" is abundantly evident.[8] In addition to the most visible contemporary cases (e.g., Iraq or Palestine), the continuing presence of resource wars in Africa and elsewhere is a further indication of the same pattern.[9] Recent reports of countries such as South Korea and the United Arab Emirates buying huge tracts of prime farmland in poor and vulnerable countries at bargain prices remind us that exocolonization also takes on subtler, less visible forms.[10] All of this makes clear that even in a supposedly postcolonial era, the externally-directed vector of colonization remains an active element in global politics with the potential to inflict tremendous damage on vulnerable communities.

At the same time, given the terrestrial, ecological and ethical realities involved in this kind of exploitation, exocolonization is always confronted by limits that threaten to derail it. The most obvious of these is the limit imposed by the size of the planet itself—at a certain point, Marlow's map contains no more "blank spaces"—but limits in the availability of specific resources, the rate of return on investment, and the willingness of populations at home to support the kind of structural violence (including, at the extreme, genocidal violence) that exocolonial projects typically inflict upon their objects may also be considered. All such projects, of course, face various forms of determined resistance from the populations being colonized. In short, colonizers who employ the mode of exocolonization never operate with an entirely free hand.

These limits help explain the existence of endocolonization, and it is worth noting from the outset that this concept overlaps to some degree with a number of other, more influential concepts in critical social analysis. These include neo-liberalism, understood as a global project of political and social transformation aimed at "freeing" society from all restrictions on capital accumulation;[11] and Foucault's concept of "governmentality," or the techniques through which modern populations are governed and rendered susceptible to social control, whether in "disciplinary societies" or the emergent "societies of control" referenced in the work of Foucault, Gilles Deleuze and others. What distinguishes the concept of endocolonization is its connection with changes in the nature of war, changes that arguably continue to be underappreciated even in critical circles. Most concisely, endocolonization can be defined as the socioeconomic logic of an era in which war is increasingly indistinguishable from the endless preparation for war and the extension of militarization throughout the social body. Endocolonization is, in short, the socioeconomic logic of pure war.[12] These overlapping processes find their home in a geopolitical environment marked by the existence of the Bomb and its associated doctrine of nuclear deterrence,[13] the growing prominence of technologies of mass communication, and the emerging role of IFIs in defining and enforcing new standards of austerity and social restructuring.

In an economic sense, endocolonization feeds the machine of pure war and the structures, profits and privileges associated with it by extracting resources from particular local populations that have already been incorporated into the postcolonial state. It constitutes a massive transfer of wealth and energy from the poor and middle classes to the wealthy and the military-industrial complex. At the extreme, it represents a kind of "suicidal state": a systematic underdevelopment not of some distant territory, but rather of one's own economy through policies of privatization and the withdrawal of social services.[14]

Endocolonization, however, is more than a strictly economic process aimed at finding new ways of generating, extracting and redistributing wealth. It also helps explain how global colonization has transformed the nature of war and, by extension, the character of human communities. Specifically, endocolonization operates by promoting a generalized militarization of identity and social consciousness (a process that is discussed in greater detail in Chapter 3) through the gradual fusion of science, technology, information and economy.[15] This unique and frightening system is hidden, albeit in plain sight, defining the horizon of observable and thinkable social reality.

As an example, consider the phenomenon that Ross Glover provocatively calls the logic of "The War on _____."[16] During the past half-century it has been evident how this logic produces open-ended global campaigns against a host of vaguely-defined enemies (poverty, crime, drugs, terrorism, etc.), and campaigns that facilitate the spread of militarized structures, practices and identities across the social field while also creating new foci for scientific research, technological innovation and the production and circulation of new discourses. These "wars on," argues Glover, ultimately serve as euphemisms for an ongoing war against the poor—that is, an endocolonization of the livelihoods, communities and the bodies of the most vulnerable.[17] Significantly, they are also built upon assumptions about the pathological nature of the "cultures" that support the vaguely-defined enemies being fought. In this sense, the reductionist arguments regularly mobilized under the banner of the "Global War on Terrorism" about the allegedly violent or undemocratic nature of Islam are close cousins of the "cultures of poverty" arguments that have long served to deflect attention from the structural nature of poverty. The central role of culture in the discourses of "The War on _____" signals the presence of an endocolonizing mode that targets the fabric of poor communities.

Endocolonization does not replace exocolonization in any absolute sense, but it does tend to emerge as the latter reaches its limits. In those moments, exocolonial processes that were always predicated upon particular kinds of social transformation "at home" find that the endocolonial begins to gain the upper hand. For metropole colonizers (e.g., the British Empire), the extraction of wealth from foreign territories may be followed by withdrawal and the inward turn of the colonizing vector (e.g., Thatcherism). For settler colonizers such as the white settlers in South Africa or North America, the successful creation of a new society is typically followed by the confinement and systematic structural exploitation of the remaining subaltern population (e.g., South Africa's black "homelands," North America's reservations, the Jim Crow South or the "prison-industrial complex"). Finally, for many of those societies that managed to gain formal independence from their colonial rulers (e.g., Argentina or Zaire), decolonization ushered in a period of endocolonization in the form of military dictatorships and kleptocracies supported and enabled (openly or covertly) by powerful external forces (e.g., Cold War patrons).

The significant distinctions between these first two modes of colonization can be mapped out usefully along a number of axes. Spatially, whereas exocolonization plays itself out in struggles over the incorporation of distant territories often viewed as "empty" (e.g., on Marlow's map), endocolonization produces desperate, often hidden struggles over spaces that are simultaneously overcrowded and abandoned: urban ghettos, decaying industrial zones, reservations, today's Gaza Strip.[18] Militarily, exocolonization's "war of milieu," enacted in the relatively isolated military theatres of land and sea, gives way to endocolonization's "war on the milieu" enacted against the habitats that host and sustain life (see Chapter 5). Likewise, the means of violence and control and their implications change dramatically: exocolonization is aided by guns, ships, maps, machetes and other implements that facilitate expansion to the ends of the earth, while endocolonization occurs under the global shadow of apocalyptic weapons and communications technologies that effectively envelop the earth, enabling the increasingly sophisticated techniques of state surveillance.

Both of these modes possess similar mechanisms of displacement, tending to displace individuals and communities from one geographical space to another through mass violence, voluntary or forced removal, the creation of diasporas, de-peasantization and urbanization, and the creation of ghettos and other confined spaces. Exocolonization, for example, removes indigenous people from the land (or from a particular kind of relationship to the land) and pushes them into cities or onto reservations. Endocolonization begins by bringing citizens under the "protective" cover of the state, only to remove that cover systematically, leaving them to flee into spaces defined by various forms of fundamentalism (including market fundamentalism).[19] In other words, both modes deterritorialize, but they also reterritorialize—albeit in ways that enact new hierarchical structures.

The Logics of Settler Colonialism

Settler colonialism has long operated at the cutting edge of the modes of colonization described elsewhere in this chapter. As a result, it is becoming increasingly difficult to deny the far-reaching impact that the deep structures put in place by settler colonial projects continue to have in shaping the contours of violence and social hierarchy across the globe. With a growing number of scholars employing the concept of settler colonialism as a key analytical category,[20] the time has certainly come for a systematic, critical history of settler colonialism as a global historical force. Such a history would need to address the role of settler colonialism in producing not only particular territorial and geo-political patterns, but also enduring structures of violence and militarization; changes in identities across all scales from the local to the global; and opportunities for new forms of transnational solidarity in the ongoing struggle for human liberation.

There is no universally accepted definition of settler colonialism—nor could there be. One of the key points of general agreement within the burgeoning literature on the topic, however, is that there are important resemblances among a number of cases of colonization involving the creation of new, settler-based societies. These are usefully distinguished from other cases, where colonizers primarily sought to gain specific benefits from a given territory before withdrawing (while leaving behind "postcolonial" political and economic structures that extended those benefits). Cases commonly invoked as part of the former group include North America, Australia, Israel/Palestine and South Africa.

Comparative and transnational analysis of these and other settler colonial cases is less about establishing isomorphisms than it is about excavating tendencies and patterns for the purpose of engaging in the critique of prevailing social realities. In any case, scholars are not the only ones who see meaningful connections between the cases just mentioned. On the contrary, these states have effectively constituted themselves as a kind of undeclared "settler international" that manifests itself in the form of long-standing diplomatic, military and cultural alliances.[21] In this light, it is evident that while the famous "special relationship" between the US and Israel may be a function of strategic decisions taken at the elite policy level, it is also grounded in a common history of settler colonialism that conditions popular attitudes towards the relationship itself. Thus many North Americans or Australians who are the descendants of white settlers intuitively feel that they have more in common with Israeli Jews than with Palestinians.

Such political and cultural patterns indicate the operation of a shared structural logic. The considerable contribution of recent scholarly work on settler colonialism has been to illuminate exactly how this logic works, how it is grounded in global history, and how it continues to shape social reality not only within settler societies, but also beyond them. One of the key findings of the literature on this topic is that settler colonialism, while undoubtedly possessing features that call to mind ancient examples, is a distinctly modern phenomenon rooted in the modern dynamics of state formation, racialization, capital accumulation and genocide. In this sense, the origins of settler colonialism belong firmly in the mode of exocolonization, with settler projects constituting important thrusts in the trajectory of imperial expansion. In some cases these projects were absolutely central to the pursuance of imperial aims, while in other cases settlement was a means to resolve the demographic, economic and political contradictions that empire produced in the metropolis. Settlers often enjoyed the crucial backing of the imperial state (particularly its military power), but occasionally found themselves at odds with that state at key moments. In all cases, however, the core dynamics of settler projects were deeply immersed in the political economy and geopolitics of exocolonization.

A second finding of the literature on settler colonialism, drawing on the wider critique of colonial discourse, is that the major ideological justifications for settler projects read like an index of imperial thought and its "imaginative geographies".[22] sovereignty was established in the act of "discovery"; the territories being settled were "empty" or "unused";[23] imperial powers and their emissaries on the ground therefore had a mission (sacred or secular) to make the land productive; civilization was inherently destined to rule over, instruct, and/or eliminate barbarism by ushering in an era of peace. These ideological constructions, together with the aforementioned geo-political dynamics, establish the modernity of settler colonialism and its centrality to many of the processes that have produced the contemporary hierarchical world-system.

In one of the most incisive contributions to the literature on the topic, Patrick Wolfe emphasizes that what makes settler colonialism distinct is its desire to create an entirely new society in place of, or on the ruins of, an existing one: it "destroys to replace."[24] All colonization is violent, but it may be posited that from the perspective of indigenous society, settler colonialism is cataclysmically violent. Wolfe demonstrates that settler colonialism is thus animated not simply by a drive for territorial control, but also by a "logic of elimination." This first logic represents the dominant settler response to a basic reality: the organized presence of other human beings on the land.[25]

Settler projects, both before and after formal statehood, enact this fundamental logic by employing mechanisms of exclusion including slavery, forced migration (e.g., the Cherokee "Trail of Tears," the Palestinian *Nakba*) to confinement (e.g., reservations in North America and Australia, bantustans in South Africa), coercive assimilation (e.g., boarding school abuses in North America, the "Stolen Generation" in Australia) and mass killing.[26] All of these are typically supplemented with mechanisms of rhetorical exclusion designed to deny the identity of the colonized ("Palestine does not exist"), their claims to the land ("they weren't making the land productive") and the legitimacy of their resistance ("they are terrorists").

The logic of elimination works in tandem with a second logic of expansion that structures settler colonialism's characteristic spatial politics, particularly the violent politics associated with the frontier. Rather than a fixed location, the settler colonial frontier is best conceived as a moving structure that facilitates territorial acquisition through the creation of paramilitary vanguards (e.g., the frontier "rabble"); the systematic fostering of fear and insecurity in the settler population as a perpetual justification for further conquest; and the strategic use of legal gray zones where "frontier justice" can be dispensed with relative impunity. Within the ideological framework of settlement, the frontier becomes the site of heroic figures and events (e.g., the Afrikaner "Great Trek," the westward migration of North America's European settlers and the reclaiming of biblical territory by Jewish settlers) that form the iconic bedrock of nationalist mythology. Within the "tradition of the oppressed," by contrast, the frontier represents a space of perpetual violence familiar to anyone who has studied the oppressive spatial dynamics set in motion by the growth of Israeli settlement colonies in the West Bank, Gaza and East Jerusalem in recent decades.[27]

Settler colonial projects are also linked by a third logic that is most famously expressed in US historian Fredrick Jackson Turner's "frontier thesis"—the logic of exceptionalism.[28] Settler movements are "chosen people" movements, regularly constructing powerful ideological concepts and metaphors (e.g., "Manifest Destiny") to demonstrate their unique missions in the world.[29] The great "American Experiment" (itself a tendentious phrase that implicitly positions indigenous people and African slaves as laboratory animals) was fueled by a powerful cocktail of exceptionalist elements, both religious and secular. Beginning from the belief that their survival was a sign of divine favor, the early American colonists quickly founded a kind of secular Holy Church built on what historian William Appleman Williams calls a "non-articulated social Darwinism."[30] John Adams captured the grandiosity and arrogance of this attitude when he argued that the colonization of North America represented "the opening of a grand scheme and design in providence for the illumination of the ignorant, and the emancipation of the slavish part of mankind all over the earth."[31]

The recurrence of such exceptionalist discourses points toward deeper cultural patterns linking settler projects. Not for nothing did Herman Melville refer to Americans in 1850 as "the peculiar, chosen people—the Israel of our time." And not for nothing did Thomas Jefferson suggest that the Great Seal of the United States should "depict the children of Israel being guided by a pillar of light."[32] Perhaps the Afrikaner ideologues who created the Voortrekker Monument near Pretoria had the same notion in mind when they constructed their temple in such a way that a pillar of light would shine down to illuminate a cenotaph at exactly noon every 16 December to commemorate the 1838 Battle of Blood River, when a small group of settlers defeated an army of 10,000 Zulu warriors. A powerful example of exceptionalist settler iconography, the monument could easily be mistaken for a celebration of New England Puritanism and its westward expansion; it features a statue honoring a bonnet-wearing Afrikaner woman and is ringed by a wall depicting sixty-four covered wagons.

The sense of uniqueness and mission animating the white settlement project in South Africa helped generate a close identification with Zionism and the state of Israel. As Benjamin Beit-Hallahmi notes, this cultural and ideological affinity did not even require Afrikaners to interrogate their own anti-Jewish feeling. "Israelis are colonial fighters and settlers, just like the Afrikaners," the logic went. "They are tough and resilient. They know how to dominate."[33] In employing this kind of sly distinction between weak Jews and strong Israelis, the beneficiaries of apartheid echoed not only the dominant imaginary of Zionism itself, but also the simultaneously philo-Semitic and anti-Semitic discourse employed by many of Zionism's evangelical Christian supporters in the US down to the present day. Breyten Breytenbach, the dissident South African writer, commented during the latter years of formal apartheid on the ironic and violent implications of the pro-Israel discourse among Afrikaners:

What a strange identification the Afrikaners have with Israel. There has always been a strong current of anti-Semitism in the land, after all—the present rulers are the result and the direct descendants of pro-Nazi ideologues. And yet they have the greatest admiration for Israel...They identify themselves with Israel—as the Biblical chosen people of God, and as a modern embattled state surrounded by a sea of enemies. Which, they believe, justify aggressive foreign military adventures.[34]

It is worth emphasizing here that at its origins, settler colonial exceptionalism takes the form of—indeed, is dependent upon—an open acknowledgement of its settler nature: the special status of the project derives precisely from its determination to engage in what is viewed as a daring, necessary and even altruistic undertaking. Over time, however, this open acknowledgement begins to come at a cost. The gradual emergence of a global human rights regime during the latter part of the twentieth century, while selectively enforced, brought with it a condemnation of the excesses associated with settler projects, particularly in South Africa. As a result, settler states now seek to exnominate a central aspect of their own identity, airbrushing their history in a way that hides what their founders once proclaimed openly: their status as settler colonizers.[35]

Indeed, it may be argued that in addition to the logics of elimination, expansion and exceptionalism, settler colonial projects share a fourth logic: the deep and pervasive logic of denial.[36] Stanley Cohen, whose critical perspective derives in part from his experience of living in both apartheid South Africa and Israel, identifies several types of denial including literal denial ("the assertion that something did not happen or is not true"), interpretive denial ("the raw facts are not being denied...[but] are given a different meaning from what seems apparent to others"), implicatory denial (denying neither the facts nor their conventional interpretation but rather "the psychological, political or moral implications that conventionally follow"), and cultural denial (when whole societies "encourage turning a collective blind eye, leaving horrors unexamined or normalized as being part of the rhythms of everyday life"). All of these types of denial are active and influential in settler societies, which by definition are built upon hidden structures of violence that extend into the present. The most basic form of denial is that which enables members of the dominant culture in settler societies to examine their surroundings and view no evidence of colonization.[37]

Despite the relatively recent critical interventions by scholars of settler colonialism, the academy has generally played the role of enabler in relation to settler colonial denial. Through its internalization of state perspectives, for example, the international relations approach that dominates the study of global politics has tended to accept at face value the self-representations of settler states (e.g., the notion that Israel may be viewed unproblematically as "the only democracy in the Middle East").[38] As a result, the recognition of settler colonial realities is only slightly more present in the scholarly record than in the political rhetoric that has emanated from these states for more than half a century. Nowhere is this clearer than in the case of Israel/Palestine, where the "conflict" approach described at the beginning of this chapter has dwarfed, and in some cases actively silenced, attempts to employ settler colonialism as an analytical category.

Palestine and Settler Exocolonization

Once the settler colonization of Palestine is understood to be an ongoing process, the dynamic relationship between Palestine and the modes of global colonization identified above comes into focus. The Zionist project of creating a Jewish homeland in Palestine emerged and grew in the midst of inter-imperial rivalry and aggressive exocolonization, a world whose culmination in genocide and world war helped lay the groundwork for the creation of the state of Israel and the near-destruction of Palestinian society in 1947–48. The rise of endocolonization and pure war in turn provided the context within which the Zionist project was consolidated in subsequent decades. Finally, throughout this period—but especially in recent years—developments in Palestine reveal the workings of new forms of colonization that are driven by the application of new technologies on bodies, communities and social relations.

Concerning exocolonization, it is worth remembering that the first major wave of Jewish emigration to Palestine is generally recognized as having begun in 1882, just two years before European powers carved up much of Africa at the Berlin Conference. This era of "high imperialism" saw not only the extension of European domination across much of the globe, but also the dawn of what came to be known as total war. Simultaneously intensive and extensive, total war collapses the local and the global into a single amalgam of ideology, industry and acceleration. Ideologically, the impulse toward total war derives from the conviction that the state itself is under existential threat, a conviction that can profoundly affect the subjectivities of political and military elites and of ordinary citizens who are collectively called upon to defend the nation.[39] The industrialization of weapons manufacturing enables the state to set the machinery of total war in motion through a powerful joining of mass mobilization and mass production.[40] Finally, total war is inseparable from the process of acceleration that renders the world increasingly dromocratic (ruled by speed). Total war and acceleration share a tendency toward the removal of political, ethical and technical limitations on movement and action, and both therefore constitute important globalizing forces.

Conditions for the emergence of total war began to emerge by the mid-nineteenth century through the rapid mass production of weapons such as the modern machine gun. Given the ideological and industrial realities of the United States during this period, the American Civil War appears as, in William McNeill's words, "the first full-fledged example of an industrialized war."[41] The inter-imperial wars of the late-nineteenth and early twentieth century, however, marked the golden age of total war, whose totalizing nature found its ultimate expression in Hitler's Telegram 71. Faced with defeat, the German leader gave his commanders instructions for the systematic destruction of Germany's logistical infrastructure and industrial plant with the pithy aphorism: "If the war is lost, let the nation perish."[42]

In addition to imperial total war and the trajectory of modern anti-Semitism, European ethno-nationalism played a key role in creating the conditions for the emergence of Zionism by not only highlighting the difficulty (and, some argued, the impossibility) of Jewish assimilation, but also shaping the form that both the Zionist response to anti-Semitism and the Arab response to European domination would take. What is less widely acknowledged is that the same environment also created the conditions for the particular way in which Zionism was actualized on the ground, namely, through the mechanisms of settler colonialism.

Despite starting toward the end of the period of open exocolonization, Zionism had more in common with older cases of what Elkins and Pederson call "new world" colonization efforts in Australia and North America, where "Republican freedom and band-of-brothers exclusivity [constituted] the entangled twin ideological poles of the settler colonial state."[43] More generally, these authors argue, all settler projects share two structural characteristics that are clearly identifiable in the case of the Zionist project in Palestine. The first is the particular four-sided set of relationships among external imperial powers, their local representatives, the settler community and the indigenous population. For exocolonizing European powers, Zionism served as a useful tool for outsourcing the "Jewish question" while simultaneously aiding broader imperial goals. At the same time, the fact that the Zionist settlers had their own exocolonial aims—the extension of Jewish settlement and sovereignty throughout as much of historic Palestine as possible—meant that, like settlers in other "new world" situations, they often came into tension and conflict with the imperial metropole. In this sense, Palestine was a site where multiple exocolonial agendas met, sometimes in harmony and sometimes in dissonance.

The second structural characteristic is the set of privileges enjoyed by the settlers vis-à-vis the colonized. As Maxime Rodinson argued in his path-breaking (if somewhat flawed) 1973 book on the subject, and as subsequent work has definitively established, the architects of Zionism were conscious and often unapologetic about their status as settler colonizers, whose right to the land superseded that of Palestine's Arab inhabitants.[44] This colonial attitude has spawned a whole series of hierarchical structures that are built upon a logic of racialization, with Palestinians serving as the primary objects of systematic discrimination and oppression.[45] In political discourse, these structures are reflected in the openly racist and militaristic discourse of right-wing Zionists who advocate the expulsion or further disenfranchisement of Israel's Palestinian population and the annexation of additional territory to the state. The determined edifice of cultural denial erected by many liberal Zionists and supporters of Israel in order to deflect the opprobrium now associated with naked colonization and its most racialized elements is further evidence of these hierarchical dynamics.[46]

The fact that Zionism was (and is), structurally and ideologically, a settler colonial project is not incompatible with the fact that individual European Jews had their own reasons for immigrating to Palestine. Zionism is the political and ideological glue that cemented these individuals into the settler project, initially by transforming them from a victimized minority into a colonizing minority. The work of the Israeli sociologist Gershon Shafir remains a crucial touchstone in illuminating the concrete conditions under which this transformation took place. In particular, Shafir identifies three related processes that animated the period of early Zionist settlement (1882–1914) and laid the foundation for Israeli state and nation formation: the "conquest of labor" strategy (often articulated in terms of "Hebrew labor") that led to the hegemony of the labor movement in Zionist/Israeli politics; the "conquest of guarding" strategy that fueled structures of vanguardist militarization; and the "conquest of land" strategy, actualized most notably in the creation of Jewish-only collective farms (*kibbutzim*) that turned workers into agricultural settlers. These three strategies of conquest, Shafir argues, combined to produce a national political culture dominated by the philosophy of militant settlement and the principle of Jewish exclusivism.[47]

If these processes constituted the Jewish population of Palestine as a settler body and a colonizing minority, the *Nakba* (known in Israel as the "War of Independence") transformed them into a colonizing majority. By 1949 more than 500 Palestinian villages and nearly a dozen urban neighborhoods were emptied of their inhabitants, and roughly 750,000 people were made refugees in what the Israeli historian Ilan Pappe calls "a clear-cut case of an ethnic cleansing operation, regarded under international law today as a crime against humanity."[48] While nationalist Israeli historiography initially managed to ignore and marginalize important Palestinian accounts of the *Nakba* and to occlude what Shafir refers to as the obvious demographic interest behind it, evidence that Israel's founders actively sought the demographic reversal that the war effected is now overwhelming. The current division is between those historians, like Pappe, who object to this ethnic cleansing on moral grounds and those, like Benny Morris, who employ an exceptionalist rhetoric of necessity to justify the massacres and expulsions without which Israel could not have been created as a majority-Jewish state.[49]

What emerges from this historical overview is a picture of Zionism as a hybrid project combining at least three major elements: nineteenth-century romantic nationalist movement, imperial safety valve and settler colonial enterprise. This picture, however, is incomplete without an understanding of how Zionism's identity politics—particularly its narrative of Jewish auto-emancipation—dovetailed with its territorial ambitions. Referring to Theodor Herzl's futurist novel *Altneuland*, Joseph Massad describes the complexity of Zionism's "identitarian" project to construct a remedy for European Jewry's "abnormal" condition:

The settler colony was going to be the space of Jewish transformation. To become European, Jews must exit Europe. They could return to it and become part of it by emulating its culture at a geographical remove. If Jews were Asians in Europe, in Asia, they will become Europeans.[50]

Zionism, from this perspective, requires the internalization of the anti-Semitism it ostensibly sought to combat. Yet the full weight of this irony only emerges when the implementation of Zionism's colonial project causes a second turn of the screw:

Upon encountering the Palestinian Arabs, Zionism's transformative project expanded. While it sought to metamorphose Jews into Europeans, it set in motion a historical process by which it was to metamorphose Palestinian Arabs into Jews in a displaced geography of anti-Semitism.

In other words—and as Massad provocatively concludes—the "Jewish question" and the "Palestinian question" are the same question, a question with its roots in European modernity's dominant cultural formation. Within such a formation, the self is always unproblematic, while other formations are reduced to the status of questions or problems. It is not for nothing that W.E.B. Du Bois framed his 1903 book *The Souls of Black Folk* by asking, "How does it feel to be a problem?"

Europe's relationship to Zionism is thus best conceived as a pedagogical one based on imitation and displacement. Zionism illustrates how settler colonial projects turn the colonized space into a laboratory for working out displaced European contradictions. When the displacement of anti-Semitism hit the ground, it spawned a system of territorial displacement that has turned Palestinians into refugees (many more than once), labor migrants, fugitives and frightened residents who spend their time furtively circumventing Israeli roadblocks. It is clear that even as Zionism attempted to create a more powerful and self-sufficient form of "Jewishness" in reaction to the perceived weakness of the Diaspora, it has been unable to escape the psychological and ideological structures that birthed it as a movement.

Palestine and Settler Endocolonization

If exocolonization culminates in exceptional and shattering periods of total war as well as cataclysmic events like the Palestinian *Nakba*, endocolonization is associated with the daily, simmering forms of social transformation that occur as war begins to disappear into the fabric of society—that is, as it turns into pure war. In the shadow of the Bomb and its associated doctrine of deterrence, officially declared wars between sovereign states are gradually replaced by "police actions" and humanitarian interventions and, as discussed above, the reorganization of society according to a logic of immanent militarization. When Dwight D. Eisenhower famously warned against the growth of the military-industrial complex upon his exit from the White House in 1960, he signaled not only the troubling political influence of the armaments industry, but also the arrival of a supposedly peacetime economy that was making it virtually impossible for anyone to opt out of the war machine.[51]

Within such a system, state violence remains as ubiquitous as ever, but most of its manifestations go under the banner of maintaining, seeking, and enforcing peace. This kind of rhetoric has long played a useful role for imperial powers and is arguably constitutive of empire itself, meaning that it spans the two modes of exocolonization and endocolonization.[52] It is in this light that one may view the 1941 address in which Franklin D. Roosevelt identified "four freedoms" as general human goals. Three of these (freedom of speech, freedom of religion and freedom from fear) were longstanding principles of the liberal tradition, but the fourth (freedom from want) represented the crystallization of a more consumer-oriented American liberalism.[53] For his part, FDR explicitly linked the freedom from want with the global pursuit of peace, referring to "economic understandings which will secure to every nation a healthy peacetime life for its inhabitants—everywhere in the world."[54]

In Virilio's unusual and provocative interpretation of the speech, the freedom from want, which he memorably describes as "slipped among the others like a marked card," meant that the State took upon itself the right to determine the meaning of "want" for those who live within, and even beyond, its borders:

> The *freedom from want* is revolutionary to the degree it substitutes man [*sic*] as recipient of health and social services, that is to say, man exposed and alone under statist and clinical scrutiny, for the man of common law with his privileges. The *free* is no longer properly spoken of as a "citizen;" he is an anonymous organism in a limited situation, since the law sees to the minimal satisfaction of need, that which is indispensable to life…[I]t is the unique precariousness of his situation in the heart of the system that binds him to this, since, for the man thus exposed, assistance has become survival, non-assistance a condemnation to death.[55]

The growing role of the State in ensuring freedom from want cannot be separated from the problems and questions posed by stateless peoples who complicate the tidy categories of the interstate system. Unsurprisingly, the postwar era coincides with a growing military involvement in previously civilian functions of policing, border control and humanitarian relief. On this reading, the logic of the freedom from want sends a chilling message to the world's subaltern populations, especially those who have suffered catastrophic dispossession or displacement: we will feed you enough to keep you alive, but we will confine you if necessary in order to do so—and we retain the right to withdraw food at any time.[56]

The same biopolitical logic informs the way the third freedom was marketed for domestic American consumption. Perhaps most notable was the intervention of Norman Rockwell, whose series of four paintings inspired by FDR's speech included "Freedom From Want," an iconic image of a family seated at the dinner table as the mother serves an enormous Thanksgiving turkey on what is the ultimate settler colonial holiday. With the Great Depression still fresh in mind, Americans could've been forgiven for responding gratefully to the promise of such bounty. While the promise was delivered for some through subsequent years of fitful progress on questions of social justice, the more restrictive face of the freedom from want continued on a parallel track leading from Jim Crow to Reaganism to the endemic structural violence laid bare in the wake of Hurricane Katrina. By

2006 American biopolitics had reached what is arguably its most logical (and horrifying) conclusion: American soldiers in Guantanamo Bay force-feeding detainees in order to keep them from exercising their last remaining source of power: the power to die.

The freedom from want provides an important context for understanding the world Palestinians confronted after 1948, coping with the shock of the *Nakba* and maintaining only a ghostly presence on the global stage. Scattered throughout the Middle East, they quickly learned that from the state's perspective, denationalized populations are, by definition, dangerous. As recipients of international humanitarian assistance, they experienced the yawning gap between the rhetoric of global human rights and the reality of a world where the democratic realization of those rights often conflicted directly with a refortified state sovereignty[57] and the decidedly undemocratic sovereignty of the transnational military class.

In his short story "The Child Goes to the Camp," Ghassan Kanafani offers a glimpse into how this situation played itself out in everyday life. Recalling a childhood spent in a refugee camp, the story's narrator describes a spirited and desperate competition among children scavenging in the market for discarded food. Even close friendships were subject to the logic of the emergency. "We worked all afternoon, Isam and I, struggling with the other children, or the shop owners or the truck drivers, sometimes even with the police," he recalls, adding matter-of-factly, "The rest of the time I fought with Isam."[58] Extraordinary strategies were necessary because, as he repeatedly asserts, "It was a time of hostilities." And what did this mean?

It was war-time. Not war really, but hostilities to be precise…a continued struggle with the enemy. In war the winds of peace gather the combatants to repose, truce, tranquility, the holiday of retreat. But this is not so with hostilities that are always never more than a gunshot away, where you are always walking miraculously between the shots. That's what it was, just as I was telling you, a time of hostilities…[but]…it wasn't a time of hostilities in the sense that you might think. That is, there wasn't really a war. In fact there was no war at all. The whole thing is that we were eighteen people from different generations living in one house, which would have been more than enough at any time. None of us had managed to find work, and hunger—

which you may have heard of--was our daily worry. That is what I call the time of hostilities. You know, there is absolutely no difference.[59]

One would be hard-pressed to find a more evocative expression of what endocolonization has meant for Palestinians.

In Palestinian poetry we find further images of how it feels to be an object of policies rooted in the freedom from want. Mahmoud Darwish's 1968 poem "A Naïve Song for the Red Cross" imagines a son questioning his father about the family's condition:

> When the sacks of flour are finished
> the full moon becomes a loaf in my eyes
> so why my father did you peddle my chants & my religion
> for crumbs & Kraft cheese
> in the warehouses of the Red Cross?
> O my father does the forest of olive trees
> shelter us when rain comes?
> & will the trees serve us better than fire?
> & will moonlight
> melt snow? or scorch off the spirits of darkness?
> I ask a million questions
> & see in your eyes the silence of the stone
> so answer me now my father: Are you my father
> or have I become a son of the Red Cross?

Here it is worth noting that refugees are what one scholar calls a "limit concept" with respect to the interstate system. By virtue of their exclusion from that system, argues Peter Nyers, refugees "make what is hidden come to light, thus 'unhinging' the nation-state-territory trinity that conventional theories of the state take for granted."[60] Similarly, refugees reveal the failure of the system to protect the factor—individual human life—that undergirds the state's sovereign power in the first place. Refugees thus perform a diagnostic function that threatens the ideological edifice of state power, and for this they are rewarded with some combination of abandonment, confinement and exploitation.

The Palestinian refugee problem was one of the first crises faced by the United Nations and thus an early test for an emerging era of international cooperation. Faced with a formidable dilemma, the UN ultimately was unable to achieve a just solution. By the middle of 1949 it had acquiesced, in effect, to the Israeli government's exceptionalist argument against the Palestinian right of return.[61] In lieu of repatriation, the organization created an entirely new bureaucratic structure, effectively displacing the refugee issue from the juridical to the humanitarian realm. The United Nations Relief and Works Agency for Palestinian Refugees in the Near East was built upon a foundation of liberal humanitarianism that had initially sought to rehabilitate refugees through involving them in public works projects.[62]

While providing employment to Palestinians and helping them avoid further social fragmentation, this approach nonetheless fit comfortably within the framework of "freedom from want." "Aid discourses," writes Julie Peteet, "implicitly classified refugees as spatially and culturally liminal; as deterritorialized people in need of humanitarian intervention."[63] This intervention, she notes, was carried out under a dense biopolitical canopy of regulations, assumptions and disciplinary practices. Consistent with the foundations of total peace, this canopy combined scientific and military elements while attempting to maintain the peace in refugee communities. The concept of minimal caloric intake provided the scientific rationale for the aid regime: each adult refugee was allotted a minimum of 1,300 calories per day to prevent starvation. Peteet reports that the United Nations Relief and Works Agency (UNRWA) also conceived of its relationship to refugees in military terms, using the Arabic word *nefar* (a military unit) to describe each registered refugee family.

Subject to the international aid regime or not, all Palestinians had to confront state power in new ways after 1948. Those remaining in Israel were suddenly defined as "non-Jews" in an explicitly Jewish state committed, as of July 1950, to a Law of Return offering Israeli citizenship to any Jew who wished to settle in the country. As with citizenship, so with land: the law of the Jewish National Fund (JNF) enabled a massive, state-enforced transfer of land into state (Jewish only) ownership, leaving the indigenous Palestinian population with a fraction of the land it had previously held.[64] Unequal treatment based on ethno-religious identity was thus built into Israeli society from its origins, both legally and in practice. As the new state was consolidating its identitarian project, it used the 1945 British emergency regulations to place the Palestinian population under military rule until 1966, presumably taking steps to ensure their freedom from want.[65]

Those Palestinians living in exile throughout the region and the wider world often found host governments less than welcoming. The majority were peasants who had been stripped of their land and their connection with Palestine's village-based agricultural economy.[66] As "sons [and daughters] of the Red Cross," these refugees often found that their own efforts at surviving and improving their situation brought them into contact with secret police, soldiers, border guards and other forces of state repression. To be a Palestinian was to risk death itself, a fate brilliantly described in Kanafani's allegorical novel *Men in the Sun*, in which a group of Palestinian labor migrants trying to cross the desert border from Iraq into Kuwait suffocate in a lorry's water tank while the border guards hassle the driver. In the end the driver dumps the bodies, leaving them to bleach in the scorching heat.[67]

Symbolizing all the repressive structures that confronted Palestinian refugees during this period, Kanafani's account of anonymous death in the desert illustrates a key fact conveniently ignored in narratives that celebrate the "successes" of Cold War nuclear deterrence: the more the superpowers deterred each other through fear, the more the poor of the Global South deterred one another through violence in a perpetual "time of hostilities." In this respect, deterrence is organically related to the process of deferral, eloquently articulated in Langston Hughes' 1951 poem on the status of the black American underclass, "A Dream Deferred." The new nations of the Third World found that the global wave of decolonization, an undeniably important world-historical shift driven in part by the mobilization of millions of people seeking to improve their lives, nonetheless came wrapped (as Fanon famously warned it might) in a political-economic package that too often translated into endless postponement of meaningful social transformation.

The post-*Nakba* experience of the Palestinians is diagnostic of this larger process. While the US pursued its policy of containing communism, Palestinian refugees were confined to camps in the hope that ensuring their freedom from want would prevent them from falling into another camp: the Soviet one. Thus the international community, despite its best intentions, effectively conspired to deter and defer the Palestinian question. Even the First World was not immune to the political implications of such policies, as the ascendance of the military-industrial complex fed a general consolidation of executive power whose consequences for the practice of democracy continue to be far-reaching. Humanity, in short, was the victim of a process through which politics itself was deterred.

All of these developments fly in the face of the rhetoric associated with the postwar international human rights regime, the stated intention of which was to establish standards that would apply to all regardless of their status as citizens. Once again, a close look at Palestine reveals a great deal. Time and again during the period since 1948, individuals and organizations who seek to advocate the rights of the Palestinian people at an international level have found their efforts frustrated by the inability of international law to trump state power in general, and the alliance between two exceptionalist settler states (the US and Israel) in particular.[68]

Palestinians and Jews emerged from the era of total war as populations whose shared vulnerability derived directly from the perpetuation of European anti-Semitism. Through the creation of the Israeli state, many Jews managed to rewrite the script of vulnerability, only to find themselves in a garrison state that incorporated most of its Jewish citizens into a permanent war machine. When that state reached the geographical limits of its exocolonial project in 1967, it did so as a new member of the nuclear club. Under the nuclear umbrella and Israel's military domination of the newly-captured territories, the lives of everyone living in Israel/Palestine were transformed in ways that are consistent with the realities of endocolonization. Already oriented toward the preparation for war, Israel's economy became partially dependent on Palestinian labor[69] and even more dependent on militarization in the form of perpetual counter-insurgency, and later, the saturating high-tech practices of "homeland security" (see Chapter 4). These later developments have built upon a turn toward neo-liberal restructuring that has had deep and predictable effects inside Israel.[70]

Palestinians living under Israeli control found that post-1967 endo-colonization initially meant being ensnared in a system of labor exploitation that involved not only the family disruption associated with migrating to work in Israel, but also the indignity of working to build a new society for others on the ruins of their own.[71] Over time, changes in Israeli economic policy, combined with the consolidation of Israel's exocolonial hold on the West Bank and East Jerusalem, left Palestinians confined to increasingly smaller areas and, in some cases (particularly in Gaza), reduced to "bare life." Equally important, as will be explored in the following chapter, having already been test subjects for the new "humanitarian" politics of total peace, Palestinians also became primary targets of the settler colonial "War on Terrorism."

3

SECURITIZATION

All of us are already civilian soldiers, without knowing it…The great stroke
of luck for the military class's terrorism is that no one recognizes it.

Paul Virilio

When Israel began the formal construction of its "separation barrier"
in 2002, comparisons to the Berlin Wall emerged almost immediately. Given the symbolic centrality of the latter to widely circulated
Cold War narratives, it was an obvious analogy, and not devoid of
some explanatory value. The more provocative analogy, however,
remained less visible. When placed in the context of the global history of settler colonialism, Israel's wall also bore echoes of the "rab-
bit-proof fence" erected in Australia at the start of the twentieth
century and later made famous by Phillip Noyce's 2002 feature film.
This alternative reading of the Israeli wall gains even more traction
in light of the fact that many of the same technologies used in its construction were also employed in the effort to build a new barrier
between Mexico and the settler colonial United States, giving a high ·
tech face to the longstanding project of controlling a border whose
legitimacy remains a point of significant contention.[1]

In a supposedly borderless world, however, the reality is that new frontiers can spring up anywhere—sometimes suddenly. In 2005, as Israel continued construction of its wall, a group of tourists, conference-goers and other individuals staying in hotels in the French Quarter in New Orleans instantly became refugees when Hurricane Katrina hit the city. Barred by law enforcement officials from entering the Superdome and Convention Center shelters that were allegedly "descending into chaos and squalor," they were told to walk to the New Orleans Bridge that spans the Mississippi River. Upon arriving at the bridge, however, they were greeted not by the promised buses waiting to take them to safety, but by police guns firing over their heads. What was normally a bustling highway bridge designed to facilitate the speedy and free flow of commerce and human traffic had suddenly become a separation barrier.

Two paramedics who were part of the French Quarter refugee group recall what happened when they tried to speak to some of the officers, who were from the nearby city of Gretna (on the west side of the river):

We questioned why we couldn't cross the bridge anyway, especially as there was little traffic on the 6-lane highway. They responded that the West Bank was not going to become New Orleans and there would be no Superdomes in their City. These were code words for if you are poor and black, you are not crossing the Mississippi River and you were not getting out of New Orleans.[2]

In desperately trying to "secure" their local community in this way, the officers were probably unaware that they were employing a classic and deeply racialized settler colonial device. Equally important, they were also blind to the ironic significance of their own upside-down statement. New Orleans, after all, had already been the West Bank for a long time.

Settler colonialism is a political creature that refuses to speak its own name. It speaks instead of security.[3] Like the magician who distracts his audience by focusing attention on his left hand while the right hand does the important work, it whispers, lectures and jokes about, and sometimes screams security in the hope of keeping the structural truths of colonization hidden. It is an ironically appropriate rhetorical move, for it reveals a deep-seated insecurity born of settler colonialism's particular mix of denial, guilt, fear, avarice and triumphalism.[4] Still living out the logic of the frontier that began with its youthful indiscretions, and haunted by its own refusal to confront its identity, settler colonialism bears a heavy responsibility for one of Global Palestine's most pervasive contemporary features: the politics of securitization.

Securitization is defined here as the growing dominance of security as the central element in an emerging, transpolitical paradigm of governance, administration and social life. This chapter will analyze how particular elements within the ongoing history of settler colonialism have helped push securitization forward in the form of what amounts to a generalized process of social militarization. If this recalls the endocolonization and "pure war" discussed in the previous chapter, this is no accident, for all of these processes exist in a kind of symbiotic relationship. The postwar shift toward endocolonization and pure war provides an ideal environment for the growth and diffusion of securitization, while the latter provides a language that gives meaning to this environment and, more generally, serves to hide the deep structures of colonization from view. At the same time, one may posit that securitization carries out its own project of colonization: a colonization of consciousness that turns everyone into "civilian soldiers."

While the age of settler colonialism extends over several centuries, the focus of this chapter is on the period that has been called the "long 1960s," extending roughly from the late 1940s to the mid-1970s.[5] In addition to the emergence of the military-industrial complex, this crucial period saw the rise of a new wave of "antisystemic movements," including resistance movements struggling against settler colonial projects.[6] It is my contention that the specific response of settler states to these movements points toward a broader understanding of the organic role that settler colonialism has played in creating the conditions for certain types of securitization whose global reach of which becomes more evident every day.

Following a brief conceptual overview of the linkages between settler colonialism and securitization, this chapter will examine the convergence of movements resisting settler colonialism during the long

1960s and the revolutionary nature of the challenge posed by these movements, both individually and through the links of solidarity among them. This is followed by a discussion of how settler states responded to these movements by designating "terrorism"—an old idea given new life during this period—as an object of study and counterinsurgency and, principally, a way to delegitimize the grievances of subaltern populations. The chapter concludes with some remarks on how the agonistic encounter between settler colonialism and its discontents has helped lay the groundwork for the current security-obsessed politics.

Settler Colonialism and Securitization

The term "security" has arguably become the most important master term of global politics in the twenty-first century, its fine ideological dust permeating every nook and cranny of social life. Powerful nation-states and social institutions appear to possess a formidable stranglehold on the discourse of security, yet evidence of the discourse's extraordinary ubiquity is visible even in those places where the powerful are being subjected to critical scrutiny. In the United Nations Human Rights Council's 2009 "Goldstone Report" (named after its lead investigator, South African Judge Richard Goldstone) on Israel's December 2008 "Operation Cast Lead" assault on Gaza, for example, the word security appears almost 400 times, effectively constituting the discursive envelope within which the entire narrative is contained. References to security include: security forces, security services, security agencies, security officers, security responsibilities, security control, security apparatus, security personnel, security institutions, security functions, security studies, security needs, security risks, security prisoners, national security, internal security, food security, economic security, military security and preventive security. All of these make their appearance along with the names of various formal institutions that are defined explicitly in terms of security: Israel's General Security Services/Israeli Security Agency, the various branches of the official Palestinian security forces and the UN Security Council.

Some of the report's references to security, of course, are rooted in the noble desire to recognize the security concerns of the Gaza residents (most of them refugees) who bore the brunt of the Israeli assault. For decades life in Gaza has been overdetermined by the macropolitics of statelessness and "de-development";[7] the spatial politics of enclosure, ghettroization and overcrowding; and the daily micropolitics of violence, poverty, and despair—in short, by a fundamental state of insecurity. The UN report, despite frantic attempts by supporters of Israel to discredit it and Judge Goldstone, played a key role in helping bring Gaza's plight into a wider public consciousness and focusing attention on the crimes that took place there during the Israeli assault. Nonetheless, it is significant that for all the references to security, it contains not a single reference to colonization. Despite its importance in helping peel away the veneer of impunity surrounding the Israeli war machine, the report also played the role of magician's assistant.

It is difficult to escape the conclusion that it is the politics of security itself—in this case, Zionism's endless settler colonial security quest and the kinds of resistance that it continues to provoke—that serves to keep Gaza in a state where, in the words of the Palestinian journalist and *Gaza Mom* blogger Leila El-Haddad, "there is no 'safe'." A regular contributor to Al-Jazeera English and *The Guardian*, El-Haddad found herself in the United States when Israel launched its attack on Gaza. Her blog entries from those days are documents of insecurity, as when she describes trying to keep tabs on her parents amidst the fighting:

When the bombs are dropped around them, they send me a quick note to inform me of what happened before running to safety. I am still not sure where "safety" is; and neither, I think, do they. It is perhaps more a mental state and place than a physical one. In any other situations, people flee to where they perceive are safer locations. In Gaza, there is no "safe." And there is nowhere to flee to, with the borders closed, the sky and sea under siege.[8]

El-Haddad's testimony illustrates that from the perspective of those who have been directly victimized by settler colonialism and its structural footprints, the politics of security provides yet more evidence to illustrate Walter Benjamin's "permanent state of emergency." Indeed, the experience of perpetual insecurity is the origin of the "tradition of the oppressed" about which Benjamin wrote so powerfully.

Yet it has also been evident in recent years that even the most privileged groups are hardly immune from the processes that a security-obsessed politics sets in motion. The wealthy South African who lives behind a massive security fence in Johannesburg, the Israeli Jewish voter who supports a right-wing party in the hope that it will bring security by continuing to build walls around Palestinians, the American who drives in and out of her gated community in a mobile gated community (a.k.a. an SUV) equipped with an On Star "Advanced Automatic Crash Response" system—all of them, whether they realize it or not, are living in a world that is increasingly shaped by the politics of securitization.

Scholars of international relations typically use the term "securitization" to designate processes through which states and other political actors make particular issues into security issues through the use of certain kinds of rhetoric.[9] So, for example, one might imagine governments designating global climate change as a national security issue (as indeed some have already done), thereby securitizing what had previously been viewed more narrowly as an environmental issue. While valuable in illuminating some of the workings of security discourse, the international relations approach is limited by the field's general tendency to privilege those phenomena that can be attributed to the intentional decisions of rational actors. The approach I have taken in this book seeks to go beyond these limitations by viewing securitization as a much broader set of processes that inevitably exceeds a narrow politics of control. It is, in other words, a deep structure that bleeds through the entire social field.

Building upon Dwight D. Eisenhower's famous warning issued as he prepared to leave the White House in January 1961, numerous critics have called attention to the profound effects of the "military-industrial complex" on the nature of US society.[10] These critiques hint at how securitization works as a kind of generalized cultural logic that helps explain, to quote the title of a documentary on the subject, "why we fight."[11] What happens, however, when we name the US a settler colonial society and connect its history with that of other, similar societies? How might this help to build a transnational understanding of securitization? And what does this indicate in regards to Global Palestine?

Settler colonialism's demiurgic, foundational impulse to replace an existing society with a new one gives it a pivotal role in one of the most important global stories of our time: the story of how the world of sovereign war waged against specific external enemies has gradually given way, as discussed in the previous chapter, to the endocolonial world of permanent war. The most influential discussion of this shift is to be found in Michel Foucault's famous 1975–1976 series of lectures at the College de France, lectures that have spurred a whole range of recent scholarly explorations into the nature of war, sovereignty and "biopower."[12] Grounded in a close reading of political philosophy and European history, Foucault's lectures do not discuss settler colonialism as such, nor do they offer anything like a detailed reading of Europe's long history of exocolonization.[13] Nonetheless, the lectures provide important conceptual clues that can aid in understanding how the deep structures of settler colonialism have left their fingerprints on today's politics of securitization.

As an artifact of what might be called mass political psychology, securitization is rooted in the desire to create, define and/or defend a "safe" space that is insulated against various kinds of "threats." As such, it seeks to preserve the possibility of a meaningful distinction between "inside" and "outside" spaces. If the threat is understood to be located inside, the securitizing impulse is to expel it, eliminate it or, if necessary, create a new inside (or at least the illusion of it) by erecting new kinds of borders. What might seem like an abstract process becomes very concrete when one considers how easily the perception of a "threat"—like the French Quarter refugees, Palestinian bombers, "illegal immigrants," or "sleeper cells"—can generate responses both immediate (e.g., the police shootings after Hurricane Katrina) and far-reaching (e.g., the construction of the Israeli wall or the creation of the US Department of Homeland Security).

All of this, however, is happening in a world where everything is now "inside," a world that is increasingly defined by the politics of (en)closure. As discussed in Chapter 2, nuclear enclosure enabled endocolonization by bringing the world under a single, apocalyptic umbrella, but other kinds of enclosure are equally salient. Neo-liberal enclosure, for example, incorporates more and more of life and social relations into a global system dominated by finance capital and the undemocratic institutions that serve its interests. The kind of planetary enclosure that is produced as technologies of communication, acceleration and violence generate new modes of enveloping the world is another example.[14]

This politics of enclosure has not stopped the powerful from strategically designating divisions between "internal" and "external" spaces in order to create optimal conditions for social control. Individuals are particularly susceptible to such manipulation today because everybody seeks "security" at a time when it appears to be increasingly elusive. This dynamic, which has become an unavoidable and often invisible part of everyday life, can be viewed through the lens of Foucault's discussion of sovereignty and permanent war. In his reading of the philosopher Thomas Hobbes, Foucault observes that sovereignty emerged (in the form of the State) as an attempt to tame the power of permanent war—a power that resided, in Hobbes time in those who saw absolute rebellion as the only legitimate way to resist the Norman conquest of England. Despite the success of that conquest (a transformation that obviously continues to structure life in England to this day in innumerable ways), the impulse toward permanent war remained active and later became racialized (in the modern sense) through the process of European exocolonial conquest.

Today one could argue that both the State and its enemies, all of whom are operating in a radically "enclosed" world, are equally invested in permanent war. This helps explain why, in Leerom Medovoi's words: "Everyone who threatens the globe's civil order is, at this point, conceived as internal to it but simultaneously also as fair game for the open warfare formerly declared only against external enemies."[15] It also helps explain how state and non-state actors have combined to produce a world where securitization is endemic but security is in shorter and shorter supply. States, of course, continue to leverage sovereignty as well, even as they try to ride the tiger of permanent war—hence the inconsistent (some might say hypocritical) relationship of certain states to international law and its application. The fact that some of the most hypocritical states are also settler colonial states, however, is a detail that has not received sufficient attention to date. This settler colonial connection offers us a clue to the deeper historical roots of the patterns described in this book.

The key to understanding the relationship between settler colonialism and the contemporary politics of securitization lies in the concept of the frontier. Settler colonial invasion does not only represent "external" colonial warfare—the extension of European power over its "outside." By its very nature, settler colonialism treats "internal" and "external" as inherently malleable categories, as "facts" to be "created" (and recreated) at will. Every time the frontier moves, the line between "inside" and "outside" changes—but the point is that it was never really a line in the first place. (In the words of a slogan that has become popular among Mexican migrants, "We didn't cross the border—the border crossed us!") The fact that the state of Israel has never officially declared its own borders is a perfect illustration of this logic: Israeli governments routinely claim the right to act anytime and anywhere in defense of a state that is the living embodiment of the peripatetic settler colonial frontier.[16]

Seen from this perspective, it is clear that settler colonial projects are always already grounded both in the discourse of sovereignty and in the discourse of permanent war. They often seek to act as sovereigns in relation to various enemies, but through the expansionist and exceptionalist operation of the "logic of elimination" they also come to employ the tools of permanent war in an effort to purge the colonized—whether through expulsion, killing, juridical exclusion or biocultural assimilation—from the expanding social body that was created by the "opening" and "closing" of the frontier.[17] In short, settler colonialism, whose actualization on the ground is almost unthinkable without some notion of a biologized other against which "society must be defended," perfectly embodies the story that Foucault so eloquently narrates.

All of this sheds light on the particular geo-political orientation of settler states that claim the "exceptional" right to ignore international law, whether using a rhetoric of necessity, or emergency,[18] or simply claiming the moral high ground. This orientation is the contemporary manifestation of a frontier mentality that combines two related elements. The first is the sovereign arrogance of the frontier sheriff who claims to respect the law but also claims, at key moments, to be the law. The second is the permanent war waged by the frontier rabble, a war whose racist and often genocidal tendencies suggest a terrifyingly simple mantra connected with the settler desire to become indigenous: "they" must die so that "we" may live.[19]

The "Settler international" and the Long 1960s

The post-WWII years have been overlaid with a wide array of geopolitical characterizations that organize history and geography in very specific and taken for granted ways. These include the binary rhetoric of the Cold War and its associated categories ("East" and "West," NATO and the Warsaw Pact, etc.); the demarcation of history according to specific armed conflicts and other crises (Korea, Cuba, Vietnam, Gulf War, etc.); and the general (and often uncritical) narrative of postwar decolonization.[20] In most cases, these constructions both stem from and continually validate the perspectives and self-fashioned identities of powerful states. The relative smoothness of such a process, however, is interrupted as soon as the political deck is slightly reshuffled. For example, shifting attention from an official alliance such as NATO to an unofficial one such as the "settler international" (a term designating the convergence of interest and action among settler colonial states) takes us beyond the self-representations of the powerful and opens up new analytical possibilities.[21]

The global shift toward permanent war gained momentum in the years after 1945, and it is worth remembering that along with a wave of decolonization, these years brought a series of settler colonial victories. Consider 1948, which is in many ways the starting point of the long 1960s. Armed with the Truman Doctrine, the United States emerged as a global power and flexed its muscles by spearheading the Berlin Airlift—an early example of the kind of militarized humanitarianism that has become ideologically seductive in our own time.[22] The list of countries that aided in the Airlift reads like a who's who of settler colonialism: Britain, Australia, Canada, New Zealand and South Africa.[23] Internally, the US was inaugurating the next phase of its settler project by moving away from the "retribalization" approach of the 1934 Indian Reorganization Act—an approach that relied explicitly on blood quantum requirements to determine the allotment each individual would receive from the state—and toward a "detribalization" approach that aimed to move the country's indigenous population into cities.[24]

In the same year (1948), the state of Israel emerged (literally) on the ruins of Palestinian society and inaugurated an eighteen-year period of military rule over those Palestinians who remained inside the borders of the new state. It is no small irony that 1948 is the same year that saw the United Nations General Assembly ratify the Universal Declaration on Human Rights (UDHR). The irony only deepens when we recall that 1948 is also the year that inaugurated the institutionalization of apartheid in settler colonial South Africa following the victory of the National Party (NP) in white-only elections. The UDHR sought to establish a global standard for human rights, including the right of all human beings to "equal protection" against all forms of discrimination. Undeterred, the victorious NP, led by D.F. Malan, began the full-scale implementation of the apartheid system with the Mixed Marriages Act (1949), followed in subsequent years by the Group Areas Act and the Population Registration Act (1950), the Suppression of Communism Act (1950), the Bantu Authorities Act (1951), the Pass Laws (1952), the Bantu Education Act (1953) and the Natives Resettlement Act (1954) (among other prominent pieces of legislation).

If 1948 marked the first chapter of settler colonialism's long 1960s, the second chapter began with the March 1960 Sharpeville massacre, in which South African police killed sixty-nine demonstrators protesting the infamous Pass Laws. The massacre and the subsequent banning of the main anti-apartheid organizations led the African National Congress (ANC) to abandon its policy of nonviolence and set up an armed wing, *Umkhonto we Sizwe*. During the next fifteen years, settler states confronted a series of armed resistance movements including the ANC, the Pan-Africanist Congress (PAC), the AIM (and related indigenous movements in North America), the Black Panther Party, Fatah, and the Popular Front for the Liberation of Palestine (PFLP).

Highlighting the co-emergence of these militant movements during the long 1960s helps to reorient one's understanding of a turbulent period that is often viewed, through the narrow prism of the US experience and its hegemonic narrative, as a story of subordinate groups seeking full inclusion within democratic systems. While not without some merit, such a view minimizes the radical nature of the global challenge that resistance movements posed to ongoing settler colonial projects during this period. These movements represented more than security threats to the democratic state; they signaled the aggressive return of those whose exclusion had enabled the state to come into existence in the first place. That is, they called attention to the precise element that settler states, through their own rhetoric of "democratic" exceptionalism, most urgently seek to deny: their past and present identity as settler states.

The long 1960s thus represented not only a crisis for democracy, but also a fundamental, albeit largely unacknowledged crisis for settler colonialism. This crisis, not coincidentally, emerged during a period when settler states were solidifying the alliances among them. Nuclear cooperation between Israel and South Africa, for example, began in the 1950s, and the apartheid regime began regular uranium shipments to Israel in 1963 in exchange for nuclear technology assistance.[25] In the same year, the Kennedy administration's sale of Hawk missiles to Israel heralded the gradual emergence of the "special relationship" that would solidify under Lyndon Johnson.[26] The US-South Africa relationship also strengthened during this period, with the Nixon administration adopting a policy designed to shore up white power against the rising tide of African nationalism.[27] These robust strategic partnerships among settler states helped Israel and South Africa cement their status as regional powers even as they increasingly came to be viewed as international pariahs.

Meanwhile, the US and the Soviet Union were busy building a machine of Mutually Assured Destruction (MAD) that animated the high-stakes screenplay of the Cold War. Once again, however, conventional categories and periodizations can hide as much as they reveal.[28] Foregrounding the deep structures of settler colonialism can decenter those Cold War chronologies that end tidily in 1989. From the western half of North America to the vast aboriginal territories of Australia, for example, it is estimated that as much as 70 per cent of the world's uranium is located on indigenous lands. Yet narratives of the Cold War period routinely downplay or ignore the question of the origin of the minerals used to fuel the MAD machine.[29] Moreover, indigenous people, particularly women, have long been impacted disproportionately by nuclear waste disposal and nuclear testing in places such as the Marshall Islands.[30]

This means that endocolonization, enabled by the aforementioned nuclear enclosure, cannot be separated from the settler colonial politics of resource extraction. Consider that at the height of the "uranium rush" in North America, members of the Navajo Nation and other indigenous groups saw some of their lands labeled by the National Academy of Sciences, without irony, as "national sacrifice areas."[31] Almost overnight, small communities like Grants, New Mexico became nuclear boom towns. Soon after, they began attracting the attention of activists in a burgeoning anti-nuclear movement that often made common cause with the growing movement for indigenous liberation. In addition to producing disastrous health consequences (water contamination, rising rates of lung cancer and radioactive waste spills), the "uranium rush" exacerbated political tensions within native communities. Some tribal leaders formed an assimilationist class that sought to profit from mining deals, while young radicals joined traditional elders in a coalition that sought to resist the exploitation of resources on native lands.

"We are unwilling to submit to either the tyranny of exploitation by energy companies," declared one Navajo Tribal Council member in 1979, "or the tyranny of regulation by federal agencies who are responsible to no one else than their own desires to experiment with the future of America."[32] To this, one can only add that in seeking to secure its own existence, the settler state was also experimenting with the future of the planet.

Globalized Resistance to Settler Colonialism

Settler colonialism establishes a series of deep structures, including pervasive systems of physical and rhetorical exclusion that seek to deny the political will of the colonized while also establishing the indigeneity of the colonizers and their descendants. When John Trudell observed in 1969 that "we have never really seen the war go away," he demonstrated that from the perspective of the colonized, the enduring and ongoing nature of colonization is an immanent, axiomatic reality. Consequently, the question of how to resist the structural violence of colonization outlasted the moment of invasion, extended into the long 1960s, and is present today.

This resistance has adopted many titles: war, rebellion, uprising, intifada, armed struggle, and of course (as will be discussed below) "terrorism." Underneath all of this, however, is the kind of permanent war with which the victims of settler colonialism have a complex, two-sided relationship. On the one hand, their presence on the land makes them targets of permanent war in the form of everything from settler attacks to organized state violence and repression. They are also, however, inheritors of what Foucault describes as the original discourse of permanent war (what he calls "race war"): the discourse of those who sought to resist the transformation wrought by the Norman invasion. Permanent war, in other words, is an artifact not of any specific actor alone, but rather of the relationships set in motion by global colonization.[33] In settler colonial spaces, some of the most aggressive settler voices are those who have their own history of victimization. The colonization of North America or Australia thus continues to occur in the long shadow of the Norman invasion, just as the colonization of Palestine perpetuates the story of European racism.[34]

Despite the shared nature of the discourse of permanent war, it is important to distinguish those who wage permanent war for purposes of conquest from those who use it for purposes of self-defense. Settlers who employ these tools are not simply acting out a script; to a significant extent they have chosen a particular path while ignoring other possible paths.[35] The path of aggressive settler violence is attractive precisely because it often presents itself as defensive: the frontier must be protected, the wagons must be circled! Such a framing is already persuasive in the early stages of the settler project, but it becomes even more so as settlers begin to view themselves as indigenous—that is, as "natives" who are engaging not in colonization, but in a simple search for security.

For those whose territory is being invaded, the picture is somewhat simpler and the defensive nature of permanent war is undeniable. The concept of popular defense, deriving from Virilio's 1978 book on the subject, is a very useful way to frame such efforts. "The principle aim of any truly popular [defense]," he writes, "is...to oppose the establishment of a social situation based solely on the illegality of armed force, which reduces a population to the status of a *movable slave*, a *commodity*."[36] On this view, popular defense is a venerable human tradition connected with the attempt to resist the particular kinds of exploitation that come with the centralization of political authority (e.g., in the form of the State).[37] It is also a useful way to frame settler colonialism's politics of violence. After all, when not seeking to eliminate indigenous people directly through mass killing, settler projects seek to turn them into "movable slaves" by displacing, confining and disenfranchising them through a diverse array of violent measures.

This framing is evocative of what Palestinians have experienced since 1948: from the original dispossession of the *Nakba* to the structural violence of Israel's domination of the West Bank and Gaza, specific episodes of state violence such as the 1982 Sabra and Shatila massacres and more recently "Operation Cast Lead." The question of whether Zionist/Israeli policy vis-à-vis the Palestinians is genocidal or merely "politicidal"—that is, seeking to eliminate permanently the conditions that would enable Palestinians to express their national political will—remains open and subject to debate.[38] There is no question, however, that in Palestine the settler colonial logic of elimination has taken the specific form of a "national delocalization," a process that created "a whole nation as movable object": the global Palestinian diaspora.[39]

Settler colonialism's permanent war produces an equally diverse array of forms of resistance. In this light, it is clear that the concept of popular defense is relevant to many acts of organized resistance to settler colonialism, from Nat Turner's 1831 slave rebellion to the late nineteenth-century Ghost Dance movement to the anti-apartheid struggle. In Palestine, resistance to the Zionist project began as soon as that project had hit the ground, with early forms of popular defense laying the groundwork for the more recent intifadas and other campaigns of mass opposition to Israeli domination.[40]

The long 1960s was an important period of global experimentation in the art of popular defense. Throughout this period—in addition to exploring a range of militant strategies for combating the ongoing effects of settler colonialism—resistance movements were exploring the possibilities for building transnational solidarity with the victims of other settler projects. The well-known ideological and organizational connections between the anti-apartheid movement and the Palestinian liberation struggle symbolize the creation of a diverse global coalition that mirrored the state-level "settler international." This coalition was inevitably unstable, uneven and prone to fissures reflecting both local colonial specificities and the varying ideological frameworks active within them (e.g., Marxism, nationalism and black consciousness). Nonetheless, the strong family resemblance shared by all settler colonial situations provided regular opportunities for bridge-building.

The Black Power movement in the US, for example, had a profound influence on the generation of Koori (Aboriginal) Australian activists who emerged in the late 1960s. According to historian Gary Foley, a member of the movement, one of the key factors in the growth of Koori "black consciousness" in Australia was the number of black American servicemen who visited Sydney on leave from their tours of duty in Vietnam. These black GIs, Foley notes, "often gravitated toward the Sydney Black community" and shared "the latest in African-American political literature and music" with their hosts. The nurturing of these "black Pacific" relationships left an indelible mark on Australia's indigenous rights activists, who found themselves reading not only Fanon and Camus, but also Angela Davis and Eldridge Cleaver.

Foley emphasizes that he and his fellow activists were equally aware of the burgeoning indigenous movement in North America. The occupation of Alcatraz Island, coming just a few months after a Caribbean scholar had given an important lecture in Melbourne on Black Power, caught the attention of Sydney's emerging black urban radicals. Referring to Dee Brown's influential history of how the "logic of elimination" unfolded in the US in the nineteenth century, Foley recalls that for Koori activists: "*Bury My Heart At Wounded Knee* was as widely read as [Cleaver's] *Soul on Ice*."[41]

Situating their own struggle firmly in a narrative of decolonization, these activists drew equally on the community defense tactics of the Black Panther Party, the potent symbolism of the Alcatraz occupation, and the political frameworks associated with the anti-apartheid struggle. A 1971 tour of Australia by the South African Springbok rugby union team—an iconic repository of white Afrikaner nationalism—provided an opportunity for Koori activists to globalize their own message of resistance. A year later, with Alcatraz fresh in their minds, they launched their most successful action: the creation of a controversial tent encampment on the grounds of Parliament House in Canberra. Known as the Aboriginal Embassy, this provocative piece of "nomadic resistance" and "collapsible architecture" generated unprecedented public attention for the indigenous rights cause.[42]

Transnational connections among resistance movements during the long 1960s were equally products of the shared experiences of both covert and overt state violence. The US government's secret Counter Intelligence Program (COINTELPRO), which targeted domestic activists throughout this period,[43] has its counterpart in the efforts of the Australian state, via the 21 Division of the New South Wales police, to undermine the work of Black Power activists there.[44] The killing of Black Panther leader Fred Hampton mirrors the targeting of anti-apartheid activists such as Steve Biko. More broadly, the open use of police violence was a regular feature of the settler state response to dissident movements across the globe, including the fire hoses of Birmingham, a police assault on the Aboriginal Embassy in Canberra, the Israeli government's heavy-handed suppression of the 1976 demonstrations subsequently known as Land Day, and the killing of hundreds of demonstrators during the Soweto Uprising in the same year.

While protesters were being killed in Israel and South Africa, the US was celebrating its bicentennial and, in a relatively unheralded move, passing the 1976 Arms Control Export Act (ACEA). Ostensibly designed to prohibit recipients of US weapons from using them outside their own borders, the ACEA may be read as a symbolic attempt to fortify the distinction between external and internal spaces of violence. As we have seen, however, settler colonialism has long rendered this distinction meaningless through its own practice.[45] In this light, John F. Kennedy's decision to declare the era of the "New Frontier" may be read (unconventionally) not as a sea change in US politics, but rather as an indication of how the long 1960s gave renewed momentum to settler colonialism both globally, and within the US.[46] By the end of that period, settler states were using their military might to openly project their power against all perceived enemies, regardless of location.

Two examples from North America reveal both the level of force concentrated in the hands of the settler state and the ideological fragility that lay beneath its persistent union of internal and external violence. In early 1973 US Marshals responded to the AIM occupation of Wounded Knee (South Dakota) by mounting a lengthy siege of the village, located near the site of the infamous 1890 massacre of Lakota Sioux by soldiers of the US 7th Cavalry. The officers sent by the Pentagon to South Dakota in 1973 had at their disposal a collection of military hardware and personnel that could easily have come right off the battlefields of Vietnam, including:

17 APCs [Armored Personnel Carriers], 130,000 rounds of M-16 ammunition, 41,000 rounds of M-40 high explosive, as well as helicopters, Phantom jets, and personnel. Military officers, supply sergeants, maintenance technicians, chemical officers, and medical teams remained on duty throughout the 71 day siege, all working in civilian clothes [to conceal their unconstitutional involvement in this "civil disorder"].[47]

The gross imbalance in the forces arrayed at Wounded Knee—the AIM activists were armed with rifles, but hardly posed a significant threat to the military might of the US government—only illustrates the depth of the American insecurities that were revealed in the government's response. From an AIM perspective, this was arguably the action's greatest success: to peel away the thin ideological veneer protecting the settler colonial war machine.

Some seventeen years later, a remarkably similar event (the "Oka crisis") took place in Quebec, where a small group of Mohawk activists responded to the planned expansion of a golf course into a sacred pine grove by occupying the territory in question and blockading a major bridge near Montreal.[48] The response of the provincial and federal authorities was predictable when seen within the trajectory of settler colonialism and its particular anxieties: "6000 soldiers of the Canadian army, complete with tanks, armored personnel carriers, and even TOW [Tube-launched, Optically tracked, Wire command data link] missiles, the greater part of the Quebec provincial police, and the RCMP [Royal Canadian Mounted Police]" converged to restore "order."[49]

The combined use of police power and heavy weaponry in these two examples illustrates the sharp militarization of settler state violence waged in response to resistance movements during the long 1960s and beyond.[50] Symbolic of this shift was the decision by South African authorities to employ the Casspir armored personnel carrier, originally designed for use in counterinsurgency campaigns in neighboring countries, for combating urban township resistance. Later used by US forces in Iraq and Afghanistan, the Casspir also inspired the creation of the US-built Buffalo armed vehicle—yet another example (like the Apache attack helicopter, the Mohawk reconnaissance aircraft or the Israeli Sabra battle tank) of settler colonial states naming their weapons through the appropriation of indigenous imagery.[51]

More than random examples bearing a passing resemblance, the kinds of actions invoked in this section reveal at least two important features of the permanent war between settler colonialism and its discontents. First, these actions are emblematic of how individual settler states sought to deal with their own problems via a highly securitized logic that saw internal and external violence as intimately connected. The apartheid government under P.W. Botha voiced this logic most explicitly, designating a "total strategy" that combined intense repression of anti-apartheid activists (indeed, of entire communities) within its own borders with the overt and covert destabilization of the neighboring "Front-Line States" that were providing support to the groups seeking majority rule in South Africa.

Beyond the level of individual state policy, however, we can also identify a second feature of this permanent war: the formation by the "settler international" of what amounted to a collaborative, globalized agenda for defending settler projects and privileges against resistance movements that were themselves globalized. Here it is perhaps helpful to cast a glance back two centuries to the American Revolution, which employed nationalism and the nation-state as a mechanism to short-circuit the revolutionary potential of working class solidarity.[52] Settler colonialism must always be on guard against this kind of possibility precisely because it creates the conditions for the emergence of such solidarities, in the first place, through its own actions. As will be discussed in the subsequent section, contemporary settler states have waged their permanent war by drawing heavily on a discursive formation they had played a central role in constructing during the latter part of the long 1960s: the discourse of something they labeled "terrorism."

The (Re)Invention of Terrorism

The Palestinian revolution's particular response to its "national delocalization" played a pivotal and prophetic role in shaping how this phase of settler colonialism's permanent war would help define the contours of transnational securitization. More than simply impacting the encounter with Zionism, the response of radical groups such as the PFLP was necessarily a global response with global implications. Crucially, this response began with a fateful decision that represented, in effect, a quantum leap not just around but beyond national sovereignty: facing an expansionist and exceptionalist settler colonial enemy, the Palestinian revolutionaries created their own "New Frontier."

The medium for the creation of this frontier was a series of hijackings, kidnappings, and other high-profile actions, some carried out in collaboration with other non-state groups. These actions were built upon a recognition that the realities of globalization made it possible—indeed essential—to fight the enemy in new kinds of "territory." To his credit, Virilio saw the significance of this move more than thirty years ago, noting that the hijackings represented "a migration gone airborne" on the part of people who had "stopped being *legal* inhabitants of the Earth."[53] Living diasporically in a hypermediated world of time-space compression, the hijackers turned the increasingly sophisticated networks of global transport and communication—airplanes, airport runways and the airwaves of the global media—to their own advantage in much the same way as anarchist revolutionaries had done with the earlier communications technologies during the period of "early globalization."[54]

In this sense, the long 1960s saw the convergence of not one, but two dialectically related occupations. First, Israeli Jews occupied Palestine, extending their settler colonial project to the remaining territories of historic Palestine following the 1967 war, a development that coincided with Israel's emergence as a nuclear power. Second, Palestinians began to occupy the world not only diasporically, but also mediatically: the media became their territory.[55] This is not to say that Palestine, the geographic location, ceased to exist, nor that its inhabitants ceased to engage in their own forms of locally grounded resistance. Nonetheless, the globalized intervention of the Palestinian hijackers had an undeniable effect on the struggle with Zionism and more generally on the global politics of securitization. In the process, the dominant image of the Palestinian was dramatically transformed from the pitiful and occasionally threatening refugee to the bomb-wielding, hostage-taking "terrorist."

It is equally hard to overestimate the global significance of the Israeli state's response to this development. In a fascinating 1982 dialogue with Sylvere Lotringer, Virilio highlights Israel's 4 July 1976 raid on Entebbe Airport in Uganda, a response to the hijacking by two Palestinians and two Germans of an Air France jet that had taken off from Tel Aviv. The rescue operation mounted by Israeli special forces was a model of settler colonial convergence, coming in the immediate aftermath of the 16 June Soweto uprising in South Africa and just hours before the official celebration of the US bicentennial. Virilio views the raid as heralding a new and frightening age of globalized state terrorism:

By what right did the Israeli air force go to Entebbe? By what right did it go to Beirut [in 1982]? This takes us far beyond the field of politics. When you see the difficulties political regimes have resisting terrorism...you can image [sic] the problems the international community has in trying to stop State terrorism...In the beginning there were the Palestinians: they hijacked a plane with 200 passengers. So what do you do? Do you kill them, and yourself along with them? From the moment that the state has strengthened itself against individual terrorism—the Red Brigades, Baader-Meinhof or the Palestinians—by developing its own brand of terrorism, you have to wonder what high court could prevent this infinite spreading of State crimes, of acts of war without war.[56]

Palestinian hijacking, of course, did not emerge "in the beginning" of anything; on the contrary, it represented the particular response of a group of revolutionaries to a set of circumstances they did not choose. The point here is that settler colonialism in Palestine generated a specific relationship between Israelis and Palestinians, and this relationship, in turn, generated a situation in which "acts of war without war" gradually became the normal mode of operation.

It is tempting to view this development as entirely expected given what is known about the dynamics that colonization typically sets in motion. The deadly colonial dance tends to produce a self-perpetuating cycle of violent reprisal, a cycle perhaps best illustrated in Gillo Pontecorvo's classic film *The Battle of Algiers*, in which the French authorities and the Algerian revolutionaries take turns escalating the conflict until the cost of occupation becomes too high and the French are forced to withdraw. The globalized process Virilio identifies, however, is something else altogether. In going "far beyond the field of politics," it represents the moment when settler colonialism and its discontents unwittingly collaborated to produce a situation in which everyone is coerced into thinking like a settler—or a native. It is, in other words, the prehistory of the more contemporary post-9/11 period in which some are claiming "we are all Israelis now"[57] while others are in the streets in Toronto, Madrid or Istanbul chanting "we are all Palestinians."

The full weight of these developments only emerges if the concept of "terrorism" and its growing centrality as a crucial ideological support for the securitization of politics and social life across the globe is closely examined. This concept has roots in earlier historical periods, most notably the French Revolution and its associated "Reign of

Terror" but also the period of global anarchist violence leading up to World War I. The "terrorism" that is now a household name, however, re-emerged during the long 1960s in the context of the ongoing struggles between settler colonial and other powerful states on the one hand, and subaltern resistance movements on the other.

Taking their cue from George Orwell's classic analysis of politics and language, numerous analysts have pointed out how the word "terrorism" functions as a simple but effective political label designed to delegitimize forms of asymmetrical political violence carried out by non-state groups against the interests of powerful states.[58] As the now-clichéd critique goes, "one person's terrorist is another person's freedom fighter." The political utility of the term is obvious: it focuses attention on the violence of the other while implicitly justifying any state action taken against the "terrorists." The discourse is successful to the extent that it hides not only the state's role in provoking "terrorist" violence in the first place, but also the fact that states themselves are guilty of perpetrating comparatively greater levels of political violence.[59]

To view "terrorism" primarily as an example of Orwellian double-speak, however, is to undersell its deeper social significance. A tremendously productive concept, "terrorism" generates a wide range of effects thanks to the formidable matrix of institutional, ideological and linguistic structures that have been combined to create knowledge about it: to name it, study it and, indeed, declare war on it. In this sense "terrorism" has much in common with drugs, crime and other concepts that have the power to spark remarkable periods of social panic and social reorganization.[60] In the case of "terrorism," the impact of the concept's circulation has been breathtaking, not least on the subjectivity of individuals who come to define themselves in terms of their vulnerability to, fear of, or, like the paranoid Vietnam veteran in Wim Wenders' 2004 film *Land of Plenty*, compulsive patriotic obligation to prevent "terrorism."[61] Similarly, the transformative impact of "terrorism" and its associated discourses on everything from the law and civil liberties to political activism and television news is of relevance here. One could gather a team of dozens of researchers, study all of these processes for years, and barely scratch the surface of their social significance.

In short, "terrorism" is an excellent example of a discursive formation: a sociolinguistic system that defines the contours of what can be said, thought and known about a particular set of social phenomena.[62] All such formations must be analyzed precisely because they impose upon a chaotic world a sense of order and regularity that can be quite seductive, particularly when backed up by the authority of powerful institutions. It is my contention that when placed in the context of the struggle between the "settler international" and the resistance movements discussed above, the current incarnation of the concept of "terrorism" can be viewed more specifically as a settler colonial discursive formation built, to a significant extent, on the inclusion and internalization of settler colonial logics and the exclusion of other logics.

Analysis of any discursive formation must begin with careful attention to the specific conditions of its emergence. In this case, the explosion of the discourse of "terrorism" during the latter part of the long 1960s constituted a virtual industry located at the intersection of key social institutions, most notably governments, the military, the academy, public policy think tanks, the news media and powerful corporations. Indeed, one of the best ways to understand the "revolving door" phenomenon marking the relations among these institutions is to examine the careers of those individuals who have spoken most authoritatively about "terrorism." Many of these individuals appear to move seamlessly between their roles as public servants, researchers, military officers, media consultants and corporate lobbyists and advisors.

Given these connections, it is not surprising that one of the first effects of the reemergence of "terrorism" discourse during the long 1960s was its contribution to a more general consolidation of executive power. The US government initially led the way, with Richard Nixon, elected in 1968 on a "law and order" platform, forming a Cabinet Committee to Combat Terrorism in 1972 and appointing a special assistant to the Secretary of State to deal with the issue. Crucially, Nixon was also responsible for launching the "war on drugs," which is best viewed as the godfather of the "Global War on Terrorism" (GWOT). Despite the post-Watergate dismantling of some domestic surveillance operations in the wake of the Church Committee's important findings, the Carter administration accelerated the state's

counterterrorism efforts by creating several new inter- and intra-
agency bodies including the Executive Committee on Terrorism. The
administration's handling of the Iran hostage crisis paved the way for
the election of Ronald Reagan, who gave his name to a new phase in
the country's endocolonization (the "Reagan Revolution"), breathed
new life into the tradition of US covert action, and launched a bombing campaign in 1986 in response to Libyan "terrorism."

An equally crucial pillar of the "terrorism" discourse was the work of
scholars, many of whom had close corporate, government and media
ties. Whereas there were relatively few books published on "terrorism"
up to the early 1970s, the years 1974–75 saw a marked increase in scholarly output. This included two books resulting from major international
conferences, and numerous works by authors who quickly became leaders in the field through their work in universities and think tanks such
as the RAND Corporation, their role as state advisers, and their regular appearances in the major news media.[63] Given the increased academic interest in "terrorism" as a distinct field of study, it is not surprising
that an intellectual journal emerged to facilitate the field's growth. *Terrorism: An International Journal*, initially published by the Institute for
Studies in International Terrorism at SUNY-Oneonta and later published by Routledge as *Studies in Conflict & Terrorism*, first appeared in
1977.[64] An examination of some of its early articles reveals a great deal
about the outlines of the emerging discourse.

The conceptual frameworks initially employed in the journal make
up what might be called the musculoskeletal structure enclosing the
object of study and enabling it to do particular kinds of social work.
These include a state-centered law and order framework emphasizing the disruptive force of "terrorism" in relation to the presumed stability of democratic states; a business framework focusing on the
security concerns of private firms; and a problem-solving framework
that constructed "terrorism" primarily as a thorny management
dilemma to be addressed through more efficient institutional cooperation and more effective policy-making.

Perhaps most striking, however, is the early popularity of psychological frameworks claiming to specify the individual traits that produce "terrorism." The inaugural issue of the journal, for example,

features one article offering a composite "profile" of "today's terrorist" that rests on thin and questionable assumptions regarding anarchist and nihilist motivations.[65] In the lead article from the same issue, an FBI Special Agent explains the actions of these "rebelling sophomores" with reference to psychoanalytic theory: "The foundations for this character type are found in the Freudian explanations for *sadism, masochism, and necrophilia.*"[66] Much of the early work on the subject replicates such arguments, foregrounding not concrete political grievances, but rather some combination of congenital character defects and young people's gullible submission to radical doctrines encountered in universities.

One of the most influential commentators on "terrorism" during this period, Walter Laqueur, added a hint of biological determinism to the discourse, informing his readers in 1978 that "it has long been known that there are some internal violence-generating factors and that some people have a lower violence threshold than others."[67] Such reductionism dovetailed nicely with the perspective of one of his book's contributors, the former Israeli chief of military intelligence Yehoshafat Harkabi, who had referred to Palestinian nationalism ten years earlier as "a world of simmering frustrated hatred and a drive for unquenchable violence."[68] Harkabi's formulation would later be sharply echoed by Benjamin Netanyahu, whose brother Jonathan was the only commando killed in the Israeli raid on Entebbe. "The root cause of terrorism," wrote the future Israeli Prime Minister, "lies not in grievances but in *a disposition toward unbridled violence.*"[69]

The fact that an openly partisan figure such as Netanyahu could be consulted regularly as a disinterested "expert" on the subject illustrates the ease with which the mainstream American news media internalized the settler colonial logic of the discourse during and after its emergence. As major media events, the hijackings and kidnappings of the long 1960s provided regular opportunities for news outlets to reinforce the prevailing assumption that "terrorists"—and not war, disease, poverty, racism or structural violence—represented the main threat to public well-being. Once again, the prominence of security went hand in hand with the invisibility of colonization.

The numerous *Time* magazine cover stories related to Israel/Palestine during this period illustrate this process, suggesting an absolutely Manichean conflict between a dignified, familiar Israel and the jagged, frightening force of Palestinian resistance. During the long 1960s, *Time* offered eleven covers devoted specifically to Israel, with the majority featuring sympathetic, artistic portraits of iconic Israeli leaders culminating in a December 1974 cover of Prime Minister Yitzhak Rabin with the headline, "Israel Besieged." By contrast, during the same period *Time* published four cover stories dealing directly with the Palestinians, and all four emphasized violence and "terrorism." The first two, from September 1970, spotlighted "Pirates in the Sky" and "The Arab Guerrillas," with the latter's artwork including a background of Arabic script and a foreground of a shadowy Arab figure wearing a *kufiya* (Arab headdress) and holding a Kalashnikov. The third cover was devoted to the 1972 Munich Olympic massacre, while the fourth ("Mid-East Massacres" from May 1974) featured images of Arabs killed by other Arabs, overlaid with faux-bloodstains in case the reader had any doubt about the content. In short, for almost the first three decades of Israel's existence, the covers of the magazine provided a pristine example of the discourse on "terrorism" and its ideological assumptions, giving readers no visible representation of any act of Israeli state violence.

The undeniable centrality of the Palestinians in the discursive formation of "terrorism" points us back to the centrality of settler colonialism. The roster of prominent expert voices within the discourse during its emergence is heavily populated with American, Israeli, South African, Australian and British voices. While these were occasionally joined by others, the overall picture is one of settler states seeking to focus global attention on those groups that most directly threatened the structures associated with settler projects. In this sense it is no exaggeration to say that the (re)invention of "terrorism" as an object of study, popular preoccupation and systematic state violence was a direct product of the crisis that settler colonialism faced during the long 1960s.

Denial and (In)Security

The reemergence of "terrorism" as a discursive formation during the long 1960s has produced a number of far-reaching social and political effects, perhaps most notably laying the groundwork for the new "epistemic community"[70] that emerged after 9/11 in the form of homeland security and the GWOT.[71] Those effects are organically related to one of settler colonialism's most basic and enduring features: its obsessive pursuit of a security that it can never deliver. Indeed, to the extent that security itself represents a complex discursive formation, it is inseparable today from the "terrorism" discourse that has been thoroughly shaped by settler colonial voices. Both of these formations, in turn, are embedded in the gradual disappearance of traditional war waged between sovereign states. Whether expressed as a return to the logic of permanent war or a shift from "war of milieu" to "war on the milieu" (see Chapter 5), it is clear that settler colonialism contains within it a tendency toward a more fundamental and all-encompassing variety of securitization.

In the settler colonial world, as analyzed in Chapter 2, the perception of threats that infiltrate the social body fuels a process of militarization that itself infiltrates the social body in the form of permanent wars on poverty, drugs, crime and terrorism, all of which are ultimately wars against the poor. Here it is worth recalling that the phrase "War on Terrorism" did not originate with George W. Bush; it was also the title of a *Time* cover story at the end of the long 1960s (31 October 1977). Within a few years the South African government was inaugurating its "total strategy" and the Israeli military was implementing its campaign of fighting "terrorism" in Beirut with overwhelming and often indiscriminate force. All of this is part of the recent lineage of permanent war.

What does permanent war (or "war on") produce? War is not only a destructive force; it also generates new identities, geo-political arrangements, social forms, and imaginaries.[72] This chapter demonstrates that the logic of permanent war contributes to the production of a politics that has been radically "securitized." This process continues to unfold today, but the tools needed to understand its full impact remain relatively elusive. Perhaps this is because securitization, to use a common metaphor in critical social analysis, is now part of the water in which we are all swimming, and therefore difficult to see with any critical distance. This makes it all the more important to ask the question: what does securitization do?

One intriguing response is to be found in the work of scholars who study the changing nature of social control in an age of highly intensified global integration. As the "horizontal" process of permanent war seems to supplant the traditional "vertical" process of sovereign war, vertical systems of social control, while still influential, seem to be giving way to what Alexander Galloway and Eugene Thacker describe as "a system of control infused into the material fabric of distributed networks."[73] They view this system as revolutionary, not least because the new distributed sovereignty "reformulates the role of governance as that of real-time security" in relation to a particular set of immanent threats.[74] The airport security agent, the antivirus programmer, the contagious disease specialist, the data mining expert, and the vigilant citizen are the twenty-first-century counterparts of the old settler colonial frontier sheriff within this system.

This logic of real-time security is evident in the infamous color-coded terror alert system devised by the US Department of Homeland Security, a system that soon became culturally omnipresent after 9/11 thanks to the cooperation of television news channels, airports and late-night comedians. The same logic is also at work in a host of other social locations that might seem less obviously political, from the ubiquitous instant alerts facilitated by mobile phone providers and news organizations, the simple premises of social media (e.g., Twitter's "what are you doing?"), to the Symantec "Internet Threat Meter" (a close cousin of the Homeland Security terror alert scale) that sits on your computer desktop and promises instant, real-time protection against viruses and other threats.

The securitization of politics and society only makes sense when we consider the central role of settler colonialism and its discontents in breaking some of the thresholds that we have seen broken during and after the long 1960s. In their refusal to become the "movable slaves" that Zionism wished them to be, for example, Palestinian revolutionaries inhabited (if only for a brief moment) the post-national territory created by the world's high-speed transportation and communication arteries, and in doing so they opened the door for others who would use global connectivity for less liberating purposes. Yet to fix blame on the global resistance movements of the long 1960s is to absolve settler states of responsibility for calling political violence into existence, both literally (through the deep structures of colonization) and discursively (through their dominance of the discourses through which "terrorism" is framed), while also laying the groundwork for a world where security is promised but never delivered.

As Patrick Wolfe reminds us, settler colonial invasion is best viewed as "a structure rather than an event."[75] Settler colonial violence, therefore, is always already an effort to perpetuate the denial of its original sins. Perhaps the supreme irony in all of this is that the factor that seems to be framing and over-determining politics most effectively today—security—is precisely the thing that settler states, in their endless search for "zero vulnerability,"[76] have always claimed as their semi-exclusive preoccupation. In this sense, to the extent that securitization brings with it the gradual militarization of identity—the creation of "civilian soldiers" who see the world as populated by an endless series of faceless threats—it seems that we are all continuing to pay the price for settler colonial denial.

Image 1. Palestinians projecting film onto the Wall in Abu Dis, © Diego López Calvin

Image 2. From *Intimacy* series, © Rula Halawani

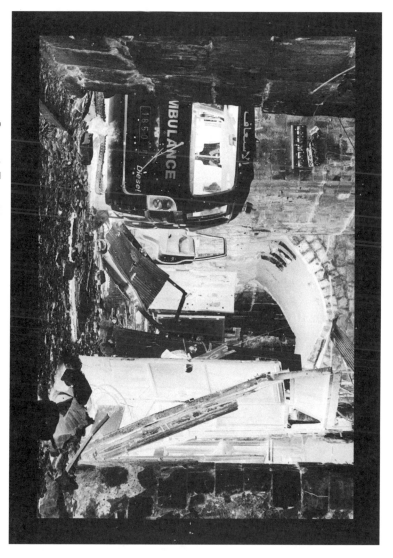

Image 3. From *Negative Incursion* series, © Rula Halawani

Image 4. Israeli soldier and West Bank ruins, © Diego López Calvin

Image 5. Palestine solidarity mural in Northern Ireland, © Chris Prener

Image 7. Solidarity march in Ramallah, © Diego López Calvin

Image 8. Jenin Refugee Camp, 2002, © Diego López Calvin

4

ACCELERATION

Taking off from the German Romantic tradition, Walter Benjamin argued that an individual work of art is monadic in relation to the larger idea of "Art." A poem or a song, in this sense, can have a global significance precisely because it contains "an image of the world." It is also true that the work of art begins a process of "decay" as soon as it is born.[1] The simple passage of time and the recursive process of interpretation continually break it down, shaving layer after layer off the whole that it once was. The task of the critic is to turn this fact into an opportunity for understanding. Indeed, it is only through this kind of decay that criticism even becomes possible, for it is the "mortification" of the work that allows the critic to take the resulting fragments and combine them with other fragments to form a new "constellation" that will reveal the monadic nature of the work.

As this book argues, Palestine may be viewed, in essence, as a "work" that bears precisely the kind of monadic character of which Benjamin wrote so provocatively. From this arises the troubling question of what is allowing its monadic character to come into view at this point in history. What is it, if not a culmination of a process of decay that began with the carving up of the Middle East after World War I? What is it, if not the mortification of Palestine that is hap-

Image 6. Use of tear gas by Israeli troops against solidarity activists in the West Bank, © Diego López Calvin

pening before our very eyes, brick by brick, acre by acre, olive tree by olive tree?

Benjamin, of course, died tragically in the Franco-Spanish border town of Portbou in 1940 after a desperate flight through the Pyrenees, hoping to escape the clutches of fascism.[2] Portbou is now the site of "Passages," a memorial to Benjamin created by the Israeli architect Dani Karavan and inaugurated in 1994. The memorial's most notable feature is a tunnel-like covered staircase that descends over a cliff and appears to open directly into the bay below, pushing visitors to think about the relationship between enclosure and release. Within the staircase, one is confined—even claustrophobic, especially at night—and yet in descent, one is increasingly open to the vastness of the sea and sky, particularly after the ceiling disappears about halfway down the stairs.

From the large metal platform Karavan placed on the hill above the staircase near the cemetery where Benjamin is buried, one's view of the Mediterranean is interrupted, curiously, by a chain-link fence.[3] Confronted with this juxtaposition, one thinks of the refugees and other migrants (how many are there?) who have died while trying to cross the same Mediterranean in recent years, prompting some members of the European Union to suggest the construction of special camps in North Africa to prevent migrants from ever reaching the dry land of Europe. Each migrant flees his or her own personal enclosure: war, disease, hopelessness and/or famine. Each enters the vast openness of the sea; in the sea, many find a place of burial. Their world, our world, is a world marked by what Sylvere Lotringer calls "confinement under an open sky."[4]

In previous chapters I have suggested that the technologies and processes which connect the far reaches of the globe—often under a hopeful rhetoric of "opening up" the world—can also be read as creating new kinds of enclosure. Lotringer's invocation of the "open sky" is thus meant to be an ironic recognition that in today's world, thanks to the invention and extension of technologies that enable accelerated forms of surveillance and violence, even the most "open" spaces are also, paradoxically, spaces of confinement. When it comes to social acceleration, the cardinal rule seems to be that the faster we go, the smaller the world feels.

Is it possible that what I label dromocolonization—the gradual colonization of humanity by techno-logic acceleration, with attendant forms of confinement spread unevenly across the social field—has been a key catalyst for Palestine's "mortification," with far-reaching global consequences? Is it possible that the deep and pervasive sense of confinement experienced by many Palestinians is a function not only of their literal enclosure within walls, camps and other physical structures, but also of the speed with which violence is often visited upon them? If so, then we need to consider the possibility that Palestine may be functioning as a kind of laboratory for some of the emerging realities that the often unacknowledged vectors of social acceleration are producing.

The contemporary global significance of Palestine in relation to these processes of acceleration and confinement calls to mind an earlier historical example: *Guernica*, Pablo Picasso's monumental homage to the Basque village that came under attack by German and Italian bombers during the Spanish Civil War. Widely recognized as one of the greatest works of art of the twentieth century, *Guernica* also remains one of the world's most stunning pieces of independent citizen journalism. Its power derives not only from the starkness of its black and white figures, but also from the viewer's recognition that the mural, like the atrocity it documents, was prophetic. The village of Guernica was used as a testing ground for a new generation of aerial weapons that would later become standard features of global warfare waged increasingly from a distance and with an ever-more frightening velocity. In this sense, the figures on Picasso's canvas—crowded into that single room as the bombs rained down—were the canaries in the coalmine that soon led to London, Dresden and Hiroshima, and later to Vietnam, Beirut and Grozny. Tragically, the particular combination of terror and confinement that aerial bombardment imposed upon the people of Guernica became one of the quintessential twentieth-century experiences.

Like the *Guernica*, part of the power of the Palestinian experience today derives from its relationship to changes in the way political violence is exercised globally through the emergence of what Achille Mbembe calls "necropolitics" or "contemporary forms of subjugation of life to the power of death."[5] The difference is that the forward-looking nature of Palestine has been scarcely recognized; if anything, discussions of Palestine traditionally tend to portray it as more of a remnant, a stubborn theater filled with actors who can't let go of the past. Yet a close look at the relationship between acceleration and confinement suggests that something more prophetic—that is, "diagnostic" of "what we are in the process of becoming"[6]—may be going on. This chapter explores how the troubling legacy of accelerated necropolitics symbolized by Picasso's mural has found its way to Palestine in a way that has implications for all of us.

Talking About Acceleration

Speed and power have always been intimately linked. When it comes to conceptualizing the nature of this relationship and its social implications, however, we have inherited a striking poverty of critical thinking. Our relative inattention to the importance of speed and acceleration sharply limits our ability to understand power as well as a host of other issues including the changing nature of war.[7] Consider, by contrast, that if we wish to explore how wealth and capital accumulation interact with power, we can draw not only on generations of sustained intellectual work within the venerable field of political economy and its cousins in the modern social sciences, but also on the lessons learned from centuries of social movements rooted in the struggle for economic justice. The same could be said for power's connection with space, identity and discourse—all areas where sustained intellectual and political work have provided a rich and growing analytical toolbox. Yet only recently have scholars in globalization studies, particularly those concerned with the phenomenon of time-space compression, begun to explore some of the outlines of what Paul Virilio, the most dogged and original theorist of acceleration, would describe as the field of political dromology (literally the logic of the *dromos* or the race): the field where power and acceleration come together.[8]

The concept of dromocolonization (introduced briefly in Chapter 2) is designed to open the door to an examination of how acceleration functions both as a colonizing tool for particular actors and as a colonizing force in and of itself. In the first place, the term refers to the fact that, like power itself, colonization is inherently dromocratic: in any colonial situation, the advantage typically lies with those who are most effectively able to control the strategic acceleration and deceleration of violence and change. In many cases, by virtue of superior technology, the colonizer is the one who has the ability to go the fastest and therefore leverage acceleration to his benefit.[9] This explains why the colonized tend to experience colonization as a process of violent acceleration, and to resist—at least in part—through the built-in advantages of local rootedness and through a variety of strategies designed to slow down the dromocratic invader.[10] In this sense, one could argue that control over acceleration is immanent to any actor-centered conception of colonization.

The notion of acceleration as a colonizing tool applies equally well to the contemporary world of neo-liberal globalization. Social acceleration is an often unacknowledged motor enabling the growth that drives the global process of capital accumulation.[11] While the "greed is good" mantra of the 1980s, made famous by Michael Douglas in *Wall Street*, may have come under critical scrutiny in subsequent years, the notion that "speed is good" is rarely questioned in the same way. Neo-liberalism's emphasis on "freeing" the flow of capital, however, is dromocratic to the core, rewarding the merchants of speed and risk[12] while encouraging the kinds of privatization and social militarization that produce involuntary migration, mass incarceration, declines in real wages and other forms of structural violence.

In short, the ability to harness acceleration does remain a fundamental, albeit somewhat hidden tool in the arsenal of a variety of actors, from the institutions created by traditional political and economic elites (e.g., states and transnational corporations) to the efforts of a variety of non-state actors (e.g., insurgents and "hacktivists"). At the same time, there is significant evidence to suggest that many of these actors are being driven by the logic of acceleration as much as (or more than) they are driving it. This is where the dromological perspective becomes valuable, for it asks us to go beyond theories of actors, their resources, and their intentions and recognize that acceleration now constitutes a relatively autonomous force in politics that evades, in many ways, the structures of human control.[13]

The dromological perspective insists that we acknowledge how the acceleration that benefits particular actors—often in ways that reproduce existing social hierarchies—also renders everyone vulnerable to new accidents and forms of disaster. These secret byproducts of acceleration represent a more abstract, but no less important, side of dromocolonization. Thus while it makes sense, on one level, to view dromocolonization as a context within which colonization more generally takes place, it is also useful to understand how the former constitutes an emergent reality in relation to which the other two modes discussed in Chapter 2 (exocolonization and endocolonization) appear increasingly "residual," co-existing uneasily with dromocolonization while always threatening to be eclipsed by it.

One important characteristic of this emergent reality is that, much like globalization itself, its effects are profoundly uneven. Saying that acceleration is colonizing humanity is not the same as saying that all human beings experience this process in the same way. For those who are immersed in the accelerated circuits of social media, compulsory multitasking, and real-time instantaneity on a daily basis, dromocolonization may appear as a nagging sense that the rhythm of life is steadily changing in a way that leaves one perpetually out of breath and unable to focus.[14] Others, however, may experience dromocolonization in a radically different way: when their village is hit without warning by a missile fired from a pilotless aircraft representing a postmodern war machine with the "ability to descend from nowhere without notice and vanish again without warning";[15] when their life savings disappear in an instant thanks to a financial crash fueled by lightning-quick computer-aided trading patterns; or when false information about them spreads like wildfire through the information superhighway faster than it can possibly be corrected.

Acceleration, Confinement and Disappearance

The history of modern warfare is a history of steady acceleration that illustrates the emergent nature of dromocolonization. In military planning circles, much as in global capitalism, the importance of speed is virtually axiomatic—even if its semi-autonomous nature is often overlooked.[16] Many of the notable military inventions of the past century—from the German *blitzkrieg* to today's satellite-guided weaponry and "infowar" weapons—have been those that achieve a significant reduction in the adversary's reaction time. Equally important, many of the same technologies also accelerate the process of decision making for those carrying out the violence—assuming the key decisions are being made by human beings at all.

Virilio's notion of the "grey ecology," which he articulates as a generalized terrestrial condition, comes into play here as a specific outcome of the acceleration of warfare and helps explain why he views acceleration itself as a form of warfare. In explaining this concept, he quotes Paul Morand: "Speed destroys color: when a gyroscope is spinning fast everything goes grey."[17] It is only fitting that these words were uttered in 1937, the year of the destruction of Guernica. Journalist G.L. Steer, who was the first to bring the details of that prophetic event to the public, describes in concise yet devastating detail the effect of the bombing: "Gernika's face was turning into ashes, everybody's face in Gernika was ash-grey..." The village was "smudged out of that rich landscape...with a heavy fist" that included blanketing the town with thermite incendiary bombs.[18] In Steer's narrative—the terms of which would apply to an even stronger degree to the subsequent Allied bombing of German cities—we see how the "grey ecology" not only hints at the psychological disorientation produced in those who are the targets of hyper-accelerated violence, but also calls on us to think about the moral disorientation present in those who deliver it.

With all of this in mind, we can see that dromocolonization brings with it distinct forms of violence, social control, and resistance, but also the growth of a frightening politics of disappearance that may be fatal for democracy. Exocolonization was, in part, about creating the conditions for the creation of democratic institutions and the selective provision of democratic privileges (e.g., to the white, male, Western, propertied citizen). Endocolonization coincided with the extension of these privileges to others (e.g., the formerly colonized, racial minorities), but it did so at precisely the time when popular sovereignty was starting to be superseded by global structures such as the Bretton Woods institutions and the superpower system of nuclear deterrence. Dromocolonization pushes humanity toward the eclipse of democracy by gradually eliminating the time for reflection on which democracy depends;[19] "the people," in turn, begin to disappear into the chaotic world of real-time, hypermediated communication as politics itself "disappears into the aesthetic."[20] Meanwhile, the purveyor of violence, shielded by distance and technology, disappears into the machine.

The traditional tools of social analysis are insufficient to make sense of this process. With their focus on territory, our frameworks for understanding politics remain geo-centric in a way that fails to grasp or explain how acceleration is changing the nature of space and arguably effecting the subordination of space to time.[21] If, as discussed in Chapter 2, exocolonization and endocolonization both displace (that is, deterritorialize) people only to reterritorialize them in ways that facilitate social control, one may posit that dromocolonization displaces people from space into time. This move is especially traumatic for indigenous communities,[22] but in a planetary sense, all human beings are indigenous people for whom dromocolonization represents a direct attack on any meaningful relationship with place. This is not to say that space and place no longer matter; on the contrary, part of what the reality of "Global Palestine" confirms is that we are all witnessing and participating in a struggle between the deterritorializing vectors of dromocratic globalization and the human desire to inhabit, defend and derive meaning from particular spaces.

Understanding these processes is crucial to understanding the importance of confinement and the particular forms it takes in a dromocratic world. To conventional interpretations that view confinement primarily in terms of overcrowding and literal enclosure, the dromological approach adds a focus on how acceleration produces forms of material, psychological and existential confinement that cut across the full spectrum of social life in much the same way that securitization, as analyzed in the previous chapter, operates as a generalized cultural logic. If securitization was enabled by the "closure" of the world through the invention of the bomb, dromocratic confinement is more a function of globalizing technologies of communication, surveillance and violence that are integral to the structures of pure war.

From this perspective, globalization is best understood as the product of a dynamic and organic relationship that has always existed among technology, acceleration, violence and confinement. Seen from one angle, satellite technology "opens" the world by enabling the rapid circulation and exchange of information. Seen from another, it envelops the world and makes everyone a potential target of war waged from orbital space.[23] Google Earth is, in this sense, the public face of the postmodern war machine in the same way that cheap nuclear energy to power consumer appliances was the public face of the age of MAD. The difference is that this time around, there is no time to duck and cover. An examination of dromocolonization, therefore, reveals new possibilities for deconstructing the dominant rhetoric of globalization and highlighting what amounts to a process of creeping claustrophobia. At the extreme, globalization represents an irreversible "pollution of distances," leading ultimately to a kind of collective incarceration as "a mass phenomenon, an apocalyptic phenomenon."[24]

In Palestine, incarceration is already a mass phenomenon. This is true, of course, in the prisons, but in a more profound sense it is true in every town, village and refugee camp and in the highly surveyed and increasingly fragmented spaces between them—the spaces constituting the "hollow land"[25] and "carceral archipelago"[26] that Palestine has become. As will be explored below, this process of "mortification" in Palestine also points us toward a series of more global dromocratic realities.

Palestine: Dromocratic Confinement in Action

The two sides of dromocolonization—colonization by the fastest and the colonization of humanity by acceleration—each have important implications for our understanding of how confinement operates today in Palestine and elsewhere. For their part, states continue to try to leverage the power of speed in order to confine particular populations, from enemy combatants to refugees and the urban poor. In the concluding chapter of *Culture and Imperialism*, Edward Said recognized this reality, identifying in the global reach of US imperialism a systematic privileging of what he called "the principle of confinement." The actualization of this principle, Said argued, is devastating for the global class of the nomadic poor who find themselves always on the move, yet always penned in.[27]

Palestine remains one place where this more traditional, geo-political notion of confinement continues to animate a profoundly hierarchical set of settler colonial structures. In spatial terms, following Patrick Wolfe's argument that settler colonialism "destroys to replace," one may contend that settler colonialism closes (or encloses) in order to open and vice-versa.[28] The language of colonization reveals much about the mentality behind such a strategy; one thinks, for example, of the "opening" and "closing" of the North American frontier. Zionism's self-fashioned mythology offers a botanical twist, speaking of the "blooming" of the desert under its new masters. The clearest illustration of the logic of (en)closure, however, lies in the tendency of settler colonial projects to produce ghettos, reservations, bantustans, "homelands," and other sites of racialized confinement as a way of "opening" expansive, comfortable and profitable spaces for settlers and their descendants.

Thanks to Zionism's particular spatial politics, confinement has been a constitutive element of Palestinian life for decades. From 1948–1966, for example, Palestinian Arab citizens of Israel lived under military rule, with Israeli authorities frequently declaring their towns "closed military zones," a technique later used in the West Bank.[29] Before the creation of the Palestinian Authority (PA) in the Oslo years and long before the construction of the Wall, many refugee camps in the Israeli-occupied West Bank bore more than a passing resemblance to prisons. I witnessed this myself in 1990 on my first visit to Palestine, when I journeyed to Dheisheh Refugee Camp outside Bethlehem to visit the elderly parents of a friend I had met while at university. I remember perfectly that the camp was encircled by a fence, and that I had to pass through a narrow turnstile in order to enter. While there was no Israeli military presence at that particular moment, there was no mistaking the intent and the implication of the limited access: Dheisheh was a confined community. On the same trip I visited Jabaliya camp in Gaza, where roughly 100,000 refugees were crowded into less than one square kilometer.

The natural population growth that has taken place since the camps were created more than a half-century ago has only intensified the effect of these spatial arrangements. Unable to expand their homes laterally, refugees are forced to build upwards, adding rooms and apartments whenever a slight improvement in the precarious economic situation allows.[30] This explains the characteristic built environment of the camps, where narrow alleyways squeeze between buildings that are perpetually unfinished. The impact of these conditions on refugees is predictable. Dheisheh residents, reports one researcher, "speak of a chronic lack of solitude, privacy, silence, especially for young girls who are often confined to overcrowded living quarters."[31]

With the benefit of hindsight, we can now see that the entire trajectory of Israel's colonization of the West Bank and Gaza has been one of extending these carceral arrangements outward from the camps to the Palestinian population as a whole through the increasingly widespread use of roadblocks, checkpoints, curfews, closure, and various types of literal imprisonment. Palestinian refugees who live elsewhere in the region have not been immune to many of these oppressive dynamics; on the contrary, host governments have generally been content to maintain the camps as "exceptional" spaces to be governed through a politics of enclosure, exclusion, and state violence.[32]

Recent history also tells us that the Israeli domination of Palestine has been a testing ground for modes of rule that are less obviously spatial in their execution. Israeli anthropologist Jeff Halper coined the term "matrix of control" to describe the "interlocking series of mechanisms, only a few of which require physical occupation of territory, that allow Israel to control every aspect of Palestinian life in the Occupied Territories." This matrix includes not only the application of force and intimidation by the military on the ground, but also the application of a "web of bureaucracy" within which the lives of Palestinians are circumscribed. Consequently, all Palestinians living in these territories—whether they live formally in camps or not—

have found themselves hemmed in by laws, orders and practices that effectively overdetermine their lives, their movements and their identities.[33]

As the reality of this matrix gradually emerged after the Oslo accords, more and more Palestinians understandably began to refer to their situation in South African and Native American terms, warning that their country was being turned into a series of disconnected "reservations" or "bantustans." After Ariel Sharon came to power in 2001, the Israeli system of spatial regulation became increasingly sophisticated and calibrated. The most visible development was been the creation of the Wall, which shadows the 1967 Green Line, snaking into the West Bank in order to effect a unilateral annexation of the territory occupied by Israeli settlement colonies.[34] The Wall is best viewed as a system that includes not only steel and concrete, but also state-of-the-art surveillance equipment, land confiscations, dramatic alterations of the political and economic environment, and a far-reaching set of psychological consequences for Palestinians and Israelis alike. The impact of such a system cannot be exhausted by a look at its most obvious spatial characteristics.

It is in Gaza, however, that the collective confinement and incarceration of Palestinians has reached its apotheosis. Beginning in the mid-1990s, the high point of the Oslo "peace process," Israel began to cut off access to its internal job market for the Gazans who had long supplied a substantial portion of the cheap Palestinian labor upon which the Israeli economy once relied. Israeli authorities severely restricted the number of work permits granted to Gazans and put up a fence around the strip, nominally for security reasons, but also to stop infiltration of workers without permits. Following the outbreak of the second intifada in the fall of 2000, the closure of Gaza tightened still further, with Israel periodically blocking the inward flow of people, goods and money as well, and since Israeli soldiers and settlers departed the strip in 2005, the closure has more often than not been total. "Open-air prison" became a trendy media descriptor for Gaza when Israel and its allies shut off the flow of aid dollars entirely after Hamas' electoral victory in 2006, but Palestinians and some prominent Israeli Jewish critics[35] had been using the term for years.

Darryl Li notes that the Strip, which constitutes a mere 1.4 per cent of British Mandate Palestine, now holds one-quarter of all Palestinians living under Israeli control. With this in mind, he argues that Gaza illustrates how the operational mantra of Zionist settler colonialism ("maximum land, minimum Arabs") has generated its own corollary: "maximum Arabs on minimum land."[36] Unable physically to remove large numbers of Palestinians from the territory entirely, the Israeli state has instead used Gaza as a laboratory in which to test out a range of spatial control mechanisms including "closure" and the creation of "buffer zones." As Li points out, these actions, along with the decision to remove Jewish settlement colonies from Gaza, have been accompanied by a rhetoric of "disengagement" as a way of reframing public discourse on the present and future of the conflict. In particular, he suggests, this strategy aims to head off the growing chorus of voices calling for a single, democratic state in Israel/Palestine.

The rhetoric of disengagement is a geo-political rhetoric that produces a form of discursive confinement, emphasizing the two-dimensional world of traditional maps and borders while hiding deeper structures of power and control. The rhetoric is misleading even in a two-dimensional sense, for it diverts attention from the question of who controls land and sea access to the territory from which Israel has supposedly "disengaged." A fuller understanding of the situation, however, requires that one take a broader view of power and consider the possibility that Gaza may be a case of dromocracy in action, a case where confinement derives not only from geopolitics, but also from chronopolitics.

Supporters of Israel have long been concerned about the possibility of a lightning-quick attack by its Arab neighbors who, the argument runs, could overrun a country whose sheer smallness and lack of strategic depth reduces reaction time to a matter of seconds. Yet Israel has regularly demonstrated its possession of the weapon of speed, whether in the 1967 Six Day War or in any of its "pre-emptive" strikes.[37] Much like the US, Israel has achieved military supremacy through mastery of the skies. Anyone who has spent time in Palestine or Lebanon knows how quickly an Israeli F-16 fighter jet or helicopter gunship can appear as if out of nowhere, whether for purposes of intimidation or violent attack. In recent years it has been evident how attacks can be accelerated further, and also miniaturized, through the use of booby-trapped cell phones that kill in the time it takes to say hello. Air power has played a pivotal role in the changing regime of control in the Gaza Strip, allowing Israel to blanket Palestinians with a thick web of surveillance and terrifying sonic booms[38] while using air-to-ground missiles to carry out extrajudicial killings.[39]

These are some of the realities that architect Eyal Weizman had in mind when he coined the phrase "politics of verticality" to describe the three-dimensional system of Israeli control over the Palestinian territories.[40] This system includes a complex combination of strategies including roads and tunnels, hilltop settlement colonies, control over underground aquifers and sewage systems, and dominance of the air. Even if the Israeli-Palestinian peace process miraculously bears fruit, this "politics of verticality" will have already transformed not only the facts on the ground, but also the facts above and below the ground.

When the dromological perspective is added to the "politics of verticality," it becomes clear that Israeli policy has already moved beyond horizontal and vertical territoriality to create what might be called a four-dimensional confinement of the Palestinians. Possession and deployment of the weapon of speed allows Israel to move rapidly in transforming the objective geo-political situation while also shrinking the existential space in which Palestinians operate. Shimon Naveh of the Israeli Army's Operational Theory Research Institute openly acknowledged the techno-logic behind this policy in a 2006 interview. "The main idea," he confirmed, "is that we can see and do what we please."[41] Naveh is a key figure in the Israeli military's increasing application of poststructuralist theory, particularly the work of Gilles Deleuze and Felix Guattari, to the strategic and tactical arenas, most notably during 2002's "Operation Defensive Shield."[42] Within the system of control they are pursuing, the Wall is simply the most visible of a wide array of measures through which Palestinian bodies are scanned, surveyed, identified, restricted and assassinated. Armed with both high-tech weaponry and the dizzying language of French theory, Weizman argues, the Israel Defense Forces (IDF) is sending a chilling message to the Palestinian population: "You will never even understand that which kills you."

Dromocracy may also be seen in more traditional military maneuvers such as the rapid tank invasions that reoccupied major West Bank towns in 2002, the ground operations in Gaza in 2006 and the regular, smaller-scale Israeli Army incursions into Palestinian areas throughout the post-1967 period. As the fastest, the party with the artillery and mechanized armor, Israel has the initiative in attempts to occupy ground. More to the point, the armament of speed gives Israel the ability to regulate the pace of daily life in the battlespace. While this ability is hardly limitless—the colonized also have ways of acting quickly—there is little doubt that well-chosen maneuvers have an important demonstration effect.

Our inability to understand the full complexity of acceleration as a social phenomenon makes it difficult to develop strategies for pursuing justice in Palestine. Outside parties attempting to assist the "peace process," for example, have a tendency to focus on traditional questions of borders and geo-political sovereignty—lines on a map. US President Bill Clinton brought the third dimension explicitly into the discussion when attempting to negotiate the diplomatic minefield of Jerusalem's Old City during the Camp David talks in 2000. His proposed solution was a vertical division of sovereignty, with Palestinians controlling the Temple Mount/Haram al-Sharif itself (with the exception of the Wailing Wall) and Israel controlling the space above and below in a prime manifestation of Weizman's "politics of verticality."

Even here, however, the dromological dimension of power remains hidden. In this light, it is interesting to note that one of the key recommendations of a 2005 RAND Corporation study on the prospects of a future Palestinian state was the creation of the Arc, a high-speed rail network designed to move people and goods quickly along a corridor stretching from the Israeli city of Haifa to Gaza in the south.[43] Despite its best intentions, this essentially neo-liberal plan (which has yet to be implemented) recalls World Bank studies that seek to facilitate trade and growth by making processes of surveillance and border control more efficient. In each case, the assumption is that "freedom of movement" can be isolated from the larger structures of power operating in Israel/Palestine and globally. From this technophilic perspective, acceleration is an unqualified solution rather than part of the problem. Yet from the dromocratic perspective of power, movement can be as productive (and confining) as lack of movement.

Even before RAND developed the idea for the Arc, Israel had already begun construction on another high-speed rail project that illustrates the relationship between Israeli dromocracy and Palestinian confinement. The A1 line, scheduled for completion in 2017, aims to connect the two metropolitan hubs of Tel Aviv and Jerusalem, enabling Israelis to reduce the travel distance between the two cities to a mere twenty-eight minutes. In yet another example of the "politics of verticality," the project will involve significant tunneling, not only inside Israel but also through a small section of the West Bank, thus adding to the disruption already produced by the construction of the Wall and Israel's many West Bank colonies. Moreover, the proposed tunneling work will require the extraction of some one million cubic meters of material (for use by the contractor) and the construction of access roads that will encroach on the agricultural lands of local villagers.[44] In short, the project contributes to the acceleration of life for Israelis at the cost of further confinement for Palestinians and the literal hollowing out of Palestine.

Reading recent accounts of Palestinian life under Israeli control, one gets the sense that people are caught between two equal and opposite forms of confinement. On the one hand, they suffer through agonizing periods of waiting: at roadblocks on their way to school and work; in long lines at heavily-fortified checkpoints; in their homes under curfew; and in the bureaucratic maze that controls access to permits and other important documents. On the other hand, they are also subject to irregular and sudden periods of hyper-accelerated terror: when the army comes pounding at the door[45] or "walking through walls";[46] when a rocket or missile hits their neighborhood; or when they frantically try to bring in the olive harvest only to be attacked by vigilante Israeli colonists. Between the hammer of state violence and the anvil of endless waiting and restrictions on freedom of movement, the entire rhythm of life of a peasant and merchant society has been disrupted.

Nowhere is this clearer and more urgent than in Saverio Costanzo's 2004 film *Private*, which chronicles in claustrophobic detail the takeover of a middle-class West Bank Palestinian home by Israeli soldiers. Seeking to use the house as a lookout point, the soldiers commandeer the top floor, forcing the family of seven to spend long nights locked inside a single room. The film's brooding, often agonizing depiction of the family's determined attempt to go about their daily lives—getting ready for school, preparing and eating meals, building a greenhouse, visiting with friends and doing homework—is repeatedly interrupted by bursts of chaotic violence as the young soldiers, mostly bored but always on the edge of exploding, suddenly arrive to exert control over the situation. Meanwhile, the oldest daughter surreptitiously makes repeated forays upstairs, hiding in a closet to spy on the soldiers as they watch football matches, tease one another and play music to pass the time.

Costanzo's film, like the intolerable situation it allegorizes, reminds us that there are many ways to confine people. It is not just speed that produces confinement; rather, the one whose hand is on the throttle (literally and figuratively), with the option of speeding things up or slowing things down at will, is the one who controls confinement. To use an ancient image, the Egyptian Pharaoh is often pictured with a whip (for accelerating the chariot) in one hand and a hook (for slowing it down by pulling on the reins) in the other.[47] There is something Pharaonic about Israel's well-calibrated settler colonial domination of Palestine. It is about more than old-fashioned control of territory; rather, in its development of cutting-edge techniques of rule, it seeks to create and maintain a much broader system of control.

Suicide Bombing and Dromocolonization

One might be tempted to conclude, therefore, that the Zionist project of settler colonialism in Palestine is as strong as it has ever been. Yet the reverse is more likely to be true. By attempting to impose such a regime on the Palestinians, Zionism has in fact brought a crisis upon itself, a crisis partly rooted in its own investment in the structures and practices of dromocolonization. Israeli policy in recent years has taken the form of a "war on the milieu" (see Chapter 5) that inevitably generates violent responses from precisely those Palestinian groups that are most likely to target Israeli civilians. That is, Zionism's control of territory, achieved through the techniques of acceleration and confinement, has been purchased at a heavy price that continues to be paid not only by Palestinians (the primary victims, to be sure) but also by Israeli Jews—and indeed, as will be discussed below, by the world as a whole.

A closer examination of the issue of Palestinian suicide bombing can help us understand the destructively dromocratic nature of the entire Israeli-Palestinian dynamic. Much as the settler state's provocation of and response to the resistance movements of the long 1960s lay the foundation for today's ubiquitous politics of securitization, the relationship between suicide bombing and Israeli settler colonialism is staking out new and frightening territory in humanity's continuing search for new modes of waging war. Understanding this relationship, however, requires many of the most popular frameworks that have been used to explain suicide bombing to be set aside.

Most fundamentally, as Ghassan Hage has argued, we must struggle against the kind of exighophobia (fear of explanation) that often leads commentators to demand "absolute moral condemnation" of suicidal bombing as a way of avoiding what would otherwise be obvious questions about the social conditions that lead people to carry out such acts.[48] Even among analysts who have sought explanations for suicide bombing, the frameworks most commonly employed leave ample room for skepticism, not least because they rarely entertain the dangerous possibility that suicide bombing may in fact be a close cousin of the kinds of suicide missions in which Western soldiers have long participated. Instead, the continuing influence of Orientalist thinking has led to numerous readings of suicide bombing that rely on questionable assumptions about Islam (as if "Islam" were a unitary, unchanging social fact), about the concept of jihad, and about Islam's supposedly unique connection with political violence.[49] Some of the most strident voices, echoing the kinds of arguments long deployed in the wars on poverty, drugs, and terrorism, have attempted to locate suicide bombing within a pathological "culture of death" that is assumed to be detachable from the socio-historical context of colonization or military occupation.[50] The latter approach ignores the obvious reality that, from the perspective of the colonized, settler colonialism might be viewed as the real "culture of death."

More generally, as numerous critics have pointed out, the public discourse on suicide bombing works exactly like, and is organically related to, the discourse on terrorism: through repetition and the fostering of excessive (one might say obsessive) public attention on suicide bombings, it serves ideologically to deflect attention from the comparatively greater levels of violence committed by the state. One of the unfortunate side effects of this process is that in the effort to counter this distorted picture and refocus attention on the pervasiveness of state violence, critics of the dominant discourse often find themselves seeking to downplay the importance of suicide bombing. Yet there is no question that suicide bombing represents an important social phenomenon, not least because it helps us diagnose the nature of the oppressive social conditions and persistent hierarchical structures that give rise to it.

It is also necessary to explore the unintended consequences of the emergence of Palestinian suicide bombing, consequences that will echo far into the future. It is my contention that, somewhat ironically, suicide bombing represents both a response and a contribution to the process of global dromocolonization. On the one hand, to the extent that acceleration brings with it a gradual disappearance of politics, and to the extent that settler colonialism in Palestine has gone hand in hand with a process of "politicide,"[51] one may posit that suicide bombing has the effect of insisting that politics remains visible. Whether this particular politics is liberating for anyone, of course, is another question; the bulk of the evidence suggests that this strategy has been counterproductive for Palestinians and, obviously, traumatic for Israelis. But there is no doubt that at a time when other forms of popular activism and resistance tend to be largely ignored by the news media, suicide bombing represents a public manifestation of (a particular version of) Palestinian political will.

On the other hand, with their decision to adopt the tactic of suicide bombing periodically during the last two decades, Palestinian groups such as Hamas and Islamic Jihad have joined their Israeli adversaries in furthering a process of violent acceleration. Suicide bombing engages the Israeli state on the dromological level by targeting ordinary Israelis, almost instantly, in their own milieu (shopping malls, buses and restaurants). The Academy Award-nominated film *Paradise Now* portrays this perfectly: at the end of the film, as the bomber sits on the bus staring straight ahead, we know that the passengers about to be blown up will have no time to react. In other words, they find themselves in the same situation as the residents of Gaza just before an Israeli missile slams through the side of their building. Incredibly, the fate of both groups makes the small amount of time once available to the villagers of Guernica seem like an eternity.

The deadly encounter between Israel's national security apparatus and militant Palestinian resistance, however, is hardly an equal one, nor does it occur in a vacuum. If we take Hage's critique of the "absolute condemnation" approach seriously, we must recognize that suicide bombing emerges in Palestine at a particular moment in the history of a settler colonial project and cannot be separated from the kinds of deep colonial structures discussed in this book. Exocolonization's catastrophic territorial dispossession, endocolonization's "de-development"[52] and pure war, and dromocolonization's politics of confinement each help construct the conditions of possibility for suicidal violence.

Following the work of Pierre Bourdieu, Hage suggests that the desire to give up one's life in the act of fighting settler colonial domination is directly and paradoxically related to the desire to achieve a kind of "meaningfulness" for one's life: "The participant deliberately faces the danger of annihilation and at the same time seeks to accumulate personal status and self-esteem."[53] The deep need for meaningfulness, in turn, is the product of a radically hierarchical and oppressive social situation, with colonization and statelessness setting in motion "a generalized form of premature social aging, even of social death: a situation where there is a quasi-complete absence of possibilities of a worthy life."[54] This notion of "premature social aging" suggests that Palestinians who choose to become suicide bombers do so, in part, because they feel that death is already on the immediate horizon; it is simply a question of finding a way to take control of how that death ultimately occurs and what kind of social meaning will be attached to it.[55]

Such a perspective also tells us something important about how acceleration mediates the relationship between colonization and suicide bombing. After all, what is "premature social aging" if not the imposition of a particularly terrifying and accelerated form of existential confinement on a vulnerable population for whom death is always nearby? Those who recruit and groom suicide bombers understand this quite well, supplementing tactics that belong in the tradition of formal military training with measures grounded in settler colonial realities. While some critics seek to focus attention on how these recruiters wield the power of suggestion (e.g., by conjuring in the would-be bomber images of celestial virgins), such interpretations downplay the extent to which the recruitment process plays upon (and obviously amplifies) real feelings of existential confinement.

The rise of Palestinian attacks inside Israel has contributed to the "mortification" of the Zionist project by revealing as naïve and unreachable the settler colonial dream of absolute security. Ordinary Israeli Jews are then put into their own desperate position, pushed to support increasingly inhumane actions in order to maintain some sense of control over their own environment as they perceive it. In this sense, every Israeli bombing of Gaza is, however unwittingly, a suicide bombing. Here it is worth noting that the maintenance of the settler project in Israel has always been linked to the possibility of collective destruction, a possibility that Israel's considerable nuclear arsenal only brings into sharper relief.[56] The suicidal logic of nuclear deterrence—"if I am going to die, I am going to take you down with me"—is really not so different from the logic of the suicide bomber.

When the issue is viewed in this way, it is evident that dromocratic settler colonialism in Palestine has produced a reality that makes it very difficult for anyone to resist the deadly logic of acceleration. While the complex feedback loop that exists between state and non-state violence (including terrorism) is beyond the scope of this chapter, the end result of this loop is not. People everywhere are subject to the tyranny of acceleration and, by extension, to the tyranny of confinement—albeit, as noted above, in uneven ways that map closely onto existing social hierarchies. Israeli settlement colonies are intensely guarded and confined zones that have been militarized through their integration and cooptation into the national security apparatus. From their carefully selected location and design to the architecture of the houses, these "panoptic fortresses" are the ideal expressions of a colonizing impulse that seeks to marginalize Palestinians, but does so by enticing its own people into "cul-de-sac envelopes" masquerading as ideal locations for the spiritual-national "regeneration of the soul."[57] Even the special network of bypass roads designed to move settlers quickly to their jobs inside Israel is double-edged, for the speed of the roads—undoubtedly a selling point for potential residents—simply makes a small territory seem even smaller. Living in what is already a garrisoned society in an ideological sense, Israelis may find that their superior technology brings only further claustrophobia.[58] Not for nothing did the prominent Israeli dissident Michel Warschawski frame the title of his 2004 book with the metaphor of an "open tomb."[59]

Toward a Global Suicidal State?

Despite enormous differences in terms of freedom of movement, it is clear that both Israeli Jews and Palestinians are victims of a semi-autonomous acceleration machine that often seems incapable of producing anything more than destruction, isolation and lost hope. When missiles, suicide bombers and drones attack with no warning, and when soldiers come "walking through walls," who (or what) is in control? Does anyone really control acceleration, or does acceleration create the conditions within which various kinds of control are enacted? If the latter, is it possible to resist dromocolonization? How?

In one of his most difficult, yet rewarding and provocative interventions, Virilio in 1976 analyzed the emergence of the "suicidal state," a concept that also appears in Deleuze and Guattari's *A Thousand Pla-*

teaus. In one sense, the suicidal state is the state that is willing to put everything at risk, including its own survival, in order to pursue its goals. Such states produce not only their own violence, but also the other's violence, whether in the form of guerrilla warfare, acts of individual desperation, or catastrophic "blowback." In Virilio's reading, however, this notion quickly bleeds into a more abstract, transcultural notion of the "suicidal state" through the observation that governments, societies and individuals are fully implicated in "the ever more advanced exploitation of our instincts for death."[60] The suicidal state, in other words, is the collectivization of the death drive and is set in motion by the revolutionary fusion of militarization, acceleration, science and technology. Shortly after the attacks of September 11 2001, Virilio extended his analysis, arguing that we are now seeing the full emergence of a "global suicidal state."[61] It is my contention that the process of dromocolonization being carried out in Palestine has already contributed a great deal to the materialization of this global reality. In the remainder of this chapter, some of the most troubling of Palestine's global reverberations will be examined; in the following chapter another, more hopeful side of the same dynamic will be explored.

Suicide bombing is one key element of Global Palestine's politics of violence that is organically related to Palestine's "local" struggle against dromocratic settler colonialism.[62] The most far-reaching reverberation of Palestine's dromocolonization, however, is to be found in the outlines of an emerging global politics of state and other institutional violence that seeks to increase the efficiency of social control through the application of new technologies, many of which have been field tested in Palestine. The use of these technologies tends to increase the distance between those carrying out the violence and those receiving it and, by extension, seeks to shield the former from critical public scrutiny. Once again, as has been evident throughout this book, we must take seriously the will to power that inheres in these efforts while also recognizing that because of their investment in dromocracy, they contain within them the potential to spin out of anyone's control.

The Wall is a useful example of a local mechanism that is directly connected with broader global trends. Through the diffusion of technology, the project has proven to be enormously productive of new realities both within and beyond the immediate area it occupies. When Israel's foremost military historian, Martin van Creveld, laid out a vision for how something like the Wall might work, he specifically referenced how creating such a system of social control would draw upon Israel's position as a world leader in the kind of "modern sensing devices" that make surveillance more effective and efficient.[63]

By 2007, journalist Naomi Klein was arguing that the Wall was one important chapter in the story of Israel's key role in the emergence of an "apartheid planet." Now the fourth-largest arms dealer in the world, Israel has effectively reorganized its economy around its emerging status as a world leader in the "homeland security" sector, foregrounding "precisely the tools and technologies Israel has used to lock in the occupied territories."[64] Far from creating a disastrous drain on what has often been viewed as an artificial, US-subsidized economy, Israel's ongoing control over Palestinian territory is now providing the raw material for a project of what Klein calls "turn[ing] endless war into a brand asset."[65]

Israeli firms continue to take full advantage of these opportunities. At a November 2010 homeland security expo held in Tel Aviv, one marketing manager confirmed Klein's analysis, arguing that his and other high-tech security firms were seeking to leverage the advantage of being able to offer products that are "field-proven."[66] A good example is Narus, which started in Israel during the initial high-tech boom and was later purchased by US-based Boeing. Narus has become a major global player in the provision of what it calls "Real-Time Cyber Defense": systems designed to help corporate and state clients carry out sophisticated and accelerated surveillance of electronic traffic. The attraction of such technology for state security purposes is obvious, and the firm's products are now at work in Egypt, Japan, the US, Pakistan, and Saudi Arabia, to name several prominent examples.[67]

The "rebranding" of Israel's economy must be situated within the global wave of neo-liberal restructuring that has gone hand in hand with a resurgent politics of confinement, a politics that produces what Andy Clarno calls "the proliferation of walled enclosures."[68] As Clarno's perceptive analysis makes clear, this restructuring has facilitated

Israel's rapid integration into the global economy while also enabling new and less costly strategies of dominating the Palestinian population. The combination of neo-liberal restructuring and dromocratic spatial enclosure represents the new, postmodern face of a much older Zionist project of settler colonialism.

This transition has paved the way for the development and deployment of new technologies that radically alter the relationship between the Palestinian population and the agents of Israeli state violence. During the first intifada, this relationship had often taken the form of direct, face-to-face confrontations between heavily armed Israeli soldiers and Palestinians, whether stone throwing demonstrators or just people going about their lives. While such interactions had always been a part of the story, they became more intensive (and generated more media attention) during the uprising, to the point that soldiers began complaining that they were being asked to carry out police work for which they had not been trained. The technologies employed in recent years are partly a response to this dilemma, partly a strategy for dealing with the public relations problem generated by media coverage of hierarchical soldier-civilian interactions, and partly a way of supporting Israel's emerging homeland security economy.

Three characteristics of these new dromocratic technologies have given them a key role in shaping Global Palestine's particular politics of violence. First, they enable Israelis to minimize direct contact with Palestinians even as they are controlling them, displacing them and, in some cases, killing them. This shift is perhaps best illustrated by the difference between the original military checkpoints set up in the West Bank in the post-Oslo years and the new, high-tech checkpoints (often called "terminals," a linguistic choice that deserves its own analysis) that have emerged more recently, beginning in Gaza. The former, while undoubtedly oppressive and humiliating, still retained an unavoidable element of human contact. The Palestinian photographer Rula Halawani captured this dynamic in stunning fashion in "Intimacy," a 2004 series of photographs that zero in on hands as they gesture, touch and exchange the all-important documents at the Qalandia checkpoint near Jerusalem.[69]

The new checkpoints, in sharp contrast, operate according to a logic of remote control aided by technologies that scan bodies from a distance; in the most extreme form of this approach, the Israeli security agents are literally miles away from the actual checkpoint. This logic extends not only to checkpoints, but also to the direct exercise of violence. By altering the "logistics of perception,"[70] such technologies make the violence more clinical and less traumatic—for the perpetrator. "The Palestinians are completely transparent to us," observed one Israeli reservist who took part in the December 2008-January 2009 "Operation Cast Lead" in Gaza. "It feels like hunting season has begun… Sometimes it reminds me of a Play Station [computer] game. You hear cheers in the war room after you see on the screens that the missile hit a target, as if it were a soccer game."[71]

This changing "logistics of perception" is shaping the practice of war and social control across the globe. An excellent example referenced in Klein's article is the Cogito 1002 "Test Station," one of several products manufactured by the Israeli firm Suspect Detection Systems. Described suggestively on the company's website as "a fully automated system not requiring human control and/or operation," the Cogito is now in use in India, Guatemala, Central Asia and elsewhere for purposes of rapid interrogation at airports, border crossings, and other locations. In addition to freeing officers from the messy, face-to-face work of interrogating suspects, the technology promises speed and efficiency: "The COGITO technology enables conducting hundred of interrogations without help of professional interrogator interviewers. In 5 minutes test the system can identify terrorists, employees who has hostile intents, criminals, smugglers or collaborators and direct further interrogation [sic]."[72]

Second, these dromocratic technologies are particularly tempting options for states seeking to control vulnerable populations that have been systematically racialized, pathologized and forced to live and work in the enclosed and abandoned spaces produced by neo-liberal globalization. From refugee camps and *maquiladoras* to the "megaslums" of the Global South[73] and the carceral spaces of the "prison-industrial complex," the politics of confinement are increasingly mediated by the intervention of technologies that facilitate surveillance and the quick, surgical exercise of punitive violence. The realities of enclosure in these areas create certain difficulties for agents of social control as overcrowding reduces visibility and enhances the ability of individuals to disappear in the crowd. At the same time, enclosure also creates the conditions within which these difficulties can be overcome—if you possess the technologies necessary to see through the clutter. The same holds for less enclosed areas often referred to in national security and law enforcement literature as "black spots," "no-go areas," and "failed states." The maritime spaces occupied by Somali pirates are one recent example drawing increasing attention from policy-makers and weapons manufacturers.

The recent emergence of drones ("unmanned aerial vehicles") as key weapons of warfare and social control, a story that continues to unfold rapidly as of this writing, symbolizes this second characteristic of global dromocolonization. The disappearance of the pilot; the acceleration of the act of violence itself; the lack of reaction time for those on the receiving end of the violence; the generalized sense of claustrophobia (recall Lotringer's "confinement under an open sky") created by the presence of the drones; and the dehumanization of victims who are positioned as either targets or collateral damage—all of these suggest the operation of a process that confines everyone within the realities it creates. Equally important is the use of drones to carry out targeted killings (a euphemism for extrajudicial assassinations) in a prime example of how dromocolonization—in this case through the merging of judge, jury and executioner in the form of the drone—effects a disappearance of politics itself.

Both Israel and the US have been at the forefront of this development.[74] Just as the US has tested out its drones in the Philippines and elsewhere, Gaza has been one of the most important "proving grounds" for the Heron drones produced by Israel Aerospace Industries (IAI) and the Hermes drones produced by Elbit Systems. "Operation Cast Lead" included numerous drone attacks that, according to the Israeli military, were aimed at killing important militants active in the area. Reports based on investigations carried out by multiple human rights organizations indicate that these drone attacks were also responsible for killing dozens of civilians.[75]

Despite the fact that drones are clearly not as surgical as their manufacturers might claim, other countries are taking notice of the new technology and its potential for meeting their security needs. In November 2009 IAI announced a $350 million sale of drones to Brazil, where authorities will use the aircraft to oversee its borders and increase security in advance of the country's hosting of two major international sporting events in the coming years. Significantly, *Haaretz* reports—noting Brazil's intention to employ the drones for law enforcement purposes in the country's vast slums—this will be "the model's first use by a police force."[76] Drones, including those built by IAI, have played key roles in the US-led wars in Iraq and Afghanistan, and continue to be used by the US in its undeclared war in Pakistan.

Finally, these technologies are particularly suited to the world of neo-liberal restructuring because they lend themselves well to privatization. While the global wave of privatization that spread to the Global South from Britain and the US in the 1980s originated in the area of public services (transport and utilities), it is now being extended to the waging of war and the broader politics of securitization.[77] Thus it is not surprising to learn that as a world leader in homeland security technologies, Israel is now experimenting with the privatization of its checkpoints. As is the case with other private military companies emerging out of the US (e.g., Blackwater/Xe), Australia (e.g., Unity Resources Group), and South Africa (e.g., Executive Outcomes), Israeli companies such as Beni-Tal Security and Global CST have been active outside the state's borders, helping to shape the changing face of global violence. Such transnational experiments represent another example of settler colonialism's far-reaching influence in the areas of securitization and dromocracy.

What are we to make of these developments? More than thirty years ago, near the end of the essay with which this final section was started, Virilio suggested that the stark realities of the "suicidal state," emerging in the context of extensive endocolonization, present us with an equally stark choice:

To live as poet or assassin?

Like many others, the 14th Arrondissement of Paris is disappearing at this time. It is in ruins like a bomb-site. In these new, indistinct terrains, wild plants grow very high. A great tree is bent over; beneath, some young people are seated, they inhabit, for a moment, poetically this provisional zone of silence and emptiness.

This great, bent-over tree has become a safe retreat.

Further off, beyond the railroad, near the boulevard, already buildings rise up, cars, noise, supermarkets, parking lots, parks...The bomb-sites maintain an uncertain hope, the newly constructed zones offer no other hope than their future destruction.

One will inhabit them as assassin.[78]

In sharp contrast to the "uncertain hope" of the young people engaged in a simple politics of habitation, he argues, the "directors of the suicidal state" possess a boundless "hatred of the everyday" which they share with the rest of us through the mass media. What we are left with is a world of "anti-objects," symbolized by the two leading industries of the post-war American economy: the cinema and the automobile, both of which represent "contempt for, abandonment of, all productive rapport with the milieu." In a world where pure war is waged not in the milieu but on it, violence constitutes the reality in which we live. Hence the question: "To live as poet or assassin?"

The assassins live amongst us; they run and they serve the war machine in which everybody is implicated. They bomb commuter trains and videotape themselves beheading "infidels." They use cluster bombs, phosphorus bombs, suicide vests, drones, "bunker busters" and shells tipped with depleted uranium. They seek quasi-legal justifications for the use of torture and invent ever more sophisticated ways of killing while keeping their hands clean. They seek to profit from every turn of a global economy that is grounded in the structures of pure war. They engage in sacred and secular jihad, believing that they can save the world by destroying it.

And who are the poets? Who are the contemporary counterparts of the young Parisians who peacefully inhabit the ruins? One thinks of those who continue to use habitation as a determined form of resistance in countless locations around the world. One thinks of blues musicians and other artists who stare straight into the face of suffering only to transcend that suffering through their art. One also thinks of the growing number of people who are responding to the global realities of dromocolonization by inventing creative ways of slowing down, defending indigenous knowledge, and insisting on a balanced relationship with the milieu.

To return to the Palestinian context, one thinks of the "uncertain hope" of Palestinians like Anwar, the eleven-year-old Dheisheh Refugee Camp resident who, during the first intifada, would goad soldiers into shooting rubber bullets in his direction so that he could gather them and use them to play marbles with his friends.[79] More recently is the curious example of Gaza Youth Breaks Out, a small group that announced its presence on Facebook in late 2010 via a manifesto that rejects not only Israel's colonial domination, but also the suffocating rule of Hamas and the corruption of the Palestinian Authority. The manifesto is articulated in terms that speak directly to the realities of dromocratic and existential confinement:

We want to scream and break this wall of silence, injustice and indifference like the Israeli F16's breaking the wall of sound; scream with all the power in our souls in order to release this immense frustration that consumes us because of this fucking situation we live in; we are like lice between two nails living a nightmare inside a nightmare, no room for hope, no space for freedom.[80]

Finally, there is the example of the Palestinian and international activists who continue to find creative ways to struggle collectively against the Wall and the destruction of homes and trees (see Chapter 5). Originating in Palestine but also building on traditions established elsewhere (Spain, Mississippi and Chiapas), this solidarity movement draws on a politics of "habitational resistance" and represents a determined response to the oppressive realities of dromocolonization. Just as Walter Benjamin once hailed the poet Charles Baudelaire for heroically parrying the "shocks" of modernity, we might say that Palestinians are some of the most important poets—and prophets—of the age of "shock and awe."

5

OCCUPATION

The previous chapter included a reference to Picasso's *Guernica* and its stunning depiction of the relationship between violent acceleration and confinement in a village that was, in G.L. Steer's words, "compact as peat to serve as fuel for the German planes."[1] The fact that the *Guernica*, despite being rooted in the experience of a single small community, has generally been housed in major international museums suggests a recognition of how it mediates the relationship between this particular experience and something more universal. Despite occasional calls by Basque nationalists to return Picasso's masterwork "home," either to Guernica or to the Guggenheim Museum in Bilbao, the Basque Country has never hosted the mural that bears the name of its iconic village.

What the village does possess, however, is one of the most famous trees in the world, a large oak that inspired the title of Steer's definitive account of the Basque fight for freedom during the Spanish civil war. The Gernikako Arbola remains both a symbol of Basque identity and a traditional site of peaceful political assembly. In a community best known for being a place where forms of violence tested out in the colonies were brought home,[2] and within a region best known as a site of violent struggle between the Spanish state and radical

Basque nationalists, the tree may also be viewed as a reminder of the more ecological (in the broadest sense) impulses that even the most determined war machines can never fully extinguish.

In Portbou, some 700 kilometers to the east, a less famous tree forms part of Dani Karavan's monument to Walter Benjamin. Between the platform and the covered staircase is another part of the monument: an olive tree planted next to the outer wall of the municipal cemetery where Benjamin is buried. Its roots reach into the earth, under the wall, bringing life to the place of the dead. The tree is open—olive trees, after all, can live for centuries unless they are cut down or uprooted by the wind[3]—in sharp contrast to the intense confinement of the cemetery, where the dead are stacked like cordwood, their coffins resembling drawers in an open-air morgue that have been decorated with flowers. Yet the tree is also tied to the earth, the earthly world from whose clutches Benjamin ultimately escaped into the openness of death.

The olive tree is a popular symbol of the Palestinian people, sprinkled throughout their poetry and nationalist iconography as a figure of interiority, home and the abiding link between generations.[4] The botanical symbol of the "new" Israel created in 1948 on the ruins of Palestinian society, by contrast, is a figure of exteriority: the *sabr* (prickly pear cactus). As a way of distinguishing themselves from the weak, victimized people they imagined their diaspora parents to be, and also as a way of constructing a new relationship with the land, the new generation of native-born Israelis began referring to themselves as *sabras*, taking their name from the *Opuntia ficus-indica* cactus that originated in Mesoamerica but has since made its way to arid and semi-arid zones across the globe.[5] Like the fruit of that plant, Israeli *sabras* are said to be sweet on the inside, but tough and prickly on the outside, ready to take on all challengers and to survive whatever the world throws at them. The name of the cactus is etymologically related to the Arabic word for patience.

Many of today's Israeli *sabras* (though not all, of course) look in the mirror and see people who are strong and defiant, not needing to coexist with or cede anything to the other. There is something oddly fitting about this attitude; the prickly pear typically grows wild, finding its home in marginal areas—such as the ruins of destroyed Palestinian villages[6]—in much the same way as Israeli colonies have appeared on hilltops throughout the West Bank. This diverges sharply from the profile of the olive tree, which is carefully cultivated in a traumatropic fashion[7] so that it may continue to provide a wealth of diverse elements (cash, oil, soap and wood) that help sustain the domestic economy.

Botanically and ecologically speaking, then, the prickly pear and the olive tree have little in common. They occupy opposite positions in the nature/culture dichotomy: whereas the former "requires no care" the latter "carries the signature of a person" much as the story bears the "traces of the storyteller" and the clay vessel bears "the handprints of the potter."[8] In Portbou, however, the two plants appear to mingle freely and patiently, partaking of the same soil and often growing out of the same rock. At the other end of the Mediterranean from Israel/Palestine, both keep watch over the memorial to the man who refused to become a Zionist.

When the Nobel Committee announced its decision to award its 2004 Peace Prize to an environmental activist who was best known for planting trees, more than a few observers raised their eyebrows. After all, wasn't the world's most prestigious peace prize typically reserved for those who have a direct hand in resolving armed conflicts (in some cases after waging them)? Wangari Maathai, the Kenyan activist who was honored with the 2004 prize, certainly did not fit that mold. In her acceptance speech, she acknowledged that the committee had done something unusual by choosing to recognize her work in founding the Green Belt Movement and championing the causes of reforestation and (literal) grassroots empowerment. "The committee, I believe, is seeking to encourage community efforts to restore the earth," she said, "at a time when we face the ecological crises of deforestation, desertification, water scarcity and a lack of biological diversity."[9]

Amidst such a global crisis, what was the world's only superpower up to? The day before Maathai accepted her Nobel Prize, the US Congress passed legislation authorizing the Federal Aviation Administration to issue permits for space tourism. Around the same time,

American officials were talking hopefully about the future colonization of Mars. Settler colonizers, it seems, are willing to pay almost any price in order to escape the grassroots.

Reclaiming Occupation

For much of the rest of the world, the importance of protecting trees is self-evidently a matter of life and death. The choice of Maathai represented a recognition of the organic relationship between the struggle for peace and the struggle to defend the biosphere, including and especially the most vulnerable communities that inhabit it, against the impact of a predatory system of global colonization that combines endless capital accumulation with dromocratic violence. This twenty-first-century impulse is the inheritor of a much longer tradition of popular defense discussed in Chapter 3: the tradition of struggle through which local communities have sought to resist the onslaught of dromocratic invaders.

While such efforts have always faced an uphill battle, the age of high globalization has seen the gap between the power of the war machine and the power of popular defense widen even further. Moreover, the shift from geopolitics to chronopolitics means that the notion of place is under siege as "time displaces space as the more significant strategic 'field'" for dromocratic elites.[10] Are there any places left to defend, or are we only inhabiting time now? From within the dromological framework, one almost gets the impression that the game is over: contemporary movements for popular defense are no more than quixotic remnants of a vanished past, and we have no choice but to play out the apocalyptic string from within the prison of "real time."

Or perhaps not. As the example of today's Palestinians and their international solidarity comrades suggests, the need to defend locality through various forms of popular defense remains a strong impulse with a growing sense of global urgency. Such efforts draw much of their motivation and their moral strength from their place-based nature—the desire to enable continued occupation of the land—and in this sense they share important characteristics with the kinds of everyday survival strategies that have long aided oppressed groups in their quest to mitigate the effect of colonization and other forms of political domination.

The conditions within which a popular defense can be mounted, however, have changed dramatically in recent decades. State repression and popular mobilization alike are now enmeshed in circuits of accelerated global violence that both use and are used by acceleration, operating both within and beyond a politics of control. These circuits, in turn, are directly connected with the widespread securitization of politics discussed in Chapter 3. Equally important, the same kinds of technologies that enable solidarity movements to communicate, educate the public, and bear witness to what is happening on the ground also threaten to obliterate the possibility of place-based resistance altogether.

In short, efforts at popular defense now inevitably find themselves confronted by and implicated in the realities of globalization in general and the "relatively autonomous" realities of dromocolonization in particular. The great value of the dromological approach, in this case, is that when combined with close attention to what is happening on the ground, it helps us understand the central dilemma facing anyone who wishes to engage in an anticolonial struggle for social justice in the twenty-first century: how to negotiate a path between acceleration and occupation without being swallowed by the former.

In framing the issue in this way, I seek to recover and reinscribe one of the key concepts typically used to frame the politics of Israel/Palestine. The conventional usage of the term "occupation" to describe Israel's military domination of the West Bank and Gaza since 1967 is built on an unstated assumption that it is the presence of soldiers, whether this presence is viewed as oppressive or defensive, that makes the territories "occupied." In fact, Palestine is the site of not one, but two occupations, both of which are occluded by this assumption. The first is the settler colonial occupation of Palestine by the Zionist project. The second is the stubborn, everyday habitation of the land by Palestinians, a human occupation that has always represented Zionism's most fundamental obstacle.

The Palestinian occupation and the diverse forms of resistance associated with it are grounded in what Arturo Escobar describes as the desire to pursue "the defense of particular, place-based historical conceptions of the world and practices of world-making"; such struggles, he insists, are "place-based, yet transnationalised."[11] They retain and seek to defend a deep connection with the land, rejecting the relentless commodification of life forms associated with neo-liberalism, the deterritorialization wrought by colonial domination and the most extreme kinds of rootlessness fostered by the increasing dominance of chronopolitics. At the same time, they also pursue their aims by tapping into the networks that globalizing technologies have helped to create.

Chapter 3 examined how, during the "long 1960s," the exiled Palestinian revolutionaries, operating in a context of radical delocalization, chose to respond by "occupying" the world's airwaves and transportation arteries. In the process, they unwittingly helped push forward the process of global dromocolonization. By contrast, today's Palestinian revolutionaries operate in a context where the struggle has literally returned to its roots: land, trees, rocks and homes. It is no accident that more of the violence in Palestine in recent years has taken place in and around these basic elements of habitation. These conditions have given rise to new forms of popular defense, particularly those associated with a robust movement of international solidarity that has arisen during the past decade, a movement that is now attracting significant participation from Israeli Jews. This movement faces the difficult task of trying to defend the rights and the integrity of Palestinian communities while contributing as little oxygen as possible to the dromocratic war machine. It is precisely this challenge, however, that creates an increasingly strong basis from which to build bridges with wider movements that are facing the same dilemma, including movements for global justice, ecological sustainability, and indigenous rights.

Understanding the challenges confronting the Palestinian occupation first requires an examination of what might be called the political ecology of Israel's own settler colonial system—in particular its ongoing war on the Palestinian milieu. As the subsequent section will explore, this war has taken as its target the fabric of everyday life, turning even the most mundane, everyday practices into opportunities for repression—and resistance.

Israel's "War on the Milieu"

In his remarkable book, *Palestinian Walks*, Ramallah lawyer and human rights activist Raja Shehadeh narrates a series of lengthy walks through the hills and valleys that make up the "vanishing landscape" of the West Bank, using each as an opportunity to explore the complex ecosystems of the area and the dramatic transformations set in motion by Israeli colonization. One of these walks takes place in 1999, well after the creation of the PA but before the outbreak of the second intifada. During this so-called "Interim Phase," Palestinian security forces were "given" nominal control over small areas of the West Bank, resulting in an even more byzantine set of checkpoints (both Israeli and PA), jurisdictions, and other structures that left the territory increasingly fragmented and militarized but still, ultimately, dominated by Israel.

As Shehadeh and his wife, Penny Johnson, are trekking through the A'yn Qenya valley, they suddenly come under sustained gunfire. Given the interim realities just described, they are unsure what to make of their predicament. Are the shots coming from Israeli soldiers, Jewish settlers, Palestinian police or other Palestinian gunmen? Are the hikers being mistaken for settlers or suspected "terrorists"? When the shots finally stop after twenty harrowing minutes, they are able to extricate themselves and return home. Later Shehadeh discusses the issue with the *Muhafiz* (the Palestinian governor of Ramallah), who suggests that the shooters had been a group of *shabab* (young Palestinian men) engaging in target practice and tells Shehadeh matter-of-factly, "You shouldn't go to the valley." For Shehadeh, a lifelong hiker and defender of Palestinian land rights, hearing this message from a fellow Palestinian is too much to bear:

"They mustn't do this," I said. "There are shepherds there and others who walk in the hills. I have been walking for twenty-five years. Nothing ever happened to me in these hills. I never had to worry. People should be encour-

aged to walk in the hills. It will increase their attachment to their country."
The Muhafiz didn't agree. "You shouldn't walk," he repeated in a concerned
paternal tone. "It's much too dangerous."[12]

Had he been a fan of American science fiction, the Muhafiz might
have realized that he was acting out the theme of "The Pedestrian,"
Ray Bradbury's classic 1951 story of a future time when the simple
act of walking in the city is enough to land the protagonist, Leonard
Mead, in the "Psychiatric Center for Research on Regressive
Tendencies."

While it may seem Kafkaesque, Shehadeh's story indicates the operation of a logic that is hard-wired into the expansionist mindset of
settler colonialism. Despite the existence of powerful patriotic discourses that invoke the beauty of the land and the need to defend it,
settler projects tend to be oriented toward the violent conquest of territory rather than the peaceful occupation of it. Drawing on the work
of Wendell Berry, Anthony Hall writes that this attitude of "transient
frontierism" has produced in North America "a pattern of sustained
hostility towards any group that wove its way of life together with its
sense of identity into the ecological fabric of a particular place."[13] The
same argument applies to the settler colonial hostility toward the
indigenous population of Palestine.

Shehadeh's surreal conversation with the Muhafiz appears prophetic
in the context of Israel's 2008 "Operation Cast Lead" assault on Gaza.
In testimony given to the Breaking the Silence organization and
quoted in a provocative report by the Public Committee Against Torture in Israel (PCATI), one Israeli soldier described the attitude of the
Israeli military toward Palestinian civilians in Gaza during the operation. In the process, he demonstrated precisely what happens when
the logic of the Muhafiz ("You shouldn't walk. It's much too dangerous") is merged with the realities of dromocratic violence described
in the previous chapter. "If we detect any thing that should not be
there—we shoot," the soldier observed. "We're told the air force distributed flyers telling everyone to go to Gaza City. If beyond this line
any people are detected—they are not supposed to be there."[14]

The soldier's testimony, while laudable for its honesty, is ultimately
redundant. After all, within the terms of the settler colonial project,

Palestinians by definition are "not supposed to be there." It is hardly surprising, therefore, to find that the policies of the settler state are geared toward reinforcing that definition. As the authors of the PCATI report point out, the confined and carceral realities of Gaza (a territory of only 139 square miles that is home to 1.6 million people) meant that the Israeli policy of pushing residents to leave their homes and flee elsewhere guaranteed that large numbers of people would find themselves on the street and therefore considered, in the words of one Israeli commander, "not innocent" and "doomed to die."[15]

What happened in Gaza during Operation Cast Lead is not simply the product of a specific and relatively recent dynamic between Israeli and Hamas violence; it is also the culmination of Israel's entire post-1967 policy vis-à-vis the Palestinians. Even as it was projecting its military reach externally toward the exiled Palestinian guerrillas, the Israeli state was establishing a strategy of perpetual counterinsurgency in the newly-captured West Bank and Gaza, a strategy that has increasingly taken the form of a war that is waged directly on a people's capacity for biological and social reproduction and on the natural and built environment that ensures their survival—in short, a war on the milieu.[16] Food, water, shelter, vegetation, education and infrastructure are some of the primary objects of this war. With its extraordinarily detailed philosophy of "another acre, another goat,"[17] the Zionist/Israeli colonization of Palestine has always had its own (colonial) ecology rooted in the careful and systematic attempt to manage the natural and built environment to its own advantage, if necessary by destroying it. In Derek Gregory's apt characterization, "It is though the very earth has been turned into an enemy."[18]

Nothing illustrates the logic of Israel's war on the milieu more clearly than the systematic destruction of olive trees. In a sustained campaign that recalls a host of US actions directed against the milieu in many places (the near-extinction of the buffalo in North America, the defoliation of Vietnam, the bombing of water treatment facilities in Baghdad, the use of graphite bombs to create widespread blackouts in Yugoslavia), the Israeli military has uprooted hundreds of thousands of olive trees since 1967. This arboricidal process has accelerated significantly during the construction of the Wall in recent years, predictably damaging Palestine's economy and also dealing a power-ful symbolic blow to Palestine's national imaginary.

An equally visible aspect of this war on the milieu has been the Israeli practice of eliminating Palestinian homes, whether through direct demolition, systematic discrimination against non-Jews in the issuing of building permits, or the kind of widespread destruction car-ried out in military campaigns. With the military's use of increasingly overwhelming force, particularly in urban environments, this aspect of the colonial project has also been extended to the full range of structures including mosques, hospitals, factories and government buildings. This development is illustrated by the difference between Ariel Sharon's 2002 "Operation Defensive Shield" in the West Bank (approximately 900 buildings destroyed) and Ehud Olmert's assault on Gaza (nearly 4,000 buildings destroyed in space roughly one-fif-teenth the size of the West Bank) only six years later.[19]

The war on the milieu has also not stopped at the ground level: a less visible aspect of the policy is the diverting of water resources from underneath the feet of Palestinians for use by Israelis, including those who live in settlement colonies. Yet while the water issue has received a fair amount of attention from scholars, journalists and political nego-tiators, the other underground issue—the politics of sewage—has remained virtually ignored. Eyal Weizman, one of the few people to address this particular issue, connects the sewage issue with "the hygienic phobia of Zionism," a phobia that "sees the presence of Pal-estinians as a 'defiled' substance within the 'Israeli' landscape…"[20] Once again, the most extreme manifestation of the issue is to be found in Gaza, where periodic sewage crises garner momentary attention as much for their "threat" to Israel as for what they say about the living conditions of Palestinian refugees.

The politics of sewage points us to an understanding of the biopo-litical nature of the war on the milieu. Gaza, in particular, has been the site of a sustained experiment in how to use freedom from want (see Chapter 2) as a tool of social control. Cut off from the outside world by the Israeli blockade, Gazans have found themselves targeted by the weaponization of food. In a move that connects directly with the broader global trend of militarized humanitarianism, Israel's control of access to Gaza proceeds through a combination of collective punishment and the occasional provision of food to prevent mass starvation. The opening paragraph of a 2006 *New York Times* report illustrates this process perfectly:

Israel reopened the main freight crossing to the Gaza Strip on Monday to allow delivery of flour and sugar to the Palestinians. But it abruptly closed the crossing after just a half-hour, citing security threats.[21]

By reducing Palestinians to "bare life," this policy bears considerable responsibility for a growing and now well-documented pattern of malnutrition, stunted growth and psychological trauma throughout the Gaza population.[22]

Equally biopolitical is the impact of Israeli domination on pregnant women and their unborn and newborn children. One of the most devastating effects of the creation of Israel's web of checkpoints during the post-Oslo years has been to place the very process of reproduction at special risk as women on their way to the hospital are forced to wait, sometimes for hours, at checkpoints. Meanwhile, perhaps owing to its ongoing national obsession with maintaining Jewish demographic superiority, Israel is also a world leader in assisted reproductive technologies, thus making it a pioneer in what amounts to the next biopolitical phase of endocolonization: the colonization of the body by technology.[23] When placed in the broader context of the processes discussed in this section, Israel's own politics of reproduction echo the settler colonial biopolitics of North America and Australia in forming an important part of its war on the milieu.[24]

The Palestinian Occupation: Existence is Resistance

The cumulative material effects of Israel's war on the milieu have dramatically altered the political horizon of Palestinian nationalism and the conditions within which Palestinians engage in the popular defense of their communities. What I am calling the Palestinian occupation has been present throughout the period of settler colonization—indeed, it represents the most implacable obstacle to the settler project and its "logic of elimination"—but it has been relatively ignored thanks to Zionism's ideological success in focusing the attention of external observers on more spectacular forms of Palestinian resistance. Recent developments, however, have given the Palestinian occupation greater visibility as the politics of survival and habitation take center stage. With its emphasis on an unhurried and grounded relationship with place, the Palestinian occupation is also opposed to the structures of dromocolonization in which the state of Israel and some of its adversaries—those who seek faster and more effective ways of visiting violence upon Israelis—are heavily invested.

Shehadeh's story of being shot at by Palestinian gunmen linked with the Palestinian Authority's extensive security apparatus reveals the importance of the Palestinian occupation by illustrating a tension between sovereignty and what might be called self-sovereignty.[25] The modern concept of sovereignty is difficult to separate from the history of the confrontation between Europe and its colonial "others," leading one to wonder whether it might be viewed as a colonial concept at its very core.[26] Self-sovereignty, on the other hand, refers to the desire to feel "at home" in the world and to feel some sense of control over one's circumstances.

Given the extent to which colonial-style hierarchies continue to structure even supposedly postcolonial relations, it is clear that the tension between sovereignty and self-sovereignty cannot be resolved simply by appealing to state-centered anticolonial nationalism. In the case of Palestine, as numerous critics have pointed out, the creation of the PA was essentially a colonial subcontracting operation, with the Palestinian leadership expected to concern itself with protecting Israeli security. What this means is that the things ordinary Palestinians are defending are less the things that make for sovereignty and more the things that make for self-sovereignty. Specifically, as the dream of a truly independent Palestinian state fades into oblivion, more and more Palestinians find themselves engaging in different forms of what might be called habitational resistance.

One of the by-products of this gradual shift is that it makes the settler colonial nature of the situation more visible to all. Within Israel, for example, the number of voices openly embracing the settler identity and the "logic of elimination" appears to be on the rise. This development is a direct result of the shrinking ideological space available to those Israeli Jews who had previously held on to the belief that Zionism could somehow be disentangled from its settler foundations. Among Palestinians, articulations of an indigenous identity—that is, a "Fourth World" identity that would suggest strong linkages with, say, the Cherokee or aboriginal Australians—have been historically rare when compared with the salience of pan-Arab, pan-Islamic or pan-"Third World" solidarity.[27] Yet the necessary shift toward a politics of habitation has left Palestinians with a growing need to prioritize one of the cardinal, near-ontological principles of indigenous identity and power in a settler colonial world: the refusal to leave the land and disappear. Existence, in this sense, is resistance.

The case of tree farmer Abdel Fattah Abed Rabbo illustrates the lengths to which a settler colonial project will go in order to oppose the existential resistance of the colonized. In November 2009 Abed Rabbo found himself facing eviction by Israeli authorities who accused him of building without a permit. What drew the attention of journalists was the fact that his supposedly illegal building was, in fact, a cave he was occupying in the hills between Jerusalem and Bethlehem, where his wife and children live in the Dheisheh refugee camp.[28] It appears that he was targeted for eviction more than once, most recently because of plans to build a new settlement, Givat Yael, as part of Israel's ongoing expansion of Jerusalem on land annexed illegally in 1980. "Don't charge me," Abed Rabbo was reported to have said. "Charge nature."[29]

Settler colonialism does both: it "charges" not only the colonized but also their "natural" connection to the land, a connection that frustrates the settler project and provokes the habitational resistance the settler state must then violently suppress. Thus did the Israeli state come to employ more than a thousand police officers, backed by bulldozers and helicopters, in a July 2010 assault aimed at demolishing al-Araqib, a village occupied by some 300 Bedouin members of the al-Turi tribe who had been temporarily relocated in the early 1950s but had continued to use the land for farming and grazing before returning to build homes there in the late 1990s.[30] This and other recent cases involving Bedouin land rights have raised for official Israel the specter of the sort of serious debate over "native title" that took place in Australia during the 1990s.

One of the most ironic and revealing aspects of the al-Araqib case is that the stated purpose of the 2010 demolition of the village was to clear space so that the Jewish National Fund could plant a forest there. Here it is important to note that the planting of trees has long served a dual purpose in Israel. First, it has provided a thin but powerful layer of ecological justification for the expropriation of land from non-Jewish owners and occupants. Equally important, however, it has provided ideological fuel for Zionism's entire settler colonial imaginary. Efforts to "make the desert bloom," after all, fit hand in glove with efforts to establish an indigenous identity for Jewish settlers by asserting their close connection to the land. Only by achieving such a reversal does it become possible to claim—as has often been claimed with respect to Bedouin communities in Israel—that they are "invaders" rather than rights-bearing inhabitants.[31]

By resisting their state-sponsored deterritorialization and the planting of the Jewish National Fund (JNF) forest, therefore, the al-Turi not only brought public attention to their immediate plight, but also implicitly called attention to the logic behind a classic settler colonial move. In each of these cases, forced removals and their attendant legal rationalizations (e.g., the doctrine of *terra nullius* or, in the case of Israel, the declaration of Bedouin lands as "dead" lands) were followed by ecological assaults—war on the milieu—that subjected indigenous communities to everything from radiation poisoning to the spraying of defoliants and other toxic chemicals on crops;[32] further efforts to displace indigenous people by moving them into urban areas (e.g., through the US postwar "detribalization" policy referred to in Chapter 3, or the Israeli creation of state-sponsored "development towns" in the Negev); and the discursive confinement of the indigenous population either as criminals or terrorists (for those who resist) or as two-dimensional "natives" who serve as tourist attractions or reminders of an idealized and sanitized past. All of this, combined with the propagation of discourses that highlight the beauty of the land and assert the settlers' love of and care for it, is designed to effect the reversal noted above.

To return briefly to the theme of the previous chapter, the examples just discussed also reveal another of settler colonialism's most dromocratic elements. With its "time-oriented" narratives of "development," Western colonization has always clashed with indigenous ways of knowing that are built upon a holistic, relational notion of place. By removing indigenous people from the land, it seeks to insert them coercively into a new, more chronopolitical arrangement—even as it seeks, ironically enough, to establish its own place-based credentials. Yet in the final analysis, settler colonialism has been remarkably unsuccessful at extinguishing the ethical and cosmological orientation of indigenous communities, an orientation that remains a key resource in the ongoing struggle to resist what Glen Coulthard describes as "the dual imperatives of state sovereignty and capitalist accumulation that constitute our colonial present."[33]

As the large literature on Palestinian refugees clearly demonstrates, the experience of violent and continuing dislocation—the ongoing *Nakba*—generates not only a deep longing for return, but also a deep attachment to the places in which the refugees have been dislocated and confined. When I worked in Balata camp in 1996–97, for example, the community's sense of collective identity and determination to defend its territory was palpable. Indeed, Balata has long been famous for resisting the entry of Israeli soldiers, a reputation that led to the "walking through walls" strategy of 2002's "Operation Defensive Shield." In a similar way, Palestinian refugees in Gaza have developed a strong sense of Gazan identity despite having been pushed to live there against their will. In short, the Palestinian occupation to which I am referring is a product not only of centuries of habitation in Shehadeh's West Bank hills, but also of the deterritorialization wrought by settler colonialism.

As a form of resistance to the settler project, this occupation has always had as its basic building block the actions of Palestinian families on the micro level. With colonization largely taking the daily, inexorable form of "another acre, another goat," Palestine is full of examples of heroic families who have spent years struggling against land confiscation within the Israeli court system and staying on their land amidst the physical encroachment of the settlement colonies. With families serving as a foundational source of social solidarity,[34] it is not surprising that settler states often seek to disrupt this solidarity through the cultivation of suspicion within families and communities; Israel's creation of a system of collaborators throughout the West Bank and Gaza since 1967 is an excellent example of such a strategy.

The politics of habitational resistance has historically found further expression in the long tradition of Palestinian nonviolent action at the community level. Perhaps the best-known example of this is the growth of popular committees (*lijan sha'biya*) during the first intifada. These committees took upon themselves a wide range of tasks related to popular defense including medical relief, clandestine education, local security and emergency food production in the form of community gardens.[35] Such efforts, however, built upon a process of popular organizing that had been steadily building throughout the first two decades of Israel's military domination of the West Bank and Gaza.[36] Women, youth, students, workers, shopkeepers and farmers have all been involved in nonviolent resistance to Israeli rule.

It would be an exaggeration to say that ecological awareness has played a major role in the Palestinian liberation movement to date. With nationalist and Islamist elements dominating the political stage throughout the past century, Palestinians seeking to work on environmental issues have mostly had to do so with little fanfare. With the growth of an indigenous consciousness, however, comes the recognition, to quote John Trudell, that "we are the land."[37] As the war on the milieu raises the ecological stakes, both locally and globally, it also produces new ways of conceiving the project of resisting the deep structures put in place by settler colonialism, and Palestine, once again, emerges as part of something much larger.

The concept of permaculture provides one focal point for local ecological activism while also providing a basis from which to build bridges between settler societies. Strongly influenced by indigenous science and philosophy, permaculture came into public consciousness in the 1970s through the work of Australian researchers David Holmgren and Bill Mollison and is best understood as the effort to build truly sustainable human communities through the application of land use strategies that are derived from a deep understanding of how natural ecosystems work. Permaculture projects are tackling a variety of issues related to food security in indigenous communities across the globe, including the Pine Ridge Reservation in South Dakota, site of the 1890 Wounded Knee massacre and the 1973 Wounded Knee siege.[38] The growth of such projects indicates the operation of a global knowledge exchange circuit that builds upon longstanding bonds of pan-indigenous solidarity, helping to keep alive popular alternatives to the state-level "settler international" discussed in Chapter 3.

Permaculture is also present in Palestine in a way that highlights the impulse toward self-sovereignty. Just as Shehadeh's simple act of walking in the hills took on added political significance, the practices of permaculture become acts of habitational resistance when they occur in a context of ongoing settler colonial domination. The Bustan Qaraaqa (Tortoise Garden) located in the West Bank town of Beit Sahour, for example, defines its mission in terms of "restor[ing] a sense of independence and dignity to people suffering under brutal military occupation."[39] In pursuing this permaculture project, from tree cultivation and rainwater conservation to environmental consultancy and a "Green Intifada" blog,[40] the community activists at Bustan Qaraaqa are following in their town's proud tradition of nonviolent resistance, a tradition forged during the tax revolt launched by its residents during the first intifada.

The politics of indigenous knowledge are notoriously complex, with legitimate concerns about cultural imperialism and appropriation never far from the surface. Ecological activism, under certain circumstances, can also take the form of "greenwashing" tactics that serve as cover for efforts to sideline questions of political rights. Such concerns are important to keep in mind at a time when efforts to bring Palestinians and Israeli Jews together to work on environmental projects are generating more public attention. The most promising of these projects are those that ground their work firmly in the work of confronting settler colonial realities and moving toward a truly democratic, post-Zionist future.

Even for those Palestinians who live in the most limited situations, permaculture is emerging as an attractive strategy of self-sovereignty and habitational resistance. In Gaza, the combination of Israel's blockade, several years of inadequate rainfall, and the arrival of an especially violent storm in late 2010 has pushed many Palestinians there to nurture a whole series of ecological practices ranging from organic pesticide production to small-scale fish farming. "Urban agriculture," a trendy topic in the aging industrial centers of the United States, is finding a home in Gaza's refugee camps. As Simon Boas notes, Gaza's solutions may be as important to the globe as Gaza's problems have been.[41]

"Gravity and Density": Solidarity and Popular Defense in Palestine

If the habitational resistance of Palestinians is finally beginning to come into the light, this is partly because of the presence of the international solidarity activists who have brought great energy and visibility to the struggles of ordinary Palestinians. Now more than ever, the popular defense of Palestinian communities is a globalized process. The growth in collaboration between these communities and activists affiliated with the International Solidarity Movement (ISM) and other groups during the past decade has coincided with the escalating process of dromocratic confinement. Writing presciently in 1993 on the "principle of confinement" animating the contemporary practices of US imperialism, Edward Said also prefigured the rise of the ISM and the broader global justice movement when he identified the emergence of an "elusive oppositional mood....an internationalist counter-articulation" closely linked with the "antisystemic movements" described in the literature on world-systems theory.[42]

Many of the movements associated with this global counter-articulation have consciously responded to the "principle of confinement" by insisting on their right as human beings to inhabit streets, abandoned buildings and other public spaces. Taking back the notion of occupation is an important component of the activist networks that are struggling to resist the violent injustices of neo-liberal globalization. To give just one example, the young people who took over an empty printing factory in the Madrid neighborhood of Lavapies in 2003 and renamed it "Laboratorio 3" were clearly engaging in habitational resistance. When I visited the site in 2003, shortly after the US launched its war in Iraq, the Laboratorio was a fully-functioning community including a kitchen, media center, public art and dance studios, concert space, as well as ample meeting space for activists. "Palestine" was a visible presence, from posters on the walls to the "intifada" chants of the crowd taking in an evening concert.

The importance of Palestine for European squatter projects like the Laboratorio 3 is part of a much longer tradition grounded primarily in the bonds of subaltern solidarity. When the poor areas of Los Angeles rose in revolt in 1992 after the Rodney King verdict, for example, community activists referred to the uprising as LA's "intifada."[43] Around the same time, John Trudell wrote and recorded "Rich Man's War," a devastating song critiquing the first Gulf War, the war in which there was, according to the Bush administration at the time, no linkage between the Iraqi invasion of Kuwait and the Israeli domination of Palestine. Situating his critique in the context of a broader critique of colonization and industrial capitalism, Trudell explicitly links Palestine with a range of places including Harlem, Pine Ridge and Belfast. The latter reference called to mind Northern Ireland's famous Republican murals that prominently reference Palestine as part of a broader anticolonial discourse.

The importance of solidarity with Palestine finds arguably its most eloquent expression in one of Said's final writings, in which the world's most famous Palestinian scholar called for a "more comparative and critical" engagement with the Palestinian struggle and offered a spirited, hopeful observation perhaps directed at those who tend to get discouraged at the often suffocating North American ideological environment:

Remember the solidarity here and everywhere in Latin America, Africa, Europe, Asia and Australia, and remember also that there is a cause to which many people have committed themselves, difficulties and terrible obstacles notwithstanding. Why? Because it is a just cause, a noble ideal, a moral quest for equality and human rights.[44]

Said's reminder highlighted the fact that the Palestinian struggle, much like the anti-apartheid struggle in South Africa did in an earlier time, forms the hub of a global web that not only connects people of diverse experiences, but also provides an idiom within which to see important commonalities among those experiences. In this sense it is hardly surprising that the Palestinian and South African liberation movements have nurtured and maintained strong bonds for decades in the form of everything from official ANC-PLO ties to popular actions such as the 1994 decision of the local ANC branch in Orange Farm, a South African squatter community of 250,000 residents, to rename the area "Palestine" as an act of transnational solidarity.[45]

In some cases, it must be noted, identification with Palestine can be a shallow and highly romanticized attachment that does not stretch beyond the exercise of political fashion statements (e.g., wearing a *kufiya*). In other cases, however, the connection with Palestine is more deeply felt and becomes the basis for life-changing decisions. The most famous example, of course, is the young American activist Rachel Corrie, who was crushed to death by an Israeli bulldozer in 2003 as she attempted to prevent the demolition of a Palestinian home in Rafah in the southern Gaza Strip. In the aforementioned article, Said used Corrie's death as an occasion to reflect on the continuing and growing power of the solidarity movement:

What Rachel Corrie's work in Gaza recognized was precisely the gravity and the density of the living history of the Palestinian people as a national community, and not merely as a collection of deprived refugees. That is what she was in solidarity with. And we need to remember that that kind of solidarity is no longer confined to a small number of intrepid souls here and there, but is recognized the world over.[46]

In choosing to invoke the ideas of gravity and density, Said called attention to the transformation that often occurs when activists cross the geographic threshold and find themselves on the ground in Palestine, feeling the weight not only of the deep structures put in place by settler colonization, but also of the tenacious occupation maintained by the colonized.

The key practices of the solidarity movement are closely allied with local Palestinian efforts at nonviolent, habitational resistance. These practices include witnessing, documenting, standing with Palestinians in their homes and at checkpoints, assisting with the harvesting of olives under the threat of settler violence and, perhaps most visibly, working in communities that are most directly affected by the construction of the Wall. By engaging in large-scale land confiscation in places such as Bil'in, a West Bank village located between Ramallah and the Green Line, the Israeli state has created specific focal points for solidarity work. The local and international activists, in turn, have seized upon the opportunity to use these locations as testing grounds for new forms of grassroots action against the Wall, including the practice of activists chaining themselves to trees. Once an unremarkable agricultural village with a population of 1800, Bil'in now hosts an annual international conference and features prominently in the burgeoning, media-savvy world of Palestinian solidarity activism.

In recent years Palestine has also generated remarkable new bodies of creative work on the part of artists and activists, both Palestinian and international, who seek to comment on changing spatial arrangements and their emotional and political implications. One famous example is the work of Banksy, the British guerrilla graffiti artist who created nine stenciled images on the concrete of the Israeli wall in 2005. During the same year, a Madrid gallery hosted a collaborative exhibition called *Mirando a Palestina* (Looking Towards Palestine) that featured the work of more than a dozen Palestinian, European, and American photographers. Whether in Diego Lopez Calvin's image of Palestinians projecting a movie onto the Wall, Peter Fryer's treatment of the barriers created by grinding rural poverty among Palestinian refugees in Lebanon, or the stunning work of Palestinian photographer Rula Halawani referred to in the previous chapter, the exhibition provided a provocative visual commentary on the everyday politics of confinement and habitation.[47] More recently the Wall Project,[48] sponsored by the Wende Museum in Los Angeles, used the occasion of the twentieth anniversary of the fall of the Berlin Wall to draw parallels with other walls including the one in Palestine.

Global Justice Between Acceleration and Occupation

This chapter has evidenced that the popular defense of the Palestinian occupation continues to be shaped not only locally, by Israel's war on the milieu, but also globally, by the considerable impact of the structures of dromocratic violence. We have also seen that evidence testifying to Palestine's large and growing significance for a variety of people around the world continues to mount—with good reason. What are the implications of these dynamics, both for Palestinians and for the rest of us who live in Global Palestine?

One place to begin an examination of this question is with the example of the Gaza tunnel system that has been targeted in recent years by the Israeli military. On the one hand, the tunnels—created as a response to the carceral conditions that prevailed after the Israeli "disengagement" from the territory—undoubtedly play a key role in the Palestinian occupation: they enable Gazans to continue to inhabit the land without running completely out of food or fuel. They also constitute a powerful symbolic device that can be mobilized and circulated globally—for example, via the many available videos that take viewers inside the tunnels—as evidence of Palestinian suffering and desperation. On the other hand, their military function of facilitating the entry of weapons indicates that the tunnels can also serve to push forward the dynamic of violent acceleration that continues to hold Gaza's population in bondage. Many Palestinians, for understandable reasons, might see this as a necessary contradiction, but it remains a contradiction—one that reveals a great deal about the starkly limited situation that settler colonization has produced in Palestine.

At a (literally) deeper level, the case of the Gaza tunnels calls our attention to how transformations in the practice of war during the past century have affected the options available to those on the receiving end of state violence. When the state controls the air, whether through traditional weaponry (planes, helicopters and missiles), satellite surveillance or the advanced tools of information warfare, those seeking to resist state violence are often forced to dig deep. To use a current example, the complex maze of anonymity and mirror sites designed to protect WikiLeaks is ultimately a radically deterritorialized version of the famous tunnels that helped the Vietnamese guerrillas prolong the war against US imperialism. Perhaps more farcically, recall the images of Saddam Hussein being dragged out of his "spider hole" by US forces who later insisted, in another set of widely circulated images, that even the Iraqi dictator's teeth be rendered visible to military doctors. In this light, the Gaza tunnels—along with recent reports of similar tunnels being found underneath the US-Mexico border—suggest a clear relationship between modern dromocratic violence and the practices of subterranean resistance.

In such an environment, engaging in a true popular defense today requires eschewing, to the greatest extent possible, the politics of violent acceleration. While it is not impossible to imagine isolated individuals affiliated with the solidarity movement who might deliberately engage in clandestine cooperation with armed Palestinian groups, or even with the Israeli state, the larger issue is that the global structures of dromocratic violence leave all activists vulnerable to unintended consequences. Even a philosophical commitment to pacifism does not guarantee that one can control the effects of one's own actions. The pro-Israeli propaganda campaign against global solidarity activists in Palestine leverages precisely this fact by taking a movement that presents itself as nonviolent and attempting to reframe it as a material supporter of the kind of terrorism (in the form of suicide bombings) that must be subject, in the dominant public discourse, to "absolute moral condemnation."[49] The networked nature of contemporary violence and the representation of violence means that solidarity activists can never refute such charges definitively.

The dilemmas facing solidarity activists, Palestinians and internationals alike, point us toward one of the most important social justice questions of the twenty-first century: how can acceleration be politicized in order to construct an effective movement of global popular defense? In the same way that Marxism and workers movements helped politicize wealth, or feminism and other "new social movements" helped politicize identity, what is needed now is a movement that makes visible the relationship between acceleration and permanent social war. Fortunately, we also see all around us evidence of what amounts to the social basis for a dynamic global occupation movement.[50]

One of the key elements of this picture is the broad, coalitional politics of the World Social Forum (WSF) and its "movement of movements"–though it is hardly an uncontested element.[51] Created primarily as a grassroots response to the claim that "there is no alternative" to the globalization of neo-liberal capitalism, the WSF has been criticized for privileging the perspectives and the leadership role of middle-class, educated populations and also for being disproportionately whiter than the larger population it claims to represent.[52] The opposition of these relatively privileged groups to the dominant system, critics suggest, is drastically undercut by their often unacknowledged investment in it, an investment symbolized by their level of comfort in inhabiting the placeless world of the internet at a time when more marginalized populations are engaged in place-based struggles.

Similarly, the Forum's origins in the critique of capitalism initially had the effect of marginalizing some of the issues (e.g., environmental sustainability and militarization) and perspectives (e.g., indigenous people) that would presumably be central to maintaining and strengthening the tradition of popular defense against the destructive and suicidal politics of dromocolonization. More recently, however, there are indications that the WSF and the many national and regional forums it has spawned are moving toward a more inclusive approach in response to both internal critiques and the emerging realities of "imperial globality" and "global coloniality" in which "the global economy comes to be supported by a global organization of violence and vice versa."[53] Boaventura de Sousa Santos, one of the most prominent intellectuals associated with the WSF, signaled this direction shortly after the launch of the US war on Iraq in 2003:

A strategic shift is required. Social movements, no matter what their spheres of struggle, must give priority to the fight for peace, as a necessary condition for the success of all the other struggles. This means that they must be in the frontline of the fight for peace, and not simply leave this space to be occupied solely by peace movements. All the movements against neoliberal globalization are, from now on, peace movements…The peace to be fought for is not a mere absence of war or terrorism. It is rather a peace based upon the elimination of the conditions that foster war and terrorism: global injustice, social exclusion, cultural and political discrimination and oppression and imperialist greed.[54]

The shift that Santos envisions is not a minor one, nor is it necessarily a palatable one for those who insist that war is simply a tool of capitalism. Nonetheless, refusing to subordinate the struggle against militarization to a narrow anti-capitalist politics is arguably more in tune with the global realities that colonization in general, and settler colonialism in particular, have fostered in the modern era. Palestinians, like all those who have been targeted, displaced and/or enslaved by settler colonial projects, have found that war on the milieu also makes ecological issues increasingly integral to the fight for peace.

In this light, it is hardly accidental that the idea of globalization from below has coincided with a renewed global politics of indigeneity, whether in national elections (e.g., the presidency of Evo Morales in Bolivia), transnational action (e.g., the series of hemispheric indigenous summits first held during the past decade), or at the level of international institutions (e.g., the passage of the UN Declaration on the Rights of Indigenous People). The WSF itself probably could not have emerged without the impetus provided by the 1994 Zapatista uprising in Chiapas, Mexico. This uprising articulated its identity and its goals explicitly in response to a 500-year system combining violent colonization and, more recently, the kind of exploitation associated with unchecked neo-liberal globalization—which is the economic face of dromocolonization.

There are indications that the "movement of movements" has begun to redress the marginalization of indigenous voices, a development that could have far-reaching consequences. The 2009 Forum in Brazil featured a much stronger emphasis on indigenous issues and a much more visible indigenous presence.[55] Such a shift can only push forward the process of exploring the linkages among militarization, neoliberalism and global climate change at a time when new thinking is needed. Indigenous people, of course, are not the only people who have good reason to mount a determined politics of occupation and popular defense; the same holds true for all those who are facing structural violence and dislocation. Without question, however, indigenous voices are of central importance in pushing for a renewed ecological politics focused on core issues of land, water, food and climate—issues that are also of concern to many within the global privileged class, including those who populate the various "slow movements" that often prioritize sustainability and a return to small-scale agriculture (particularly organic agriculture) within wealthy countries.

The political convergences evident on the level of Escobar's "place-based yet transnationalised" social movements suggest a step away from the kind of "Third Worldist" approach rooted firmly in modernity. In reaching toward something that is beyond modernity, they have much in common with the "Fourth World" thinking that has always been suspicious of the kind of linear, hierarchical thinking imposed by colonial projects and internalized by many anti-colonial nationalists.[56] At the same time, as Escobar rightly notes, "many of the conditions that gave rise to Third Worldism have by no means disappeared."[57]

This gray area between Third and Fourth World realities and responses is precisely where the Palestinian struggle is currently located. For those who see it as the last remaining struggle against colonialism, it is the quintessential Third World issue, one that still awaits resolution in the form of Palestinian statehood. For others, however, Palestine's primary importance lies in its connection with wider struggles for social, economic and even environmental justice.[58] This may explain why Palestine continues to be one of the most unifying issues within the lively, diverse, and often contentious global justice movement. While moments of confrontation with supporters of Israel (e.g., during the 2001 World Conference Against Racism in Durban) remain unavoidable in the context of continuing settler colonization in Palestine, the primary debates within the movement (e.g., at the 2005 WSF meeting) have concerned strategic questions such as the relative value of government sanctions on Israel vs. the civil society-based approach that has produced growing calls for divestment and boycotts in recent years.[59]

Defending Solidarity

With Palestine's status as *cause célèbre* for global justice activists, of course, come a number of dangers. Not least of these is the danger of romanticization. While there are undoubtedly many activists who are both cognizant of the complex realities facing Palestinians on the ground and committed to changing those realities, there are also undoubtedly others whose engagement with Palestine consists of something considerably less grounded. Perhaps even more concerning, however, is the danger of oppressive orthodoxy. To the extent that an undifferentiated notion of "Palestine" becomes an article of faith within the global justice movement, it becomes more difficult for anyone to ask critical questions about the relationship between Palestinian resistance, international solidarity, and the deeper structures within which both are embedded.

What these dangers highlight is the importance of ensuring that solidarity does not, as Said famously warned, have the effect of blinding its adherents and silencing the kind of critical reflection that is the lifeblood of any struggle for social justice.[60] Regardless of the exact path that the global justice movement takes, there is little doubt that solidarity will provide the glue holding together these efforts and enabling them to connect productively with the global movement for justice in Palestine. As political struggle becomes more entwined with ecological struggle, we have been conditioned to fear that humanity will conform to the cinematic portrayals of Hobbesian, post-apocalyptic wastelands. Yet this is not what has happened in Palestine. In the face of growing desperation and suffering, Palestinians have managed to maintain a strong sense of internal solidarity without eliminating the space for democratic debate.

Similarly, through their work with international solidarity volunteers, Palestinians have been able to expand outward their network of popular defense. In this sense, as many commentators have noted, these volunteers are, despite important differences in circumstance, the twenty-first century counterparts of the International Brigades that descended on Catalonia during the Spanish Civil War—a war whose dates (1936–39) match exactly the dates of Palestine's first major anticolonial uprising. Perhaps some of the *brigadistas* came via France, passing through the beautiful train station in Portbou after crossing the frontier, much as today's solidarity activists make their own difficult passage through the Tel Aviv airport or the Allenby Bridge across the Jordan River on their way to help with the olive harvest in the West Bank or stand as witnesses as Israeli soldiers force young Palestinian men to lift their shirts (or to be "remotely" scanned) at military checkpoints. When dromocratic confinement reaches such a point that suicide becomes thinkable, solidarity and the politics of occupation appear, in Benjamin's words, to "blast open the continuum of history."[61]

6

DECOLONIZATION

"At this moment in history, the Palestinian case takes on the shape of things to come..."[1] This 1978 observation from Paul Virilio, serves as the epigraph for this book and expresses one of its core analytical impulses. The book has sought to construct an argument around this impulse by situating Palestine within the context of broader processes of global colonization (and settler colonization in particular), securitization, acceleration and occupation. The central idea is that Palestine is both embedded in these processes and at the vanguard of some of their most important global effects. Palestine, in short, maintains a relationship with the global that is both microcosmic and prophetic. It is this relationship that the book's title, Global Palestine, is designed to capture.

Are we all becoming Palestinians? Are the processes associated with global colonization inevitably speeding, like war itself, toward a post-political, apocalyptic essence? Where are the spaces that might serve as points of resistance to such a trend? If Palestine has often been a prophetic laboratory for many of these global processes, can it also be a laboratory for a different, more liberating set of social arrangements? Asking these questions takes us directly and inevitably to one of the most important unresolved issues of the past century: the issue of decolonization.

What follows here, far from constituting a conclusion, is instead a set of necessarily preliminary and schematic thoughts about the politics of decolonization—in Palestine and in Global Palestine—in light of the analysis presented in the foregoing chapters. They are notes toward a broader discussion, and I offer them in the form of four basic propositions about decolonization:

1. Decolonization today requires a direct engagement with the long-term structural impact of settler colonialism and with the perspectives of those who have borne the brunt of its impact.
2. Decolonization in Palestine means not simply the creation of a new set of institutional arrangements, but also the transformation of the entire territory into a single society that pushes beyond a colonizing multiculturalism to a politics of real cohabitation and self-sovereignty.
3. Decolonization today requires addressing the interwoven vectors of dromocratic violence, neo-liberalism and ecological destruction.
4. Decolonization today requires that we reaffirm and continue to struggle for the right to imagine and practice "dangerous solidarities."

Taken together, these propositions speak not only of the enormity of the challenge facing those who seek to create a world that is at least relatively liberated from the most pervasive and dehumanizing colonial structures, but also of the role that Palestine might play in bringing about such a future. Needless to say, this is an exercise in utopian thinking, for which I make no apologies. The world has had enough of the "realistic" approaches associated with the peace process; these only perpetuate hierarchical structures both within Palestine and beyond. Instead of writing timidly from within the prison of this oppressive dynamic, we need to write boldly from the exit.

Unsettled Colonization

In this book I have employed a structural approach to colonization rather than an event-based approach. The logical companion to an event-based approach to colonization is a belief that colonization can be reversed through some sort of formal political transition, usually a transfer of political authority from one ruling class to another. A structural approach, by contrast, leads one to the realization that as the product of permanent structural transformations rather than temporary colonial relationships, the problems created by settler colonial projects were never meant to be solved—at least not in the conventional sense of that term. Ironically enough, they remain perpetually unsettled.

In a useful overview of the issues at stake in thinking about settler colonial decolonization, Lorenzo Veracini points us toward a series of patterns that illustrate the depth of the challenges facing anyone who might seek to foster a serious conversation about how to bring about meaningful passages from settler colonialism to a new reality that would deserve the label postcolonial.[2] Four of his observations, in particular, can help us begin to imagine a framework for thinking about decolonization not only in Palestine, but also in Global Palestine.

Veracini argues, first, that settler colonialism's own resistance to decolonization is fueled by a refusal to deal seriously with the question of real indigenous sovereignty, and that this refusal has helped produce a general marginalization of indigenous perspectives within the literature on decolonization. Second, he notes that while there is an "acceptable narrative" of Third World decolonization—albeit one that is based on problematic assumptions about development—there is not (yet) a comparable narrative that would provide a logic for settler colonial decolonization. To date, the latter has been largely unthinkable because settler projects view themselves as already having decolonized (far in the past, when they broke away from the "mother country"); and because admitting indigenous claims in the present would undermine the entire ideological basis of the project. Third, given these realities, most settler colonial societies have tended to deal with the question of decolonization either through denial (see Chapter 2) or through highly circumscribed processes of reconciliation that do little to alter deeper colonial hierarchies.[3] Finally, argues Veracini, the widespread failure of settler colonial decolonization requires that we develop a new language and a new set of imaginaries that would enable us to pursue the goal of decolonizing colonial relationships at all levels, not just pieces of territory.

Just as the limitations of Third World decolonization tell us something very important about the persistence of global hierarchies in the post-WWII period, I believe that the limitations of settler colonial decolonization reveal a great deal about the contours of the emerging world I am calling Global Palestine. Third World decolonization is associated with a time when the logic of endocolonization came to saturate the world both horizontally (across societies) and vertically (within societies), resulting in a progressive "Third-Worlding" of the world as a whole. Contemporary dromocolonization, on the other hand, may be viewed in terms of a progressive "Fourth-Worlding" of a world where everyone is becoming increasingly indigenous in relation to the colonizing machinery of dromocratic violence and surveillance.

Consequently, just as settler colonial decolonization in a particular polity (e.g., Palestine) requires a true engagement with the question of indigenous sovereignty in the present, global decolonization must begin with a sustained engagement with the perspectives of those who have been the primary victims of settler colonization. As will be explored below, such an approach offers much in terms of helping develop a new imaginary of decolonization that stretches beyond political change at the state level to encompass the many interlocking structures of global colonization.

Decolonizing Palestine

A sign of the times: At a 2009 conference on Palestine hosted by an NGO in Madrid, Spain, two full days of panels featuring Palestinian, Israeli, and international speakers came and went without a single reference to the possibility of Palestinian statehood. The absence of what would previously have been the core political objective animating the entire discussion revealed how much has changed on the ground, and also how activists have responded to these changes by rearticulating the struggle in anti-apartheid terms. There was much discussion of the growing repression faced by Palestinian citizens of

Israel,[4] and the general focus was on civil and human rights rather than on national liberation. To the extent that participants were thinking about political futures, they were thinking about the "one-state solution": the creation of a single, democratic state for all who live in Israel/Palestine.

This perspective represents a definitive rejection of the two-state solution that has long been advocated by a broad stratum of the world's policy elites as the proper way forward in Israel/Palestine. This solution, however, is based upon a set of dominant twentieth-century geopolitical models (e.g., the misleading "conflict" model discussed in Chapter 2) and narrative scripts (e.g., the narrative of Third World decolonization) that either deny or misunderstand the settler colonial realities that prevail in Palestine.

In any case, as a growing number of analysts have argued in recent years, Zionism itself has rendered the two-state solution thoroughly unworkable by settling its Jewish population throughout historic Palestine, a process that continues at the time of writing through the expansion of Jewish colonies in and around East Jerusalem. In so doing, the state of Israel has created a single polity marked by the differential provision of rights to its inhabitants on the basis of ethnoreligious identity. Carving a viable, truly sovereign Palestinian state out of this territory, as even the most well-meaning political negotiators have discovered, appears to be an impossible task. The only imaginable result is a hierarchical political arrangement in which Palestinians remain subject to Israeli political, economic and military domination and Israeli Jews find their country increasingly subject to comparisons with apartheid South Africa. These developments have produced what Ilan Pappe calls a sense of "navigation fatigue" among liberal Israeli Jews who find themselves occupying a shrinking ideological space as they are forced to confront the exclusivist nature of their national project.[5] Some traditional liberal supporters of Israel (both inside and outside the state) are moving to the right, but others are starting to join international activists in rejecting Zionism altogether and supporting the one-state solution.

In other words, as Palestine becomes even more globalized, and as the globe arguably becomes more Palestinianized in ways detailed in this book, the conditions of possibility for a transformation of current realities in Palestine are inevitably being altered. With its nineteenth and twentieth-century approach rooted in the logic of ethnonational separation and partition, the two-state solution emerges not only as unworkable, but also as a political anachronism. The one-state solution, by contrast, emerges as a much more forward-looking, twenty-first-century vision. The former offers only surface-level decolonization (statehood for all), whereas the latter holds out the possibility of a much more revolutionary decolonization (social transformation for all). The global impact of such a process could stretch far beyond a mere cessation of local hostilities.

Critics of the one-state solution typically argue that Israeli Jews and Palestinians cannot possibly live together in peace, or that Jews will inevitably end up as second-class citizens (or worse) in such a state. Such arguments are built upon the assumption that the only desirable solutions are those whose future story can be written in advance. Yet, as analyzed in this book, settler colonialism does not create problems that can be "solved" in this way. In such contexts, real decolonization is no more of an event than colonization itself; rather, it must take the form of a collective commitment to the transformation of settler colonial structures.

In this sense, perhaps the term "one-state solution" is a misnomer; perhaps we should be discussing post-Zionism. Chapter 2 explored how Zionism, in attempting to resolve the "Jewish question," only succeeded in displacing it by creating the "Palestinian question," thereby perpetuating the logic of anti-Semitism. This logic has always been built on the denial of the right to occupation, habitation and self-sovereignty—that is, the insistence that Jews (or in a Zionist context, Palestinians) must not be allowed to feel at home. The one-state solution is revolutionary in the sense that it ratifies the realities of human occupation—it would force no one in Israel/Palestine to move—and supports the human desire for self-sovereignty while treating everyone in Israel/Palestine, in effect, as indigenous within a multicultural framework. The attraction of the one-state solution, in other words, lies in its connection with the values that animate today's broader movements for global justice.

Moreover, given Palestine's ongoing status as a prophetic political laboratory, a successful shift toward a logic of decolonization in the form of the one-state solution could have significant global consequences. It would not be the first time that settler colonialism has played such a role. Older settler colonial cases, for example, have given the world a complex and ongoing legacy in a number of areas, two of which are worth highlighting here. First, white settler societies such as the US and Australia have been sites of experimentation in a politics of multiculturalism that has often ratified colonial structures rather than transforming them. Even if viewed as well-intentioned but unsuccessful efforts at meaningful social change, such cases represent important cautionary tales. As Ghassan Hage argues, such a colonizing multiculturalism is only possible once the threat of indigenous sovereignty has been neutralized. In the case of Israel/Palestine, however, one wonders whether an awareness of these troubling histories, combined with the different demographic realities produced by the relatively late arrival of the settler population and its relative failure to remove most of the indigenous population, might create a space for a more egalitarian form of multiculturalism.

The second lesson in settler colonial decolonization comes from South Africa, site of a sustained process of confronting the realities of past violence, most notably through the Truth and Reconciliation Commission (TRC). Once again, we see that this process has come under considerable scrutiny from critics who question whether it has actually done anything to dismantle the structural legacy of colonization. Yet there is little doubt that for all its limitations, the TRC has had important ripple effects throughout the world. By offering a very public, institutionally-supported step toward challenging the politics of denial, it outstrips the limited nature of the "apologies" offered to the victims of colonization by leaders in the US and Australia in recent years.

In this light, it seems that the challenge in Palestine will be to learn from these earlier examples and to create a truly multicultural society that actively seeks to leave behind, to the greatest extent possible, the structural legacies of colonization. No one would claim that this is an easy task—but unlike the two-state solution, at least it is not afraid to aim high.

Decolonizing Global Palestine

The move toward a real process of decolonization in Palestine would need to confront much more than simply the legal and quasi-legal structures that privilege Jews over non-Jews. It would also need to confront the deep impact, on Israeli Jews and Palestinians alike, of the interwoven vectors of dromocratic violence (including its semi-autonomous aspects), neo-liberal restructuring, and ecological destruction. Once again, however, what is undoubtedly a formidable challenge also represents an opportunity for Palestine to be transformed into a different, more liberating kind of global laboratory. As John Trudell's observation about permanent war ("we have never really seen the war go away") indicates, indigenous people never had the luxury of making artificial distinctions among colonization, predatory capitalism, and war on the milieu. Equally important, indigenous people have long been ahead of their time in developing a phenomenological understanding of the global realities of time-space compression and dromocratic violence. Globalization and global colonization, in this sense, provide an opportunity for all of us to "catch up" to those who have never stopped being indigenous.[6]

What might this mean, in practice, for Palestine? It would mean continuing to foster connections between the "place-based yet trans-nationalised" struggle on the ground in Palestine and the broader movement for global justice. It would mean searching for liberating alternatives to the models that continue to inform the actions of nationalist elites who seek state power in Palestine at the cost of meaningful social transformation. It would mean fighting to make sure that when the Wall comes down, it isn't simply replaced with other barriers (visible and invisible) that only serve to make the world safe for capital accumulation. It would also mean supporting the efforts of those who are experimenting with new forms of ecological (in the broadest sense) resistance to Israeli colonization.

Perhaps most importantly, it would mean listening to Palestinians in a new way. For too long, Palestinians have been consigned to a peculiarly oppressive space in the economy of global discourse. To the extent that they are given the chance to be heard, it is only (with rare exceptions) because of their connection with Israel. As a result, their voices are valued primarily insofar as they provide evidence to be fed into the Israeli-Palestinian grist mill or to discussions of a narrow range of global issues (e.g., terrorism or anti-Semitism). Outside of this, they are largely voiceless and invisible. Once we begin to see Palestine as a monadic and prophetic space vis-à-vis the global, however, we are forced to recognize that Palestinians might have something very important to say about what is happening elsewhere. In other words, the decolonization of Palestine requires not only freeing Palestinians from the prison of their immediate conditions, but also freeing them from epistemological and discursive prisons we have tended to impose upon them.

What might decolonization mean, in practice, for Global Palestine? It would mean working to make settler colonialism more visible so that its effects across all scales can be examined and debated, while also insisting that the issue of indigenous sovereignty remains as vital as ever. It would mean affirming that the critique of dromocracy is as important as the critique of capitalism. It would mean urgent dialogues between those struggling against the destruction of the biosphere and those struggling against militarization. It would mean refusing to be blinded by the celebratory narratives that enable new technologies to be accepted uncritically without a sustained examination of their deeper social effects.

Finally, the decolonization of Global Palestine would mean a sustained, critical and creative search for new approaches to the question of resistance. On the one hand, given what we know about dromocratic violence and how it is hard-wired into the circuits of technology, science and politics, it is difficult to imagine an effective and ethical path forward that would not be rooted primarily in a strategy of nonviolence. On the other hand, one wonders, what does nonviolence mean in the twenty-first century? The philosophy of nonviolence, after all, emerged in a world dominated by the actor-centered politics of control; the point of nonviolence was to respond in a principled way to deliberate acts of violence in an effort to get the oppressor to act differently. But what happens when we move beyond a politics of control? How does one act nonviolently in response to dromocolonization?

Here the important question may be the one that Arundhati Roy, the gifted Indian writer and anti-imperialist critic, posed in a video submitted to the Dropping Knowledge project. "Between nonviolence resistance and armed struggle," she asked, "where do we go? What is effective? What is the right thing to do? Or do we need a biodiversity of resistance?"[7]

Decolonization and Dangerous Solidarities

Solidarity is arguably the single most important concept animating the great movements for social justice in recent centuries, from transnational workers' and women's movements to the great anticolonial struggles following World War II. In the twenty-first century, we are seeing both a growing awareness of the need for transnational solidarity and growing opportunities for engaging in effective solidarity work. Despite changing conditions of possibility, however, the basic elements of the solidarity impulse remain the same: a recognition that common humanity can and must be a bridge across all the social divisions that power creates and exploits; the conviction that (in Martin Luther King's famous words) "injustice anywhere is a threat to justice everywhere"; a profound sense of hope rooted in the belief that another world is (indeed, must be) possible; and a commitment to collective action in order to transform dominant social structures.

At the same time, the ideological and institutional pressures to deny transnational connections in favor of narrower identities remain strong. In this sense, transnational solidarity in the pursuit of global justice has always been, and continues to be, a dangerous impulse. This is particularly the case for those individuals whose own social location leaves them especially vulnerable to reprisals from those who seek to police the borders of acceptable political identifications. What I am referring to as dangerous solidarities are those identifications that deliberately stretch beyond the bounds of one's own experience, and beyond the acceptable affiliations that are validated by hegemonic structures, in order to make connections between experiences and struggles that might otherwise appear disconnected.

Palestine is an interesting case for examining the politics and possibilities of solidarity because it embodies the tension between narrower solidarities—chiefly those of nationality and religion—and the kinds of transnational solidarities that are required for the pursuit of global justice. In a sense, of course, the particularly fraught politics of Israel/Palestine mean that all solidarities with the Palestinian people are dangerous by definition, especially in those places (e.g., the US or Australia) where support for Israeli settler colonialism has traditionally been strong. The most dangerous solidarities, however, are those associated with the growing movement in favor of the one-state solution, a movement that threatens not only the Zionist project, but also the nationalist framework that has historically dominated the struggle for Palestinian liberation.

It is worth noting that Zionism itself was and is built upon a certain kind of transnational solidarity that seeks to organize both a global diasporic community and the support of sympathetic non-Jews in the service of a national project. Whether viewed positively as a triumph of democratic, humanistic values or, more polemically, as an "industry" designed to exploit the memory of the Holocaust in order to justify colonization,[8] there is no question that the material success of Zionism owes a great deal to its ideological success in cultivating, framing and mobilizing feelings of transnational solidarity. The role of international worker solidarity in the early period of Zionist settlement, while certainly romanticized in the collective memory of liberal Jews in Israel and elsewhere, also contributed to the project's success. At the center of this liberal nationalist narrative lies the kibbutz, which served historically as a focus for social organization in the Yishuv and, later, as a magnet for idealistic visitors who imagined Israel to be a semi-utopian socialist experiment. In light of critical sociological literature on the topic, we can see that this image of the kibbutz was always built upon a denial of its a priori exclusivity.[9] Thus the kibbutz actually is an apt symbol of the Zionist project—but not in the way that its admirers would acknowledge.

The example of the kibbutz illustrates how easily the solidarity impulse can be yoked to political projects that are considerably less liberating. Regardless of the idealistic and progressive claims that are made on behalf of Zionism—and it would be a mistake to deny that belief in these claims is deeply felt by many—the historical reality is that the project was, and continues to be, actualized through the exclusivist, expansionist and exceptionalist mechanisms of settler colonialism. Consequently, Jews who wish to express solidarity with Palestinians have no choice but to take the dangerous step of breaking, to a significant extent, with the deep ideological structures of Zionism itself.

The structures in place to render such solidarities unthinkable, and to punish those who dare to think them, are considerable; moreover, they become more aggressive in moments of ideological crisis. These structures of ideological policing include attacks on academic freedom;[10] direct state repression of individuals and organizations that engage in a solidarity-based politics of working side by side with Palestinian communities living under Israeli domination; and the familiar accusations of romanticization, treason and naïveté that are typically leveled against anyone advocating radical social change.

Arguably the most fundamental ideological structure working against the formation of dangerous solidarities with Palestinians, however, is the structure of exceptionalism that seeks to preempt any critical examination of settler colonialism itself. Here it must be emphasized that those who deny the settler colonial realities in Palestine are engaging not only in an act of political imposition (by implicitly or explicitly justifying the destruction of Palestinian society in 1948), but also an act of epistemological imposition (by silencing the knowledges that are rooted in the experience of dispossession). The overall effect is to reinforce deep colonial structures and the privileges associated with them. This only confirms the notion that making settler colonialism visible is an absolutely essential act of solidarity precisely because it insists upon the need to take seriously the voices and experiences of the colonized.

As an example of someone who made a commitment to dangerous solidarities, particularly in settler colonial contexts, consider Jean Genet, the French playwright and activist. Genet famously spent time with Palestinian revolutionaries in Lebanon and Jordan and with Black Panther activists in the United States during the latter part of the long 1960s, championing both causes and writing powerfully about the violent structures to which they were responding. For

Genet, the connection between the two struggles was self-evident, yet many have criticized his attachment to such youthful and rebellious causes. The critique says a great deal about how settler colonialism operates as an ideological force. The attachments that Genet and others develop to resistance movements are precisely the kinds of thoughts that must be policed if settler colonialism is to preserve its aura of exceptionalism.

The death of Rachel Corrie in Gaza provided another opportunity for the policing of dangerous solidarities, with strongly pro-Israeli forces criticizing the slain activist for being young and "naïve" in her approach to the Palestinian struggle. What we have seen in recent years, however, is a growing chorus of young people who are increasingly unafraid to voice their solidarity with the Palestinian people. This includes the young Jewish activists throughout North America who have thrown their support behind the Boycott, Divestment and Sanctions (BDS) movement and engaged in previously unimaginable actions such as the disruption of speeches by senior Israeli political leaders. More generally, the emergence of groups such as Jewish Voice for Peace suggests a fraying of the bonds that have longed served to silence anti-Zionist voices within the Jewish community.

All those who practice such dangerous solidarities, of course, are acting within a long and proud tradition that includes not only past activists but also present role models like Amira Hass, the Israeli journalist who has lived in and reported from the West Bank and Gaza for many years. If we are to move in the direction of real decolonization—in Palestine and in Global Palestine—the space for such voices must be protected and enlarged.

NOTES

1. APPROACHING GLOBAL PALESTINE

1. For a now classic critique of this sort of discourse, in this case focusing on the discipline of anthropology, see Johannes Fabian, *Time and the Other: How Anthropology Makes Its Object* (New York: Columbia University Press, 1983).
2. See, *inter alia*, Simha Flapan, *The Birth of Israel: Myths and Realities* (New York: Pantheon, 1987); Benny Morris, *The Birth of the Palestinian Refugee Problem, 1947–1949* (Cambridge: Cambridge University Press, 1987); Ilan Pappe, *The Ethnic Cleansing of Palestine* (Oxford: Oneworld, 2006); Gershon Shafir, *Land, Labor, and the Origins of the Israeli-Palestinian Conflict, 1882–1914* (Berkeley: University of California Press, 1996); and Avi Shlaim, *Collusion Across the Jordan: King Abdullah, the Zionist Movement, and the Partition of Palestine* (New York: Columbia University Press, 1988).
3. Some noteworthy recent interventions include: Avraham Burg, *The Holocaust Is Over: We Must Rise From Its Ashes* (New York: Palgrave Macmillan, 2008); Yitzhak Laor, *The Myths of Liberal Zionism* (London: Verso, 2009); Gabriel Piterberg, *The Returns of Zionism: Myth, Politics, and Scholarship in Israel* (London: Verso, 2008); Shlomo Sand, *The Invention of the Jewish People* (London: Verso, 2009); and Oren Yiftachel, *Ethnocracy: Land and Identity Politics in Israel/Palestine* (Philadelphia: University of Pennsylvania Press, 2006).
4. Arjun Appadurai, "Grassroots Globalization and the Research Imagination," *Public Culture*, 12, 1 (2000), pp. 6–8.
5. Arjun Appadurai, *Modernity At Large: Cultural Dimensions of Globalization* (Minneapolis: University of Minnesota Press, 1996), p. 33.

6. See Laleh Khalili, *Heroes and Martyrs of Palestine: The Politics of National Commemoration* (Cambridge: Cambridge University Press, 2007); and Julie Peteet, *Landscape of Hope and Despair: Palestinian Refugee Camps* (Philadelphia: University of Pennsylvania Press, 2005).
7. Edward Said, *Culture and Imperialism* (New York: Alfred A. Knopf, 1993), p. 309, original emphasis.
8. Olivier Roy, *Globalized Islam: The Search for a New Ummah* (London: Hurst, 2004).
9. Faisal Devji, *Landscapes of the Jihad: Militancy, Morality, Modernity* (London: Hurst, 2005).
10. See Marc Lynch, *Voices of the New Arab Public: Iraq, al-Jazeera, and Middle East Politics Today* (New York: Columbia University Press, 2006); and Philip Seib (ed.), *New Media and the New Middle East* (New York: Palgrave Macmillan, 2007).
11. See Tarak Barkawi, *Globalization and War* (Lanham, MA: Rowman & Littlefield, 2006), pp. 151–166.
12. For an early overview of this activism, see Nancy Stohlman and Laurieann Aladin (eds), *Live From Palestine: International and Palestinian Direct Action Against the Israeli Occupation* (Boston: South End Press, 2003).
13. Gargi Bhattacharyya, "Globalizing Racism and Myths of the Other in the 'War on Terror'," in Ronit Lentin (ed.), *Thinking Palestine* (London: Zed Books, 2008), p. 48. Bhattacharyya also argues that associations with the intifada can be double-edged, as when opponents of multiculturalism in Britain seek to discredit the political mobilization of Muslim immigrant communities, and to argue in favor of heavy-handed state repression of those communities, by raising the specter of "stone-throwing youths... [that represent] a threat to "our way of life" and the harbinger of future violence and destruction" (p. 55).
14. On the "one-state solution," see Ali Abunimah, *One Country: A Bold Proposal to End the Israeli-Palestinian Impasse* (New York: Metropolitan Books, 2006); Saree Makdisi, *Palestine Inside Out: An Everyday Occupation* (New York: Norton, 2008); and Virginia Tilley, *The One-State Solution: A Breakthrough for Peace in the Israel-Palestine Deadlock* (Ann Arbor: University of Michigan Press, 2005).
15. See Yiftachel, *Ethnocracy*, op. cit.; and Baruch Kimmerling, *Politicide: Ariel Sharon's War Against the Palestinians* (London: Verso, 2003).
16. Piterberg, *The Returns of Zionism* (see note 3), p. 55.
17. Walter Benjamin, "Theses on the Philosophy of History," in Benjamin,

Illuminations: Essays and Reflections, Hannah Arendt (ed.) Introduction; trans. Harry Zohn (New York: Schocken Books, 1978), p. 257.

18. John Collins, *Occupied By Memory: The Intifada Generation and the Palestinian State of Emergency* (New York: New York University Press, 2004).

19. Similarly, the notion of "relative calm" has its analogue in the work of scholars who routinely skip over decades, even centuries, when narrating history as a series of eruptions of violence or political upheaval—periods that are "exceptional" only when viewed from an elite point of view.

20. For one of many critiques of this discourse of "relative calm" in the Palestinian context, see Allison Weir, "The LA Times" notion of 'relative calm'," *Electronic Intifada*, 25 February 2005, http://electronicintifada. net/v2/article3638.shtml.

21 Achille Mbembe, "Necropolitics," *Public Culture*, 15, 1 (2003), p. 23.

22. Susan Buck-Morss, *Thinking Past Terror: Islamism and Critical Theory on the Left* (London: Verso, 2003).

23. See Alexander Galloway and Eugene Thacker, *The Exploit: A Theory of Networks* (Minneapolis: University of Minnesota Press, 2007), pp. 1–22.

24. George Marcus, "Ethnography in/of the World System: The Emergence of Multi-Sited Ethnography," *Annual Review of Anthropology*, 24 (1995), pp. 95–117.

25. For Hall, one corollary of this perspective is that the Fourth World—the world of indigenous people in all their linguistic, cultural and ecological diversity—has always represented a fundamental obstacle to the "monocultural" impulses of European colonization and remains today the last line of resistance against unchecked corporate globalization. See Anthony J. Hall, *The American Empire and the Fourth World* (Montreal and Kingston: McGill-Queen's University Press, 2003).

26. Ella Shohat, "Rethinking Jews and Muslims: Quincentennial Reflections," *Middle East Report*, 178 (1992), pp. 25–29.

27. Paul Virilio & Sylvere Lotringer, *Pure War*, trans. Mark Polizzotti (New York: Semiotext(e), 1997 [1983]).

28. Der Derian, "The Conceptual Cosmology of Paul Virilio," *Theory, Culture & Society*, 16, 5–6, p. 219. Readers seeking additional assistance in navigating Virilio's work and its relationship to larger bodies of theory in postmodernism and international relations may consider consulting Der Derian, "The (S)pace of International Relations: Simulation, Surveillance and Speed," *International Studies Quarterly*, 34 (1990), pp. 295–310; and idem., *Virtuous War: Mapping the Military-Industrial-Media-Entertainment Network* (Boulder: Westview Press, 2001).

2. COLONIZATION

1. Caroline Elkins and Susan Pederson, "Settler Colonialism: A Concept and Its Uses," in Elkins and Pederson (eds), *Settler Colonialism in the Twentieth Century* (New York: Routledge, 2005), p. 3.
2. As Jonathan Nitzan and Shimshon Bichler note, the issue of what happened to the land vacated by Palestine's indigenous Arab population has never been sufficiently acknowledged or studied. All indications, however, are that "redistribution was massive and probably differential," with significant chunks of land going to the *kibbutzim* (collective farms). The sudden and massive influx of land annexed after 1948, they argue, was one key factor that allowed the state to function as "a cocoon for differential accumulation" and, ultimately, the formation of the ruling class that dominates the country to this day. See Nitzan and Bichler, *The Global Political Economy of Israel* (London: Pluto Press, 2002), pp. 96–97.
3. For an exhaustive look at the long shadow of apartheid structures ten years after the formal end of minority rule, see John Daniel, Roger Southall and Jessica Lutchmann (eds), *State of the Nation: South Africa, 2004–2005* (Cape Town: HSRC Press, 2005).
4. To give just one example, access to adequate maternal health care services in the US continues to be drastically unequal in ways that correlate closely with racial/ethnic identity. In a 2010 report, Amnesty International laments the chronic underfunding of the Indian Health Service and documents how Native American and Alaska Native women suffer from a striking lack of access to prenatal care when compared with white women. See Amnesty International, *Deadly Delivery: The Maternal Health Care Crisis in the USA* (2010). For a courageous and provocative reading of how these and other socioeconomic patterns affecting indigenous women fit into the broad sweep of colonization in North America, see Andrea Smith, *Conquest: Sexual Violence and American Indian Genocide* (Boston: South End Press, 2005).
5. The growing literature that examines Israel/Palestine in a comparative settler colonial context includes Gabriel Piterberg, *The Returns of Zionism: Myth, Politics, and Scholarship in Israel* (London: Verso, 2008); Gershon Shafir, *Land, Labor, and the Origins of the Israeli-Palestinian Conflict, 1882–1914* (Berkeley: University of California Press, 1996); Lorenzo Veracini, *Israel and Settler Society* (London: Pluto Press, 2006); and Patrick Wolfe, "Settler Colonialism and the Elimination of the Native," *Journal of Genocide Research*, 8, 4 (2006), pp. 387–409.

6. Cole Harris, "How Did Colonialism Dispossess? Comments from an Edge of Empire," *Annals of the Association of American Geographers*, 94, 1 (2004), p. 179.

7. From a poststructuralist perspective, the frequent use of binary oppositions in this literature reveals the inherently problematic nature of the strict taxonomic approach to studying colonialism. Udo Krautwurst argues that such taxonomies betray the desire to establish a "pure positivity [that] also requires an act of exclusion." See Krautwurst, "What is Settler Colonialism? An Anthropological Meditation on Frantz Fanon's 'Concerning Violence'," *History and Anthropology*, 14, 1 (2003), p. 56.

8. Derek Gregory, *The Colonial Present: Afghanistan, Palestine, and Iraq* (Malden: Blackwell, 2004).

9. See, *inter alia*, Michael Klare, *Resource Wars: The New Landscape of Global Conflict* (New York: Henry Holt, 2002).

10. While some might argue that such actions fall outside the realm of colonization, it is worth remembering that "legal" land purchases have long played a role in many colonial projects (including the Zionist project in Palestine). This is an excellent example of why it is important to shift one's angle of vision toward the "tradition of the oppressed" (see Chapter 1). The land purchasers, in this case, are not engaged in a full-scale process of colonizing the distant territory and would thus dispute the application of the colonial label to their actions. For smallholders in that territory, however, the situation may look familiar. The global structures that constitute the conditions of possibility for such a situation are, in and of themselves, colonial structures.

11. For a useful overview, see David Harvey, *Spaces of Global Capitalism: Towards a Theory of Uneven Geographical Development* (London: Verso, 2006).

12. Paul Virilio and Sylvere Lotringer, *Pure War*, (transl. by Mark Polizzotti) (New York: Semiotext(e), 1997 [1983]).

13. The centrality of the Bomb here reminds us that endocolonization is not merely international, but also global, achieving its ends partly through the overt and suicidal threat of planetary annihilation. The invention of the Bomb is thus a decisive break with the past: the nuclear genie cannot be put back in the bottle. In framing the issue in this way, Virilio connects directly with Foucault's work on sovereignty and biopower (the regulation of whole populations through sovereign control over the production, distribution, and maintenance of life). Foucault notes that atomic weaponry suggests both a traditional sovereign power ("the power

to kill…millions and hundreds of millions of people") as well as an unprecedented, suicidal power ("the power to kill life itself"). To engage in apocalyptic, full-scale atomic warfare, therefore, would be to undermine or abdicate the biopolitical "power to guarantee life," negating the idea of human sovereignty even while performing what some might view as the very apotheosis of it. See Foucault, *"Society Must Be Defended": Lectures at the College de France, 1975–76*, (M. Bertani and A. Fontana [eds], transl. by D. Macey) (New York: Picador, 2003), p. 253.

14. See Virilio, "The Suicidal State," in James Der Derian (ed.), *The Virilio Reader* (Malden: Blackwell, 1998), pp. 29–45; and Virilio and Lotringer, *Pure War*, op. cit., p. 95.

15. In Arthur Kroker's words, this fusion produces "the crystallization of science as the language of power, of the depletion of the energies of society, and their draining away into the war machine." See Kroker, "The Mohawk Refusal," *ctheory.ney*, 25 October 1995, http://www.ctheory.net/articles.aspx?id=153.

16. See Glover, "The War on _____," in Collins and Glover (eds), *Collateral Language: A User's Guide to America's New War* (New York: New York University Press, 2002).

17. For a fascinating discussion of the body as a site of endocolonial struggle, see Allen Feldman, *Formations of Violence* (Chicago: University of Chicago Press, 1991), Chapter 4.

18. Such abandoned zones are often described in the "violent cartographies" of elite policy discourse in striking, often racialized terms that recall Marlow's classic exocolonial map, where the "blank" place quickly becomes a place of "darkness" and "horror." This results in growing references to "black spots," "no-go areas," and the like. See Michael J. Shapiro, *Violent Cartographies: Mapping Cultures of War* (Minneapolis: University of Minnesota Press, 1997).

19. See Philip McMichael, *Development and Social Change: A Global Perspective*, 3rd edn. (Thousand Oaks: Pine Forge Press, 2004), pp. 239–246.

20. A full examination of this growing literature is beyond the scope of this chapter. Readers seeking a more detailed overview may consider consulting Chapter 3 of Piterberg's excellent *The Returns of Zionism*, in which he addresses a number of the key texts on settler colonialism, from the classic work of D.K. Fieldhouse to more recent contributions by Gershon Shafir, Patrick Wolfe, Caroline Elkins and Susan Pederson. The Fall 2008 issue of *South Atlantic Quarterly* is devoted entirely to settler

colonialism and contains a number of useful contributions. Other notable recent efforts include the Fifth Galway Conference on Colonialism (2007) and the "New Worlds, New Sovereignties" held in Melbourne (2008). Both of these conferences will be generating edited volumes addressing the general topic of settler colonialism from a range of disciplinary, interdisciplinary and comparative perspectives. Finally, a new journal devoted to the subject, *Settler Colonial Studies*, was launched at the Swinburne University of Technology in 2010.

21. See Lorenzo Veracini, "The Fourth Geneva Convention: Its Relevance for Settler Nations," *Arena Journal*, 24 (2005), pp. 101–114.

22. For an extended meditation on how these "imaginative geographies" continue to structure post-9/11 realities, see Gregory, *The Colonial Present*.

23. Palestinian lawyer Raja Shehadeh addresses this issue as he recalls his many battles with an Israeli counterpart named Dani, battles in which Shehadeh sought to prevent West Bank land from being expropriated by the Israeli state for its colonization project. "Dani knew few Arabic words. Natsh [poterium thorn] was one of them. How often I have heard him stand up before the judge in the military land court and declare: "But, Your Honor, the land is full of natsh. I saw it with my own eyes." Meaning: What more proof could anyone want that the land was uncultivated and therefore public land that the Israeli settlers could use as their own?" See Shehadeh, *Palestinian Walks: Forays Into a Vanishing Landscape* (New York: Scribner, 2007), p. 53.

24. Wolfe, "Settler Colonialism," p. 388.

25. This is not to say that all settlers subscribe equally to this belief. In any settler colonial situation there are important minority voices ranging from the liberal (e.g., advocating some form of indigenous self-government within a colonial order) to the radical (e.g., advocating the assimilation of settlers into polities organized under indigenous sovereignty). At the same time, the historical record demonstrates that such voices rarely if ever succeed in toppling fully the hegemonic logic of elimination.

26. In his thorough exploration of the issue, Wolfe notes that settler colonialism cannot be described as inherently genocidal but is often the initiator of what he calls "structural genocide" (a category that includes strategies of biocultural assimilation). Given its "logic of elimination" and its historical track record, he argues, it should be viewed most accurately as an "indicator" that signals the real possibility of genocide.

27. See, *inter alia*, Andy Clarno, "A Tale of Two Walled Cities: Neo-liberalization and Enclosure in Johannesburg and Jerusalem," *Political Power and Social Theory*, 10 (2008); John Collins, "Confinement Under an Open Sky: Following the Speed Trap from Guernica to Gaza and Beyond," *Globalizations*, 5, 4 (2008), pp. 555–569; Honaida Ghanim, "Thanatopolitics: The Case of the Colonial Occupation of Palestine," in Ronit Lentin (ed.), *Thinking Palestine* (London: Zed Books, 2008), pp. 65–81; Gregory, *The Colonial Present*, Alina Korn, "The Ghettoization of the Palestinians," in Lentin, *Thinking Palestine*, pp. 116–130; and Eyal Weizman, *Hollow Land: Israel's Architecture of Occupation* (London: Verso, 2007).

28. The gradual decline of the United States as a global empire is beginning to produce an important debate on the past, present, and future of "American exceptionalism." See, *inter alia*, Andrew Bacevich, *The Limits of Power: The End of American Exceptionalism* (New York: Metropolitan Books, 2008).

29. See Hilton Obenzinger, "Naturalizing Cultural Pluralism, Americanizing Zionism: The Settler Colonial Basis to Early-Twentieth-Century Progressive Thought," *South Atlantic Quarterly*, 107, 4 (2008), pp. 651–669.

30. William Appleman Williams, *Empire As a Way of Life* (New York: Ig Publishing, 2007 [1980]), p. 32.

31. Ibid., p. 41.

32. Ibid., pp. 75 and 48.

33. Benjamin Beit-Hallahmi, *The Israeli Connection: Who Israel Arms and Why* (New York: Pantheon, 1987), p. 161.

34. Quoted in Ibid., p. 161.

35. The logic of exceptionalism, however, lives on in the form of claims by settler states that they reserve the right to wage "preventive" war, ignore UN resolutions and international law, employ torture against "enemy combatants" and suspected "terrorists," and engage in other actions that would be unacceptable for other states.

36. Stanley Cohen, *States of Denial: Knowing About Atrocities and Suffering* (Malden: Blackwell, 2001).

37. In his critical examination of Michael Walzer's *Arguing About War*, Talal Asad notes that Walzer's strident defense of Israel's actions against the Palestinians suggests a desire to elevate certain feelings (chiefly "the feeling of vulnerability among Israelis and their supporters") over others ("a suppressed sense of guilt...at the destruction of Palestinian society

wrought by the establishment of a Jewish state"). He also hints at one of the key characteristics of settler colonial denial when he points out Walzer's failure to recognize that "the guilt may be accompanied by deep resentment against those whom one has wronged." See Asad, *On Suicide Bombing* (New York: Columbia University Press, 2007), p. 24.

38. There is some evidence to suggest that a new space is beginning to open up for questioning this assumption. A key development was the publication of John J. Mearsheimer and Stephen M. Walt, *The Israel Lobby and U.S. Foreign Policy* (New York: Farrar, Straus & Giroux, 2007), written by two very prominent international relations scholars. See also Saree Makdisi, *Palestine Inside Out: An Everyday Occupation* (New York: W.W. Norton, 2008), pp. 143–150.

39. On total war, see Tarak Barkawi, *Globalization and War* (Lanham, MA: Rowman & Littlefield, 2006),pp. 34–37; and Jonathan Schell, *The Unconquerable World: Power, Nonviolence, and the Will of the People* (New York: Henry Holt, 2003).

40. See William McNeill, *The Pursuit of Power: Technology, Armed Force and Society Since A.D. 1000* (Chicago: University of Chicago Press, 1982).

41. McNeill, *The Pursuit of Power*, p. 242.

42. Foucault, *"Society Must Be Defended"*, p. 264; and Virilio, "The Suicidal State," p. 40.

43. Elkins and Pederson, "Settler Colonialism," p. 18.

44. See Rodinson, *Israel: A Colonial-Settler State?*; Edward Said, *The Question of Palestine*; Joseph Massad, "The Persistence of the Palestinian Question," *Cultural Critique*, 59 (2005), pp. 1–23; and the many sources listed above.

45. In this sense, the growing discussion of apartheid-like realities in Israel/ Palestine is a belated recognition of structures and processes that have been in place for years. For a recent examination of some of these issues, see Human Rights Watch, "Separate and Unequal: Israel's Discriminatory Treatment of Palestinians in the Occupied Palestinian Territories" (New York: Human Rights Watch, 2010), http://www.hrw.org/en/reports/2010/12/19/separate-and-unequal-0.

46. For the latter group, the concept of colonization is only relevant, if at all, in discussions of Israel's expansion into the West Bank, Gaza and East Jerusalem.

47. While Shafir views the category of settler colonialism as eminently applicable to the case of Zionism, he also distances himself from authors such as Said and Rodinson, accusing them of placing too much emphasis on

an allegedly inexorable logic of settler colonialism. For Shafir, the Zionist settler colonization of Palestine was not inevitable but rather the result of a contingent and complex set of material processes addressed in his book.

48. Ilan Pappe, *The Ethnic Cleansing of Palestine* (Oxford: Oneworld, 2006), p. xiii.

49. See Ari Shavit, "Survival of the Fittest? An Interview with Benny Morris," *Logos*, 3, 1 (2004).

50. Massad, "The Persistence," p. 4.

51. For a provocative commentary on how this logic of pure war has transformed the United States, see Eugene Jarecki's documentary film *Why We Fight*, which takes as its starting point Eisenhower's warning about the "military-industrial complex" and draws heavily on the critical work of Chalmers Johnson and other critics of US empire. See also, Andrew Bacevich, *The New American Militarism: How Americans Are Seduced By War* (New York: Oxford University Press, 2006).

52. See Michael Hardt and Antonio Negri, *Empire* (Cambridge: Harvard University Press, 2000).

53. See K.G. Dohonue, *Freedom From Want: American Liberalism and the Idea of the Consumer* (Baltimore: The Johns Hopkins University Press, 2003).

54. The speech also has a dromocratic element (see Chapter 4), with FDR referring multiple times to the need for speed in the mounting of an effective national defense. "Whatever stands in the way of speed and efficiency in defense preparations," he argued, "must give way to the national need."

55. Virilio, "*The Suicidal State*," p. 32 (original emphasis).

56. This message will be familiar to anyone who has read Giorgio Agamben's groundbreaking work on biopolitics and "bare life." See Agamben, *Homo Sacer: Sovereign Power and Bare Life* (Stanford: Stanford University Press, 1998).

57. See Seyla Benhabib, *The Rights of Others: Aliens, Residents and Citizens* (Cambridge: Cambridge University Press, 2004).

58. Ghassan Kanafani, *Palestine's Children: Returning to Haifa and Other Stories*, (transl. by Barbara Harlow and Karen Riley) (Boulder: Lynne Rienner, 2000), p. 101.

59. Ibid., pp. 99–100.

60. Peter Nyers, *Rethinking Refugees: Beyond States of Emergency* (New York: Routledge, 2006), p. 41.

61. Under the terms of UN Resolution 194, Palestinian refugees have the right to return to their homes or, should they choose not to return, to be compensated for their losses. International agreements including the Geneva Conventions and the UDHR provide further support for the general principle behind the right of return. The Israeli counter-argument, therefore, has always been based on an implicit claim of exceptionalism, one of the core ideological pillars of settler colonial projects in general. In this case, opponents of the right of return do not dispute the general principle, only its application to the case of Israeli dispossession of the Palestinians.

62. The Agency's mission was to "prevent conditions of starvation and distress among [the refugees] and to further conditions of peace and stability," with the explicit proviso that these responsibilities would ultimately be passed on to "interested Near Eastern Governments...when international assistance for relief and works projects is no longer available." UNRWA, whose mandate has been regularly extended ever since, continues to provide basic services to more than four million registered Palestinian refugees throughout the region. On UNRWA and liberal humanitarianism, see Julie Peteet, *Landscape of Hope and Despair: Palestinian Refugee Camps* (Philadelphia: University of Pennsylvania Press, 2005).

63. Peteet, *Landscape of Hope and Despair*, p. 51.

64. See Ilan Pappe, *A History of Modern Palestine*, 2nd edn. (Cambridge: Cambridge University Press, 2004), pp. 159–160.

65. On the period of military rule for non-Jews in Israel, see Shira Robinson, "Occupied Citizens in a Liberal State: Palestinians Under Military Rule and the Colonial Formation of Israeli Society, 1948–1966" (unpublished PhD dissertation, Stanford University, 2005).

66. See Walid Khalidi, *Before Their Diaspora: A Photographic History of the Palestinians, 1876–1948* (Washington: Institute for Palestine Studies, 1984); and Rosemary Sayigh, *Palestinians: From Peasants to Revolutionaries* (London: Zed Books, 1979).

67. Ghassan Kanafani, *Men in the Sun and Other Palestinian Stories* (transl. by Hilary Kilpatrick) (Boulder: Lynne Rienner, 1999).

68. In addition to the striking number of Palestine-related United Nations resolutions either vetoed by the US or left unimplemented, we might consider the unsuccessful attempt to bring Ariel Sharon to justice for his role in the 1982 Sabra and Shatila massacres during the Israeli invasion of Lebanon. See Laurie King-Irani, "International Human Rights:

One day out of 365 is not enough," *Electronic Intifada*, 9 December 2004, http://electronicintifada.net/v2/article3422.shtml (accessed 12 December 2009). See also Veracini, "The Fourth Geneva Convention."

69. This dependence has always been much less pronounced than was the case in apartheid South Africa. Israel began a gradual reduction of its reliance on Palestinian labor after the outbreak of the first intifada, replacing many Palestinians with workers from the former Soviet Union and elsewhere.

70. For a provocative exploration of this theme, see Nitzan and Bichler, *The Global Political Economy of Israel*. They note that by 1995 Israel had become "the most unequal of all industrialized countries," with the top 20 per cent of the population earning 21.3 times as much as the bottom 20 per cent (pp. 350–351).

71. See Salim Tamari, "Building Other People's Homes: The Palestinian Peasant's Household and Work in Israel," *Journal of Palestine Studies*, 11, 1 (1981), pp. 31–66.

3. SECURITIZATION

1. This project entered a new phase in the 1990s and gained additional momentum after the attacks of September 11. For more on the security politics of this border in an age of "global apartheid," see Joseph Nevins, *Operation Gatekeeper and Beyond: The War on "Illegals" and the Remaking of the U.S.-Mexico Boundary*, 2nd edn. (New York: Routledge, 2010).

2. Larry Bradshaw and Lorrie Beth Slonsky, "Hurricane Katrina—Our Experiences," *EMS Network News*, 6 September 2005, http://www.ems-network.org/cgi-bin/artman/exec/view.cgi?archive=56&num=18427.

3. Israel is an excellent example. The dominant public discourse on Israel/Palestine reflects Zionism's ideological success in limiting what can be said and thought about the issue. All significant bilateral and multilateral efforts to reduce regional tensions and resolve Palestine's political status implicitly begin from the assumption that only one party (Israel) has "security concerns." The fact that Palestinians might have far more urgent reasons to be worried about their security must be constantly deflected or denied within this discourse. The international community is expected to make the settler state's "security concerns" its top priority, and the ultimate goal is to find a Palestinian leadership that will agree with this logic and "make peace" by signing a final agreement that formally terminates the conflict, thereby ending all indigenous claims against the settler state.

Here the parallels with North American settler colonialism are obvious and striking.

4. Ghassan Hage's work is essential to understanding the collective political psychology of settler colonialism. An excellent starting point is his *Against Paranoid Nationalism: Searching for Hope in a Shrinking Society* (London: Pluto Press, 2003). Some three decades ago the radical US historian William Appleman Williams identified the "paranoid conceptions of security" that easily lent themselves to aggressive, militaristic action such as Andrew Jackson's genocidal campaign against the Cherokee and other Native Americans. See Williams, *Empire As a Way of Life* (New York: Ig Publishing, 2007 [1980]), p. 58. Finally, David Theo Goldberg refers to the "pathological insecurity" of settler colonial racism that "calls for the most pulverizing responses to any resistance as a way to cover over its own insecurities." See Goldberg, "Racial Palestinianization," in Ronit Lentin (ed.), *Thinking Palestine* (London: Zed Books, 2008), p. 38.

5. Maurice Isserman and Michael Kazin, *America Divided: The Civil War of the 1960s*, 3rd edn. (New York: Oxford University Press, 2007).

6. See Giovanni Arrighi, Terence K. Hopkins and Immanuel Wallerstein, *Antisystemic Movements* (London: Verso, 1989).

7. See Sara Roy, *The Gaza Strip: The Political Economy of De-Development* (Washington: Institute for Palestine Studies, 1995).

8. Leila El-Haddad, "Safety is a State of Mind," *Gaza Mom: The Writings of a Mother From Gaza*, 31 December 2008, http://www.gazamom.com/2008/12/.

9. This approach is especially associated with the Copenhagen School of international relations theory, which puts a heavy emphasis on the role of "speech acts" in "securitizing" particular issues. See Michael C. Williams, "Words, Images, Enemies: Securitization and International Politics," *International Studies Quarterly*, 47 (2003), pp. 511–531.

10. Much of this work focuses on the corrosive effect of militarism and imperial overstretch on American democracy. See, *inter alia*, Andrew Bacevich, *The New American Militarism: How Americans Are Seduced By War* (New York: Oxford University Press, 2005); and Chalmers Johnson, *The Sorrows of Empire: Militarism, Secrecy, and the End of the Republic* (New York: Metropolitan Books, 2004).

11. *Why We Fight*, dir. Eugene Jarecki (Culver City, CA: Sony Pictures Home Entertainment, 2006).

12. See Michel Foucault, *"Society Must Be Defended": Lectures at the College*

de France, 1975–76, (M. Bertani and A. Fontana, eds; transl. by D. Macey) (New York: Picador, 2003). In their useful overview of Foucault's work on the shift from "disciplinary society" to the "society of control," Michael Hardt and Antonio Negri define biopower as "a form of power that regulates social life from its interior, following it, interpreting it, absorbing it, and rearticulating it." See Hardt and Negri, *Empire* (Cambridge: Harvard University Press, 2000), pp. 23–24.

13. As Leerom Medovoi and many others have pointed out, this lacuna is a recurring feature of Foucault's work in general. See Medovoi, "Global Society Must Be Defended: Biopolitics Without Borders," *Social Text*, 91 (2007), p. 61.

14. Virilio uses the term "polar inertia" to designate this general process of planetary enclosure, a process that accompanies the eclipse of geopolitics by chronopolitics. See Virilio, *Polar Inertia*, (transl. by Patrick Camiller) (London: Sage, 2000 [1990]).

15. Medovoi, "Global Society Must Be Defended," p. 55.

16. For an alternative and well-argued perspective on this issue, see James Ron, *Frontiers and Ghettos: State Violence in Serbia and Israel* (Berkeley: University of California Press, 2003). Employing a framework that emphasizes the institutional settings for state violence rather than the role of settler colonial structures, Ron contends that in the case of Israel/ Palestine, ghetto is a more applicable category than frontier.

17. Here we see the full significance of Patrick Wolfe's observation that "the full radicalization of assimilation policies in both the US and Australia coincided with the closure of the frontier." See Wolfe, "Settler Colonialism," p. 400. In this sense we can say that settler colonial projects have been pioneers of what Medovoi (building upon Foucault's discussion of the transition from disciplinary politics to biopolitics) calls "biopolitics without borders."

18. See Giorgio Agamben, *State of Exception* (transl. by Kevin Attell) (Chicago: University of Chicago Press, 2006); Derek Gregory, *The Colonial Present: Afghanistan, Palestine, Iraq* (Malden: Blackwell, 2004); and many of the essays collected in Ronit Lentin, *Thinking Palestine* (London: Zed Books, 2008).

19. On the role of the "frontier rabble" in settler colonial expansion and state-formation, see Wolfe, "Settler Colonialism."

20. For a more critical perspective on decolonization and historical periodization, see John D. Kelly and Martha Kaplan, *Represented Communities: Fiji and World Decolonization* (Chicago: University of Chicago Press, 2001), pp. 3–6.

21. On the "settler international," see Lorenzo Veracini, "The Fourth Geneva Convention: Its Relevance for Settler Nations," *Arena Journal*, 24 (2005), pp. 101–114.

22. Interestingly, 1948 is also the year the United States first became a net importer of oil, a development that has had profound consequences for US policy in the Middle East and, indeed, for the world.

23. The continuing power of settler colonial solidarity was revealed in the debate over the United Nations Declaration on the Rights of Indigenous Peoples in 2007. All four nations voting against the Declaration were settler states (the US, Canada, New Zealand and Australia). Israel did not vote.

24. See Donald Fixico, *Termination and Relocation: Federal Indian Policy 1945–1960* (Albuquerque: University of New Mexico Press, 1986). Ironically, this policy would serve to spur the growth of political consciousness among a new generation of Native American youth.

25. These early connections represented the beginning of what would become a long strategic alliance, including in the nuclear realm. See Sasha Polakow-Suransky, *The Unspoken Alliance: Israel's Secret Relationship with Apartheid South Africa* (New York: Pantheon, 2010).

26. See Warren Bass, *Support Any Friend: Kennedy's Middle East and the Making of the U.S.-Israel Alliance* (Oxford: Oxford University Press, 2003).

27. See Adrian Guelke, *Rethinking the Rise and Fall of Apartheid: South Africa and World Politics* (New York: Palgrave Macmillan, 2005).

28. Many critics have noted, for example, that the policy of nuclear deterrence enabled the two superpowers to outsource their conflict to the Global South in the form of proxy wars whose effects have far outlived the Soviet Union itself. At the conclusion of Angola's nearly thirty-year proxy war, to give just one example, the country had more landmines than people.

29. See Doug Brugge, Timothy Benally and Esther Yazzie-Lewis (eds), *The Navajo People and Uranium Mining* (Albuquerque: University of New Mexico Press, 2006); Peter Eichstaedt, *If You Poison Us: Uranium and Native Americans* (Santa Fe: Red Crane Books, 1994); and Winona LaDuke, "Uranium Mining, Native Resistance, and the Greener Path," *Orion*, January/February 2009, http://www.orionmagazine.org/index.php/articles/article/4248.

30. See Andrea Smith, *Conquest: Sexual Violence and American Indian Genocide* (Boston: South End Press, 2005), Chapter 3.

31. Dorothy Nelkin, "Native Americans and Nuclear Power," *Science, Technology & Human Values*, 6, 35 (1981), p. 3.

32. Ibid ., p. 3.

33. In a 2003 interview, Trudell addressed this issue through the lens of "civilization." Discussing the contemporary erosion of democracy, he made a shrewd observation based upon a long reading of history: "None of this is new to the natives. But if the non-natives could remember, none of it's new to them either. If the non-natives could remember, they've been "civilized" a whole lot longer than us. And all of these things I'm talking about happened—inquisitions and all of that—that's the "civilizing" process. Nothing new happening here." See Trudell, "Democracy" (mothersworldmedia, 2003), http://www.youtube.com/watch?v=qRO8 CjzFIh8.

34. It is important to note that despite sustained attempts by Zionist ideologues to separate anti-Semitism from Orientalism, the two are inextricably linked. As Edward Said argues, Orientalism is a kind of "strange, secret sharer of Western anti-Semitism," and both have collided in a variety of ways in the colonization of Palestine. See Said, *Orientalism* (New York: Vintage, 1978), pp. 27–28; and Said, "In the Shadow of the West," in Gauri Viswanathan (ed.), *Power, Politics, and Culture: Interviews With Edward W. Said* (New York: Pantheon, 2001), p. 48. For a further elaboration of this theme, see Joseph Massad, "The Persistence of the Palestinian Question," *Cultural Critique*, 59 (2005), pp. 1–23.

35. For an extended discussion of some of these paths in the colonization of North America, see Anthony J. Hall, *The American Empire and the Fourth World* (Montreal and Kingston: McGill-Queen's University Press, 2003).

36. Paul Virilio, *Popular Defense & Ecological Struggles* (transl. by Mark Polizzotti) (New York: Semiotext(e), 19990 [1978]), p. 54, original emphasis.

37. Virilio's essentially anarchist perspective views the state as a "permanent conspiracy" and a kind of "military protection racket" that is engaged primarily in the business of domination and resource extraction. He distinguishes domination from the sort of "pure power" that stretches beyond the control of politics and manifests itself, for example, in processes of runaway militarization.

38. See Baruch Kimmerling, *Politicide: Ariel Sharon's War Against the Palestinians* (London: Verso, 2003), p. 4.

39. Virilio, *Popular Defense & Ecological Struggles*, p. 55.

40. See, *inter alia*, Rashid Khalidi, "Palestinian Peasant Resistance to Zionism before World War I," in Edward W. Said and Christopher Hitch-

ens (eds), *Blaming the Victims: Spurious Scholarship and the Palestinian Question* (London: Verso, 1988), pp. 207–234; Zachary Lockman and Joel Beinin (eds), *Intifada: The Palestinian Uprising Against Israeli Occupation* (Boston: South End Press, 1989); Jamal Nassar and Roger Heacock (eds), *Intifada: Palestine at the Crossroads* (New York: Birzeit University and Praeger Publishers, 1991); Rosemary Sayigh, *Palestinians: From Peasants to Revolutionaries* (London: Zed Books, 1979); Yezid Sayigh, *Armed Struggle and the Search for State: The Palestinian National Movement, 1949–1993* (New York: Oxford University Press, 1997); and Ted Swedenburg, *Memories of Revolt: The 1936–1939 Rebellion and the Palestinian National Past* (Minneapolis: University of Minnesota Press, 1995).

41. Gary Foley, "Black Power in Redfern 1968–1972," *The Koori History Website*, http://kooriweb.org/foley/essays/essay_1.html (accessed May 2008).

42. See Cowan, "Nomadic Resistance: Tent Embassies and Collapsible Architecture," *The Koori History Website*, http://kooriweb.org/foley/images/history/1970s/emb72/embarchit.htm (accessed May 2008).

43. See Ward Churchill and Jim Vander Wall, *The COINTELPRO Papers: Documents from the FBI's Secret Wars Against Dissent in the United States* (Boston: South End Press, 1990).

44. Foley, "Black Power in Redfern."

45. The December 2008-January 2009 Israeli assault on Gaza brought this issue to the fore once again as critics of the action saw Israel as having violated the ACEA by employing US helicopters and other weapons in Gaza.

46. When Virilio remarked in the mid-1970s on what he saw as the growing tendency of governments to confuse external and internal security, he arguably undersold the extent to which this "confusion" had long been an integral element of global politics thanks to the impact of settler colonial relations in particular, and imperial relations more generally. At the same time, Virilio was prescient in identifying the far-reaching and anti-democratic effect of the generalization of this frontier logic. See Virilio, "The Suicidal State," in James Der Derian (ed.), *The Virilio Reader* (Malden: Blackwell, 1998), pp. 29–45.

47. Rex Weyler, *Blood of the Land: The U.S. Government and Corporate War Against the American Indian Movement* (New York: Vintage, 1984), quoted in Churchill and Vander Wall, *The COINTELPRO Papers*, p. 244.

48. The role of golf in the Oka crisis, I would argue, is more than incidental. Golf, which requires extensive land and water resources, may be

viewed as the ultimate settler colonial sport, as evidenced by its consistent popularity in the US, Australia, and South Africa, particularly among white male elites who have been the primary beneficiaries of the system of property relations imposed by settler projects.

49. Arthur Kroker, "The Mohawk Refusal."

50. Another prominent example is the decision by law enforcement authorities in Philadelphia to employ military-grade explosives when attacking the headquarters of MOVE, an Africanist black liberation group, in 1985, with devastating results.

51. See Hall, *The American Empire and the Fourth World*; Barry Steven Mandelker, "Indigenous People and Cultural Appropriation: Intellectual Property Problems and Solutions," *Canadian Intellectual Property Review*, 16 (2000), p. 368; and Susan Staiger Gooding, "Narrating Law and Environmental Body Politics (In Times of War) in "Indigenous America/America"," *Law & Society Review*, 39, 3 (2005), p. 707. On the politics and the military usage of the "Sabra" image in Israel, see John Collins, "From Portbou to Palestine, and Back," *Social Text*, 89 (2007), pp. 70–74.

52. See Peter Linebaugh and Marcus Rediker, *The Many-Headed Hydra: Sailors, Slaves, Commoners, and the Hidden History of the Revolutionary Atlantic* (Boston: Beacon Press, 2000).

53. Virilio, *Popular Defense & Ecological Struggles*, p. 56, original emphasis.

54. See Benedict Anderson, *Under Three Flags: Anarchism and the Anti-Colonial Imagination* (London: Verso, 2005).

55. This mediatic component also demonstrates how Palestinians became non-state pioneers in the emergence of terrorism-as-spectacle. For Douglas Kellner, such spectacles—whether committed by the state (e.g., the US "shock and awe" campaign in Iraq in 2003) or by non-state actors (e.g., the 9/11 attacks)—are differentiated from other acts of political violence by their authors' decision to build the ripple effects of their mass-mediated actions into the act itself. See Kellner, "Spectacles of Terror and Media Manipulation: A Critique of Jihadist and Bush Media Politics," *Logos*, 2, 1 (2003), pp. 86–102.

56. Virilio and Sylvere Lotringer, *Pure War* (transl. by Mark Polizzotti) (New York: Semiotext(e), 1997 [1983]), p. 33.

57. Martin Peretz, "Israel, the United States, and Evil," *The New Republic*, 14 September 2001

58. See Eqbal Ahmad, *Terrorism: Theirs and Ours* (New York: Seven Stories, 2001); Noam Chomsky, "Terrorism and American Ideology," in Edward

Said and Christopher Hitchens (eds), *Blaming the Victims: Spurious Scholarship and the Palestinian Question* (London: Verso, 1988); John Collins, "Terrorism," in John Collins and Ross Glover (eds), *Collateral Language: A User's Guide to America's New War* (New York: New York University Press, 2002), pp. 155–173; and Edward Herman, *The Real Terror Network: Terrorism in Fact and Propaganda* (Boston: South End Press, 1998).

59. This state violence includes high levels of precisely those kinds of violence that fit the dominant description of "terrorism" (e.g., indiscriminate violence against non-military targets for the purpose of achieving some sort of political effect). In this sense "terrorism" is closely related to denial, and both are, to quote Stanley Cohen, "built into the ideological façade of the state." See Cohen, *States of Denial: Knowing About Atrocities and Suffering* (Malden: Blackwell, 2001), p. 10.

60. One of the most important texts analyzing how these particular dynamics work is Stuart Hall et al., *Policing the Crisis: Mugging, the State, and Law and Order* (London: Macmillan, 1978), a classic work in British cultural studies. For other critiques focusing on media constructions, see David L. Altheide, *Terrorism and the Politics of Fear* (Lanham, MD: AltaMira Press, 2006); David Holloway, *Cultures of the War on Terror: Empire, Ideology, and the Remaking of 9/11* (Montreal: McGill/Queen's University Press, 2008); Jimmie L. Reeves and Richard Campbell, *Cracked Coverage: Television News, the Anti-Cocaine Crusade, and the Reagan Legacy* (Durham: Duke University Press, 1994); Danny Schechter, *Media Wars: News at a Time of Terror* (Lanham: Rowman & Littlefield, 2003); and Virilio, *City of Panic* (transl. by Julie Rose) (Oxford and New York: Berg, 2005).

61. For a provocative reading of one of the many ancillary panics generated immediately after the 9/11 attacks, see R. Danielle Egan, "Anthrax," in John Collins and Ross Glover (eds), *Collateral Language: A User's Guide to America's New War* (New York: New York University Press, 2002), pp. 15–26.

62. The classic reference on discourse and discursive formations is Michel Foucault, *The Archaeology of Knowledge* (transl. by A.M. Sheridan Smith) (New York: Pantheon, 1972).

63. See M. Cherif Bassiouni (ed.), *International Terrorism and Political Crimes* (Springfield, IL: Thomas, 1975); J. Bowyer Bell, *Transnational Terror* (Washington: American Enterprise Institute, 1975); David Carlton and Carlo Schaerf (eds), *International Terrorism and World Security* (New

York: Wiley, 1975); Richard Clutterbuck, *Living With Terrorism* (London: Faber & Faber, 1975); Brian M. Jenkins, *International Terrorism: A New Kind of Warfare* (Santa Monica: RAND Corporation, 1974); and Paul Wilkinson, *Political Terrorism* (New York: Macmillan, 1974).

64. A second major journal devoted specifically to the subject, *Terrorism and Political Violence*, emerged in 1989. More recently in 2007, Routledge launched *Critical Studies on Terrorism*, which seeks to "encourage fruitful intellectual engagement between critical and orthodox accounts of terrorism."

65. Charles A. Russell and Bowman H. Miller, "Profile of a Terrorist," *Terrorism: An International Journal*, 1, 1 (1977), pp. 17–34.

66. Conrad V. Hassel, "Terror: The Crime of the Privileged—An Examination and Prognosis," *Terrorism: An International Journal*, 1, 1 (1977), p. 5.

67. Walter Laqueur, *The Terrorism Reader* (Philadelphia: Temple University Press, 1978), p. 263.

68. Ibid., 149.

69. Quoted in Edward Said, "The Essential Terrorist," in Edward Said and Christopher Hitchens (eds), *Blaming the Victims: Spurious Scholarship and the Palestinian Question* (London: Verso, 1988), p. 154, emphasis added.

70. Talal Asad uses the term "epistemic community" to refer to the ways in which "[t]he *discourse* of terror enables a redefinition of the space of violence in which bold intervention and rearrangement of everyday relations can take place and be governed in relation to terror, a space that presupposes new knowledges and practices." In particular, Asad has in mind the emergence of the concept of "homeland security" as an institutional and cultural scaffolding for the GWOT, a scaffolding that already includes a significant reorganization of the federal government, the creation of new academic journals and think tanks, and the ongoing proliferation of related concepts and discourses. See Asad, *On Suicide Bombing* (New York: Columbia University Press, 2007), pp. 28–29. It must be noted that this "epistemic community" is only superficially new; its roots lie in the emergence of "terrorism" as a discursive formation during the long 1960s and, more generally, in the deep structures of settler colonialism.

71. In a provocative 2010 series of reports ("Top Secret America") bolstered by dynamic maps and a searchable database of companies, the *Washington Post* described "a national security and intelligence system so big, so complex and so hard to manage, no one really knows if it's fulfilling its

most important purpose: keeping its citizens safe." In its visual presentation of its data, however, the series privileged the national context, arguably occluding the ways in which US-based agencies, companies, and practices are themselves embedded in transnational networks. The networks of the "settler international" in particular are hidden: neither Israel nor South Africa, both of which have longstanding "security" ties with the US, appear anywhere in the database accompanying the series.

72. The productive nature of war is one of the cardinal principles of the "war and society" approach that provides an important corrective to classical social science approaches in which war plays a relatively minor role. See Tarak Barkawi, *Globalization & War* (Lanham, MA: Rowman & Littlefield, 2006), pp. 27–57.

73. Alexander Galloway and Eugene Thacker, *The Exploit: A Theory of Networks* (Minneapolis: University of Minnesota Press, 2007), p. 3.

74. Ibid., p. 74, emphasis added.

75. Wolfe, "Settler Colonialism," p. 402.

76. See Ghassan Hage, "'Comes a Time We Are All Enthusiasm': Understanding Palestinian Suicide Bombers in Times of Exighophobia," *Public Culture*, 15, 1 (2003), p. 81.

4. ACCELERATION

1. See Graeme Gilloch, *Walter Benjamin: Critical Constellations* (Cambridge: Polity Press, 2002), pp. 27–56.

2. The exact circumstances surrounding Benjamin's last hours have always been murky, but the standard narrative has been that when confronted with the possibility of being sent back to Nazi-occupied France, he chose to take a lethal dose of morphine in his hotel room. *Who Killed Walter Benjamin?*, a 2005 documentary by David Mauas (www.whokilledwalterbenjamin.com), raises the possibility that Benjamin's death was not a suicide at all.

3. In his project sketchbook, Karavan described the purpose of the platform: "On the steep hill, above the boulders that have to be clambered over to walk around the cemetery, a wall, a fence, a barrier, the graves behind. A long way away, below the horizon, framed by the high dark and mountains of the Pyrenees, the blue sea, the clear sky, freedom. I decided to construct a platform with a seat from where, through the fence, beyond the cemetery, freedom could be seen." See "The Memorial in Karavan's Own Words," *Walter Benjamin in Portbou*, http://walterbenjaminportbou.cat/en/content/el-memorial-segons-karavan (accessed 11 January 2011).

4. Paul Virilio and Sylvere Lotringer, *Crepuscular Dawn* (transl. by Mike Taormina) (Los Angeles and New York: Semiotext(e), 2002), p. 75.
5. Mbembe, "Necropolitics," pp. 11–40.
6. Gilles Deleuze, "What is a *dispositif?*," in *Michel Foucault, Philosopher* (transl. by Timothy J. Armstrong) (New York: Routledge, 2003), p. 164.
7. See Paul Virilio, *Speed and Politics* (transl. by Mark Polizzotti) (Los Angeles: Semiotext(e), 2006). Note that speed and acceleration are closely related, but are not the same thing. Speed, like wealth, is a kind of state or property; acceleration, like capital accumulation, is a process.
8. For a useful overview of some of the most important interventions the topic of social acceleration, see William E. Scheuerman, *Liberal Democracy and the Social Acceleration of Time* (Baltimore and London: The Johns Hopkins University Press, 2004), pp. 1–25.
9. On the role of technology in the ideology and practice of colonization in North America, see Michael Adas, *Dominance By Design: Technological Imperatives and America's Civilizing Mission* (Cambridge, MA and London: Belknap Press of Harvard University Press, 2006).
10. See Cole Harris, "How Did Colonialism Dispossess? Comments from an Edge of Empire," *Annals of the Association of American Geographers*, 94, 1 (2004).
11. For the most elaborated exploration of this theme, see David Harvey, *The Condition of Postmodernity* (Cambridge: Blackwell, 1989).
12. See Randy Martin, "War, by All Means," *Social Text*, 91 (2007), pp. 13–22.
13. See John Collins, "Dromocratic Palestine," *Middle East Report*, 248 (Fall 2008); Collins, "Confinement Under an Open Sky: Following the Speed Trap from Guernica to Gaza and Beyond," *Globalizations*, 5, 4 (2008), pp. 555–569; and Scheuerman, p. 19.
14. Such experiences among relatively well-to-do members of the global community have produced a range of efforts designed to slow down the pace of life. See Carl Honoré, *In Praise of Slowness: How a Worldwide Movement is Challenging the Cult of Speed* (San Francisco: HarperCollins, 2004).
15. Zygmunt Bauman, "Wars of the Globalization Era," *European Journal of Social Theory*, 4, 1 (2001), p. 15, quoted in Mbembe, "Necropolitics," p. 31.
16. Recall FDR's observation, in his 1941 "Four Freedoms" speech, that "[w]hatever stands in the way of speed and efficiency in defense preparation must give way to the national need."
17. Virilio, *Open Sky* (transl. by Julie Rose) (London: Verso, 1997), p. 59.

18. Steer, *The Tree of Gernika: A Field Study of Modern War* (London: Faber & Faber, 2009 [1938]), pp. 238–239.

19. Scheuerman's *Liberal Democracy and the Social Acceleration of Time* offers an extended meditation on how acceleration has disrupted the basic structures of liberal democracy.

20. See James Der Derian, "The Conceptual Cosmology of Paul Virilio," *Theory, Culture & Society*, 16, 5–6 (1999), p. 222.

21. See James Der Derian, "The (S)pace of International Relations: Simulation, Surveillance and Speed," *International Studies Quarterly*, 34 (1990), pp. 295–310.

22. For a suggestive meditation on how this logic informs state violence against indigenous people and their "vital sense of sedentariness," see Arthur Kroker, "The Mohawk Refusal."

23. On the growth of "technoculture" and its role in shaping recent US military action in Afghanistan and Iraq, see Derek Gregory, *The Colonial Present: Afghanistan, Palestine, and Iraq* (Malden: Blackwell, 2004), pp. 49–56 and 196–214.

24. Ibid., p. 63.

25. Eyal Weizman, *Hollow Land: Israel's Architecture of Occupation* (London: Verso, 2007)

26. Gregory, *The Colonial Present*, p. 125.

27. See Said, *Culture and Imperialism* (New York: Alfred A. Knopf, 1993).

28. Wolfe, "Settler Colonialism and the Elimination of the Native," *Journal of Genocide Research*, 8, 4 (2006), p. 388. In a fascinating article, Cole Harris highlights how the considerable "disciplinary technologies" possessed by settler colonizers in British Columbia led to "the emergence of a new, immigrant human geography, which became native peoples' most pervasive confinement." See Harris, "How Did Colonialism Dispossess?," p. 178.

29. See Shira Robinson, "Occupied Citizens in a Liberal State: Palestinians Under Military Rule and the Colonial Formation of Israeli Society, 1948–1966" (unpublished PhD thesis, Department of History, Stanford University, 2006).

30. Raja Shehadeh, who has spent years struggling to defend the rights of Palestinian landowners, recalls his conversations with an "ideologically dedicated" Israeli settler who was head of the Planning Council for the West Bank: "When I asked [him] how the village was expected to provide plots for the future expansion of its inhabitants," writes Shehadeh, "he would answer with a straight face that they could build up." See She-

hadeh, *Palestinian Walks: Forays Into a Vanishing Landscape* (New York: Scribner, 2007), p. 99.

31. Borcila, "Learning alongside—notes from "Turning our Tongues: Audio Journals from Dheisheh Refugee Camp"," http://6plus.org/third_text. html.

32. One of the most provocative interventions in recent discussions of power and violence, Giorgio Agamben's concept of *homo sacer*, has direct implications for our understanding of how Palestinian refugee populations have been positioned both within particular nation-states and within a larger global system. Agamben famously identifies the camp as an "absolute space of the exception." See Agamben, *Homo Sacer: Sovereign Power and Bare Life* (transl. by Daniel Heller-Roazen) (Stanford: Stanford University Press, 2005), p. 20. Agamben's work has become a virtual cottage industry for scholars who write on Palestine. See, *inter alia*, Derek Gregory, *The Colonial Present*, pp. 117–138; and the essays collected in Ronit Lentin (ed.), *Thinking Palestine* (London: Zed Books, 2008).

33. Jeff Halper, "The 94 Percent Solution: A Matrix of Control," *Middle East Report*, 216 (2000), pp. 14–19.

34. See Michael Sorkin (ed.), *Against the Wall: Israel's Barrier to Peace* (New York and London: New Press, 2005).

35. See Tanya Reinhart, *Israel/Palestine: How to End the War of 1948*, 2nd edn. (New York: Seven Stories, 2004).

36. Darryl Li, "The Gaza Strip as Laboratory: Notes in the Wake of Disengagement," *Journal of Palestine Studies*, 35, 2 (2006), pp. 39–40.

37. See Creveld, *Defending Israel: A Controversial Plan Toward Peace* (New York: St. Martin's Press, 2004).

38. Donald Macintyre, "Palestinians "terrorised" by sonic boom flights," *The Independent* (London), 3 November 2005.

39. Li, pp. 48–50.

40. Eyal Weizman, "The Politics of Verticality," *open Democracy*, April 2002, http://www.opendemocracy.net/conflict-politicsverticality/article_801. jsp.

41. Nicolai Ouroussoff, "A Line in the Sand," *New York Times*, 1 January 2006.

42. Weizman, "The Art of War," *Frieze* 99 (2006), http://www.frieze.com/ feature_single.asp?f=1165. For his part, Naveh claimed in a 2007 interview that his efforts to infuse Israeli military culture with his ideas had largely failed. See Yotam Feldman, "Dr. Naveh, or, how I learned to stop worrying and walk through walls," *Haaretz*, 25 October 2007, http://

www.haaretz.com/weekend/magazine/dr-naveh-or-how-i-learned-to-stop-worrying-and-walk-through-walls-1.231912 (accessed 6 January 2011).

43. Doug Suisman et al., *The Arc: A Formal Structure for a Palestinian State* (Santa Monica: RAND Corporation, 2005).

44. Coalition of Women for Peace, *Crossing the Line: The Tel Aviv–Jerusalem Fast Train* (Tel Aviv: Who Profits from the Occupation, 2010), http://www.whoprofits.org/articlefiles/WP-A1-Train.pdf (accessed 6 January 2011).

45. See John Collins, *Occupied By Memory: The Intifada Generation and the Palestinian State of Emergency* (New York: New York University Press, 2004), pp. 111–124.

46. "Walking through walls" refers to a particular strategy used by Israeli troops during "Operation Defensive Shield," particularly in crowded refugee camps like Balata, located on the outskirts of Nablus. According to Eyal Weizman, "Soldiers avoided using the streets, roads, alleys and courtyards that define the logic of movement through the city, as well as the external doors, internal stairwells and windows that constitute the order of buildings. Rather, they were punching holes through party walls, ceilings and floors, and moving across them through 100-metre-long pathways of domestic interior hollowed out of the dense and contiguous city fabric." See Weizman, *Hollow Land*, pp. 185–218.

47. Virilio and Lotringer, *Crepuscular Dawn*, p. 65.

48. Ghassan Hage, "Comes a Time We Are All Enthusiasm," pp. 65–89.

49. For a thoughtful overview of many of these frameworks and the often unstated assumptions encoded within them, see Talal Asad, *On Suicide Bombing* (New York: Columbia University Press, 2007).

50. See, for example, Israel Charny, *Fighting Suicide Bombing: A Worldwide Campaign for Life* (Westport, CT: Praeger Security International, 2007).

51. See Baruch Kimmerling, *Politicide: Ariel Sharon's War Against the Palestinians* (London: Verso, 2003).

52. See Sara Roy, *The Gaza Strip: The Political Economy of De-Development* (Washington: Institute for Palestine Studies, 1995).

53. Hage, p. 77.

54. Ibid., p. 78, emphasis added.

55. Later in the article, Hage quotes a Lebanese interlocutor and Hizbullah member: "The Americans pretend not to understand the suicide bombers and consider them evil. But I am sure they do…I know that the Americans fully understand this because this is exactly what they

were celebrating about the guy who downed the Philadelphia flight [United 93] on September 11, the one where the hijackers failed to hit their target. Isn't that exactly what he must have said when he decided to kill himself and everyone else by bringing the plane down? Didn't he say to those hijacking him: "I'd rather kill you on my own terms and kill myself with you rather than be led to my death like a sheep on your own terms"? They made a hero out of him" (pp. 84–85).

56. See Nachman Ben-Yehuda, *The Masada Myth: Collective Memory and Mythmaking in Israel* (Madison: University of Wisconsin Press, 1995); and Yael Zerubavel, "The Death of Memory and the Memory of Death: Masada and the Holocaust as Historical Metaphors," *Representations*, 45 (1994), pp. 72–100.

57. Weizman, "The Politics of Verticality."

58. "We have dozens of atomic bombs, tanks and planes. We confront people possessing none of these arms," argues the Israeli novelist David Grossman. "And yet, in our minds, we remain victims. This inability to perceive ourselves in relation to others is our principal weakness." Quoted in Roger Cohen, "A Mideast Truce," *New York Times*, 16 November 2009.

59. Michael Warschawski, *Toward an Open Tomb: The Crisis of Israeli Society* (transl. by P. Drucker) (New York: Monthly Review Press, 2004).

60. Virilio, "The Suicidal State," p. 43.

61. "After the crash of the *Net economy* in 2000 and the crash of the Pentagon's 'Net strategy,' brought about by a handful of crazed suicide attackers, we find ourselves, in fact, facing an unprecedented situation, since it is one which is globally suicidal." Virilio, *Ground Zero* (transl. by Chris Turner) (London: Verso, 2002), p. 37, emphasis added. See also Boaventura de Sousa Santos, "Collective Suicide"?, *Bad Subjects*, 63 (2003), http://bad.eserver.org/issues/2003/63/santos.html.

62. It is important to emphasize that suicide bombing was not invented in Palestine. At the same time, it is clear that the use of suicide bombing in Palestine, combined with the extensive media attention these actions have received, has influenced the choices made by groups struggling against the US military presence in Iraq and Afghanistan.

63. See Creveld, *Defending Israel*. pp. 66–80.

64. Naomi Klein, "How War Was Turned into a Brand," *Guardian*, 16 June 2007. For another reading of the same developments, in this case more sympathetic to Israel's strategic goals, see Creveld, *Defending Israel*, Creveld notes that Israel was far ahead of the curve on the "revolution in military affairs," having started to experiment with RMA in the late

1980s. As a result, he argues, Israel "has pulled ahead not only of many NATO members but even of the United States" (p. 84).

65. When Klein's analysis is combined with the historical depth provided in the work of Shimshon Bichler and Jonathan Nitzan (*The Global Political Economy of Israel*, London: Pluto Press, 2002) on Israeli political economy, it is evident that the post-9/11 shift to a "homeland security" economy provided renewed opportunities for differential capital accumulation in Israel. As Bichler and Nitzan explain, dominant capital and its political backers in Israel have always been quite adept at responding to changing global conditions of possibility. The relative optimism of the Oslo years provided "a cover-up for corporate peace dividends," while the move toward a high-tech economy (driven especially by opportunities in the telecommunications and information technology sectors) provided "a way to redistribute income and wealth" (p. 349). They conclude their book by noting that the 9/11 attacks had an "immediate and brutal" impact on Israel (p. 357). Yet as subsequent events have demonstrated, dominant capital in Israel appears to have seized upon that moment to promote the transition to an economy that is remilitarized, but with a high-tech face.

66. Quoted in Edmund Sanders and Batsheva Sobelman, "Israeli firms see a global market for their anti-terrorism know-how," *Los Angeles Times*, 27 November 2010, http://www.latimes.com/news/nationworld/world/la-fg-israel-homeland-security-20101128,0,823166,print.story.

67. See Timothy Karr, "One U.S. Corporation's Role in Egypt's Brutal Crackdown," *Huffington Post*, 28 January 2011, http://www.huffingtonpost.com/timothy-karr/one-us-corporations-role-_b_815281.html?ref=fb&src=sp. As Karr notes, using the January 2011 popular uprising against the Mubarak regime as an example, the same kinds of technologies that "connect, organize and empower protesters can also be used to hunt them down."

68. See Andy Clarno, "A Tale of Two Walled Cities: Neo-liberalization and Enclosure in Johannesburg and Jerusalem," *Political Power and Social Theory*, 19 (2008).

69. For a brief artist's statement and some images from Halawani's series, see "Rula Halawani: Intimacy," *Nafas Art Magazine*, October 2006, http://universes-in-universe.org/nafas/articles/2006/rula_halawani.

70. The phrase "logistics of perception" derives from Virilio's work on the intersections of war and cinema. See Der Derian, "The Conceptual Cosmology of Paul Virilio," p. 222.

71. Quoted in Amos Harel, "Cast Lead expose: What did the IDF think would happen in Gaza?," *Haaretz*, 2 April 2009, http://www.haaretz.com/hasen/spages/1074218.html.

72. Suspect Detection Systems, "Technology," http://www.suspectdetection.com/tech.html.

73. See Mike Davis, *Planet of Slums* (London: Verso, 2006).

74. On the role of drones in Israel's current and future defense posture, see Creveld, *Defending Israel*, op. cit., pp. 98–107. It is important to note that Israeli weapons manufacturers regularly operate inside the US for political and economic reasons; as a result, it is often hard to distinguish Israeli and American involvement in the development and deployment of new weapons technologies. A recent example is the 2009 decision by Israel Aerospace Industries to begin assembling drones in Mississippi via an American subsidiary, Stark Manufacturing. See Ora Coren, "Israel Aerospace Industries moving production to Mississippi," *Haaretz*, 18 November 2009, http://www.haaretz.com/hasen/spages/1128760.html.

75. See Human Rights Watch, *Precisely Wrong: Gaza Civilians Killed by Israeli Drone-Launched Missiles* (New York: Human Rights Watch, 2009), http://www.hrw.org/sites/default/files/reports/iopt0609web_0.pdf.

76. Yossi Melman, "Brazil to buy $350 million worth of drones from Israel," *Haaretz*, 11 November 2009,http://www.haaretz.com/hasen/spages/1127471.html.

77. See Robert Mandel, *Armies Without States: The Privatization of Security* (Boulder: Lynne Rienner, 2002); Jeremy Scahill, *Blackwater: The Rise of the World's Most Powerful Mercenary Army* (New York: Nation Books, 2007); and P.W. Singer, *Corporate Warriors: The Rise of the Privatized Military Industry* (Ithaca: Cornell University Press, 2008). It is worth noting that proponents of military privatization often cite speed as a primary argument in making their case. See Marion E. "Spike" Bowman, *Privatizing While Transforming* (Washington: Center for Technology and National Security Policy, National Defense University, 2007).

78. Virilio, "The Suicidal State," p. 43.

79. Janet Varner Gunn, *Second Life: A West Bank Memoir* (Minneapolis: University of Minnesota Press, 1995), pp. 43–44.

80. Almost immediately the manifesto became the subject of a revealing debate between Western observers attracted to the social media angle and pro-Palestinian observers who questioned the political authenticity and utility of the group's call for liberation. As is often the case with young Palestinians, adult preoccupations and interpretive impositions

had the effect of hiding the substance of what the young Gazans were actually saying.

5. OCCUPATION

1. Steer, *The Tree of Gernika: A Field Study of Modern War* (London: Faber & Faber, 2009 [1938]), p. 240.
2. Aerial bombardment was used heavily by Spanish forces during the country's colonial war in Morocco (1909–1927), a conflict in which Spain's future fascist dictator, Francisco Franco, played a prominent role. Among the tactics employed by the colonial air force was the dropping of chemical bombs on heavily populated areas. See Sebastian Balfour, *Deadly Embrace: Morocco and the Road to the Spanish Civil War* (New York: Oxford University Press, 2002). Balfour reports that Franco seriously considered bringing this tactic back to Spain after the anti-Republican military rebellion that sparked the Spanish Civil War in 1936. In response to a request from Franco, Italy sent two shipments of mustard gas bombs, along with troops trained in their use, to Nationalist forces in Spain, supplementing the chemical materials that Germany had supplied during the Moroccan war. There is no evidence that these chemical weapons were ever used in the Civil War.
3. In her ethnography of Inner Mani (Greece), C. Nadia Seremetakis notes that the cultivation of olive trees is a profoundly future-oriented act; consequently, the olive tree bears a complex relationship with death. "A word commonly used by mourners when referring to someone's death is *anakóloma*," she writes. "The same word means the uprooting, the turning upside down, of a tree by bad weather. Strong winds are associated with the open road, the outside, states of exposure, and the absence of sheltering interiors." See Seremetakis, *The Last Word: Women, Death, and Divination in Inner Mani* (Chicago: University of Chicago Press, 1991), p. 204.
4. See Barbara McKean Parmenter, *Giving Voice to Stones: Place and Identity in Palestinian Literature* (Austin: University of Texas Press, 1994).
5. See Joseph Massad, "The "Post-Colonial" Colony: Time, Space, and Bodies in Palestine/Israel," in Fawzia Afzal-Khan and Kalpana Seshadri-Crooks (eds), *The Pre-Occupation of Postcolonial Studies* (Durham and London: Duke University Press, 2000), p. 337.
6. See Walid Khalidi (ed.), *All That Remains: The Palestinian Villages Occupied and Depopulated by Israel in 1948* (Washington: Institute for Palestine Studies, 2006).

7. In botany, "trauma-tropism" refers to the ability of plants and other organisms to alter their own growth after suffering a wound. Olive tree cultivation makes use of this principle, as trees are regularly pruned in order to help improve the following year's crop. Allen Feldman uses the notion of "trauma-tropism" to understand the ways in which communities and societies reorganize themselves around selected historical "wounds," thereby opening up new possibilities for the future. See Feldman, "Strange Fruit: The South African Truth Commission and the Demonic Economies of Violence," *Social Analysis*, 46, 3 (Fall 2002), pp. 234–265.

8. See Seremetakis, *The Last Word*, p. 215; and Walter Benjamin, "The Storyteller: Reflections on the Works of Nikolai Leskov," in Hannah Arendt (ed.), *Illuminations*, (transl. by Harry Zohn) (New York: Schocken, 1968), 92.

9. Wangari Maathai, "Nobel Lecture" (Oslo, 10 December 2004), http://nobelprize.org/nobel_prizes/peace/laureates/2004/maathai-lecture-text.html (accessed 7 December 2009).

10. James Der Derian, "The (S)pace of International Relations: Simulation, Surveillance and Speed," *International Studies Quarterly*, 34 (1990), p. 308.

11. Arturo Escobar, "Beyond the Third World: Imperial Globality, Global Coloniality and Anti-Globalisation Social Movements," *Third World Quarterly*, 25, 1 (2004), pp. 222–223.

12. Raja Shehadeh, *Palestinian Walks: Forays Into a Vanishing Landscape* (New York: Scribner, 2007), p. 92.

13. Anthony Hall, *The American Empire and the Fourth World* (Montreal and Kingston: McGill-Queen's University Press, 2003), p. 24.

14. Quoted in Public Committee Against Torture in Israel, *No Second Thoughts: The Changes in the Israeli Defense Forces" Combat Doctrine in Light of "Operation Cast Lead"* (Jerusalem: PCATI, 2009), 18, http://www.stoptorture.org.il/files/no%20second%20thoughts_ENG_WEB.pdf.

15. Ibid., p. 19.

16. See Virilio, "The Suicidal State," in Derian (ed.), *The Virilio Reader*, p. 30. Elsewhere Virilio uses the term "ecological war" to refer to the same process, specifically in the context of the U.S. war in Vietnam. See Virilio, *Popular Defense & Ecological Struggles*, p. 52. While Virilio distinguishes "war on the milieu" from an earlier model ("war of milieu") in which war was waged within a specific arena (e.g., the "Pacific theatre"),

it is also clear that "war on the milieu" accurately describes longstanding practices of colonial violence.

17. Edward Said, "The Acre and the Goat," in *The Politics of Dispossession: The Struggle for Palestinian Self-Determination, 1969–1994* (New York: Pantheon, 1994), pp. 33–42.

18. Derek Gregory, *The Colonial Present: Afghanistan, Palestine, Iraq* (Malden: Blackwell, 2004), p. 131.

19. PCATI, *No Second Thoughts*, p. 24.

20. Weizman also notes that thanks to the chaotic building and destruction that has taken place in the "wild frontier of the West Bank," raw sewage has proven to be quite uncontrollable, often ending up in Israel despite the intentions of Israeli authorities to keep it contained in Palestinian areas. See Weizman, *Hollow Land: Israel's Architecture of Occupation* (London: Verso, 2007), p. 20.

21. Greg Myre, "Israel Briefly Reopens a Gaza Crossing to Send in Food," *New York Times*, 21 March 2006.

22. In early 2011 a Norwegian newspaper released a WikiLeaks document that shed light on this "bare life" policy. The March 2008 US diplomatic cable revealed that Israeli officials had indicated "on multiple occasions" their intention to "keep the Gazan economy functioning at the lowest level possible consistent with avoiding a humanitarian crisis." See "3.11.2008 Cashless in Gaza?," *Aftenposten*, 5 January 2011, http://www.aftenposten.no/spesial/wikileaksdokumenter/article3972840.ece (accessed 14 January 2011).

23. On this emerging process of corporal colonization—essentially the creation and exploitation of a new "blank space" that Joseph Conrad's Marlow never could have imagined—see Virilio and Lotringer, *Crepuscular Dawn* (transl. by Mike Taormina) (Los Angeles and New York: Semiotext(e), 2002), p. 101. For a detailed discussion of Israeli "nationalist biopolitics," including the aggressive provision of contraceptives and abortion services for Palestinians who live in Israel, see Rhoda Ann Kanaaneh, *Birthing the Nation: Strategies of Palestinian Women in Israel* (Berkeley: University of California Press, 2002).

24. See Andrea Smith, *Conquest: Sexual Violence and Native American Genocide* (Boston: South End Press, 2005); and Patrick Wolfe, "Settler Colonialism and the Elimination of the Native," *Journal of Genocide Research*, 8, 4 (2006), pp. 387–409.

25. I owe this distinction to Ghassan Hage, and in particular to his plenary lecture at the 2008 "New Worlds, New Sovereignties" conference held

in Melbourne. In Hage's reading, colonial sovereignty is inherently linked with ecological domination and the desire to domesticate the colonial "other" by denying and/or killing the other's political will.

26. See Antony Anghie, *Imperialism, Sovereignty and the Making of International Law* (Cambridge: Cambridge University Press, 2004).

27. For a provocative comparison of the Palestinian and Cherokee cases, see Norman Finkelstein, "History's Verdict: The Cherokee Case," *Journal of Palestine Studies*, 24, 4 (Summer 1995), pp. 32–45.

28. "Palestinian cave-dweller fights Israeli eviction," *Haaretz*, 12 November 2009, available at http://www.haaretz.com/hasen/spages/1127461.html.

29. Oakland Ross, "The caveman's day in court," *The Star* (Toronto), 12 April 2009, available at http://www.thestar.com/comment/columnists/article/617187.

30. Isabel Kershner, "A Test of Wills Over a Patch of Desert," *New York Times*, 25 August 2010, http://www.nytimes.com/2010/08/26/world/middleeast/26israel.html (accessed 15 January 2011). As Kershner notes, the removals of the early 1950s were carried out in order to declare land occupied by Bedouin villages as state land. What she fails to note is that these removals fit perfectly within a longer settler colonial trajectory that includes the forcible expulsion of Bedouin communities during the 1947–48 war. In an interview for the film *Route 181*, one Israeli man who fought with the Palmach in that conflict recalled his participation in "Operation Matate" (using the Hebrew word for "broom"), during which he and his comrades "swept out" the inhabitants of many Bedouin camps as part of a broader effort to, in his words, "create Jewish territorial contiguity." See Saree Makdisi, *Palestine Inside Out: An Everyday Occupation* (New York: W.W. Norton, 2008), pp. 223–226.

31. See Oren Yiftachel, "The horror show at al-Araqib village: from removal to approval," *Jews for Justice for Palestinians*, 2 August 2010, http://jfjfp.com/?p=16132 (accessed 15 January 2011).

32. See Yiftachel, "The horror show"; and Makdisi, *Palestine Inside Out*, p. 236. It is also worth noting here that the Negev is a highly militarized area whose population faces a host of environmental hazards due to the presence of numerous Israeli military bases; the Negev Nuclear Research Center near Dimona; toxic waste facilities; and a variety of petrochemical factories.

33. Glen Coulthard, "Place against Empire: Understanding Indigenous Anti-Colonialism," *Affinities: A Journal of Radical Theory, Culture, and Action*, 4, 2 (Fall 2010), pp. 79–83.

34. In *Popular Defense & Ecological Struggles* (80–82), Virilio pushes this logic further, describing the family as the original "commando group."

35. On the popular committees in general and the social basis of the first intifada in general, see Zachary Lockman and Joel Beinin (eds), *Intifada: The Palestinian Uprising Against Israeli Occupation* (Boston: South End Press, 1989); and Jamal R. Nassar and Roger Heacock (eds), *Intifada: Palestine at the Crossroads* (New York: Birzeit University and Praeger Publishers, 1991).

36. Lisa Taraki, "The Development of Political Consciousness Among Palestinians in the Occupied Territories, 1967–1987," in Nassar and Heacock, *Intifada*, pp. 53–71.

37. Trudell, "Crazy Horse," in *Lines From a Mined Mind: The Words of John Trudell* (Golden: Fulcrum, 2008), p. 224.

38. Juliana Birnbaum Fox, "Indigenous Science," *Cultural Survival Quarterly*, 33, 1 (Spring 2009), http://www.culturalsurvival.org/publications/cultural-survival-quarterly/australia/indigenous-science.

39. Bustan Qaraaqa, "Why Permaculture?," available at http://www.bustanqaraaqa.org/al2/web/page/display/id/8.html.

40. See http://www.greenintifada.blogspot.com/

41. Simon Boas, "Growing Things in Gaza," *3QuarksDaily*, 10 January 2011, http://www.3quarksdaily.com/3quarksdaily/2011/01/growing-things-in-gaza.html.

42. Edward Said, *Culture and Imperialism* (New York: Alfred A. Knopf, 1993), p. 311.

43. Cindi Katz and Neil Smith, "L.A. Intifada: Interview with Mike Davis," *Social Text*, 33 (1992), pp. 19–33. For more on the L.A.-West Bank parallels, see Ted Swedenburg, *Memories of Revolt* (Minneapolis: University of Minnesota Press, 1995).

44. Edward Said, "Dignity, Solidarity and the Penal Colony," *Counterpunch*, 25 September 2003, quoted in Barbara Harlow, "Remember the Solidarity Here and Everywhere," *Middle East Report*, 229 (Winter 2003), p. 4.

45. See "The Highway of Zinc," *Weekly Mail and Guardian*, 30 September 1994.

46. Edward Said, "The Meaning of Rachel Corrie: Of dignity and solidarity," in Sandercock et al. (eds), *Peace Under Fire: Israel/Palestine and the International Solidarity Movement* (London: Verso, 2004), p. xv.

47. See John Collins, "Looking towards Palestine: Photographic projects in Madrid," *Electronic Intifada*, 16 February 2006, available at http://electronicintifada.net/v2/article3622.shtml.

48. See http://www.wallproject.org/

49. See Ghassan Hage, "'Comes a Time'," pp. 65–89.

50. With its focus on the non-violent politics of habitation, a global occupation movement might be viewed as the actualization of Martin Luther King, Jr.'s concept of the "world house," introduced in his 1964 Nobel Peace Prize lecture, and would have the potential to alter the course of the "global suicidal state" discussed in Chapter 4. See King, "The World House," *The World House Project*, http://www.theworldhouse.org/whessay.html.

51. Readers seeking an introduction to the WSF, its global significance, and its internal politics now have a large and growing literature to consult. An excellent starting point is Boaventura de Sousa Santos, *The Rise of the Global Left: The World Social Forum and Beyond* (London: Zed Books, 2006).

52. See Teivo Teivainen, "The World Social Forum and Global Democratisation: Learning from Porto Alegre," *Third World Quarterly*, 23, 4 (2002), p. 626.

53. Escobar, "Beyond the Third World," p. 214.

54. de Sousa Santos, "Collective Suicide"? *Bad Subjects*, 63 (2003), http://bad.eserver.org/issues/2003/63/santos.html.

55. See Janet Conway, "Indigenizing the global at the World Social Forum," *Alternatives International*, 13 March 2009, http://www.alterinter.org/article3069.html.

56. For a very useful overview of "Fourth World" philosophy and its contemporary relevance in the context of neo-liberal globalization, see Hall, *The American Empire and the Fourth World*.

57. Escobar, "Beyond the Third World," p. 207.

58. The marketing of Palestinian olive oil as part of the global "solidarity economy" in recent years is a good example of how international activists who are well-connected on the ground in Palestine have been able to build bridges with wider ecological struggles. The same olive tree that has nationalist significance for Palestinians and political significance for activists who lend their hands to the annual olive harvest campaign in the West also has ecological significance for consumers who may not necessarily be personally involved in the Palestinian liberation struggle.

59. See "Palestinian Strategic Options: An Attempt at Analysis to Inform Action," *Journal of Palestine Studies*, 35, 1 (2005), pp. 91–102.

60. In his classic essay on "Secular Criticism," Edward Said argues that "solidarity before criticism means the end of criticism." Though this formu-

lation might itself be critiqued for privileging the position of the cosmopolitan intellectual, it nonetheless cautions wisely against the dangers of a solidarity that closes itself off from the fresh air of critical dialogue. See Said, *The World, the Text and the Critic* (Cambridge: Harvard University Press, 1983), p. 28.

61. Walter Benjamin, "Theses on the Philosophy of History," in Benjamin, *Illuminations: Essays and Reflections*, Hannah Arendt (ed.), Harry Zohn trans., (New York: Schocken Books, 1978), p. 262.

6. DECOLONIZATION

1. Paul Virilio, *Popular Defense & Ecological Struggles* (transl. by Mark Polizzotti) (New York: Semiotext(e), 1990 [1978]), p. 55.

2. Lorenzo Veracini, "Settler Colonialism and Decolonisation," *Borderlands*, 6, 2 (2007), http://www.borderlands.net.au/vol6no2_2007/veracini_settler.htm.

3. Periods of limited reconciliation, Veracini notes, are often accompanied by the construction of "retrospective utopia" narratives that relegate meaningful indigenous political agency to a mythologized past, simultaneously highlighting selective examples of settler-indigenous "partnership" in the present. Even such limited processes, it should be noted, provoke significant anxieties among settler populations in the form of backlashes against native title laws, affirmative action policies, and the like.

4. One of the speakers at the conference who addressed this issue in depth was Ameer Makhoul, a key leader of Palestinian civil society inside Israel. In a confirmation of the conference's marked emphasis on issues "inside the Green Line," Makhoul was subsequently arrested in April 2010 and charged with having contact with a foreign agent (in this case, a representative of Hizbullah). Several months later he agreed to a plea deal, arguing that he had no choice given that the "Israeli court and legal system are mere manifestations of the Israeli state's injustice." See Jillian Kestler D'Amours, "Plea deal 'only option' for political prisoner Ameer Makhoul," *Electronic Intifada*, 5 November 2010, http://electronicintifada.net/v2/article11611.shtml.

5. Ilan Pappe, "The *Mukhabarat* State of Israel," in Ronit Lentin (ed.), *Thinking Palestine* (London: Zed Books, 2008).

6. In a 2003 interview, Trudell pushes this argument to its logical conclusion, raising the possibility that one of the important unacknowledged effects of colonization has been to make colonizers think they can deny

their own indigeneity—that is, their own history of having been "civilized" themselves. See Trudell, "Democracy," mothersworldmedia.

7. Dropping Knowledge, "Copyleft Video: Arundhati Roy," *Dropping Knowledge* http://www.droppingknowledge.org/bin/media/show/66. page.

8. Norman Finkelstein, *The Holocaust Industry: Reflection on the Exploitation of Jewish Suffering* (London: Verso, 2000).

9. An excellent starting point is Gershon Shafir, *Land, Labor, and the Origins of the Israeli-Palestinian Conflict, 1882–1914* (Berkeley: University of California Press, 1996).

10. It is worth noting that three of the dissident scholars who have been attacked most vociferously in the post-9/11 years—Norman Finkelstein (subject of a highly politicized tenure case at DePaul University), Ward Churchill (fired from a tenured position at the University of Colorado), and Ilan Pappe (forced to leave the University of Haifa amid death threats and public calls for his resignation)—share the distinction of having made explicit linkages in their work between settler colonial projects in Israel/Palestine and the United States.

BIBLIOGRAPHY

"3.11.2008 Cashless in Gaza?" *Aftenposten*, 5 January 2011, http://www.aften-posten.no/spesial/wikileaksdokumenter/article3972840.ece (accessed 14 January 2011).

Abunimah, Ali, *One Country: A Bold Proposal to End the Israeli-Palestinian Impasse*, New York: Metropolitan Books, 2006.

Adas, Michael, *Dominance By Design: Technological Imperatives and America's Civilizing Mission*, Cambridge, MA: Belknap Press of Harvard University Press, 2006.

Agamben, Giorgio, *Homo Sacer: Sovereign Power and Bare Life* (transl. by Daniel Heller-Roazen), Stanford: Stanford University Press, 1998.

——— *State of Exception* (transl. by Kevin Attell), Chicago: University of Chicago Press, 2005.

Ahmad, Eqbal, *Terrorism: Theirs and Ours*, New York: Seven Stories, 2001.

Altheide, David L., *Terrorism and the Politics of Fear*, Lanham, MD: AltaMira Press, 2006.

Amnesty International, *Deadly Delivery: The Maternal Health Care Crisis in the USA*, New York: Amnesty International Publications, 12 March 2010, http://www.amnesty.org/en/library/asset/AMR51/007/2010/en/926e361c-4941–45c5–9368-ab18859254fd/amr510072010en.pdf.

Anderson, Benedict, *Under Three Flags: Anarchism and the Anti-Colonial Imagination*, London: Verso, 2005.

Anghie, Antony, *Imperialism, Sovereignty and the Making of International Law*, Cambridge: Cambridge University Press, 2004.

Appadurai, Arjun, *Modernity At Large: Cultural Dimensions of Globalization*, Minneapolis: University of Minnesota Press, 1996.

BIBLIOGRAPHY

Appadurai, Arjun, "Grassroots Globalization and the Research Imagination," *Public Culture*, 12, 1 (2000): 1–19.

Arrighi, Giovanni, Hopkins, Terence K., and Wallerstein, Immanuel, *Antisystemic Movements*, London: Verso, 1989.

Asad, Talal, *On Suicide Bombing*, New York: Columbia University Press, 2007.

Bacevich, Andrew, *The New American Militarism: How Americans Are Seduced By War*, New York: Oxford University Press, 2005.

———— *The Limits of Power: The End of American Exceptionalism*, New York: Metropolitan Books, 2008.

Balfour, Sebastian, *Deadly Embrace: Morocco and the Road to the Spanish Civil War*, New York: Oxford University Press, 2002.

Barkawi, Tarak, *Globalization and War*, Lanham, Rowman & Littlefield, 2006.

Bass, Warren, *Support Any Friend: Kennedy's Middle East and the Making of the US-Israel Alliance*, Oxford: Oxford University Press, 2003.

Bassiouni, M, Cherif (ed.), *International Terrorism and Political Crimes*, Springfield: Thomas, 1975.

Bauman, Zygmunt, "Wars of the Globalization Era," *European Journal of Social Theory*, 4, 1 (2001).

Beit-Hallahmi, Benjamin, *The Israeli Connection: Who Israel Arms and Why*, New York: Pantheon, 1987.

Bell, J. Bowyer, *Transnational Terror*, Washington: American Enterprise Institute, 1975.

Benhabib, Seyla, *The Rights of Others: Aliens, Residents and Citizens*, Cambridge: Cambridge University Press, 2004.

Benjamin, Walter, *Illuminations: Essays and Reflections* (edited by Hannah Arendt, transl. by Harry Zohn), New York: Schocken Books, 1978.

Ben-Yehuda, Nachman, *The Masada Myth: Collective Memory and Mythmaking in Israel*, Madison: University of Wisconsin Press, 1995.

Bhattacharyya, Gargi, "Globalizing Racism and Myths of the Other in the 'War on Terror'," in Ronit Lentin (ed.), *Thinking Palestine*, London: Zed Books, 2008, pp. 46–61.

Boas, Simon, "Growing Things in Gaza," *3QuarksDaily*, 10 January 2011, http://www.3quarksdaily.com/3quarksdaily/2011/01/growing-things-in-gaza.html.

Borcila, Rozalinda, "Learning alongside—notes from 'Turning our Tongues: Audio Journals from Dheisheh Refugee Camp'," *6+: A Women's Art Collective*, http://6plus.org/third_text.html (accessed 30 January 2008).

Bowman, Marion E, *Privatizing While Transforming*, Washington: Center for Technology and National Security Policy, National Defense University, 2007.

BIBLIOGRAPHY

Bradshaw, Larry, and Lorrie Beth Slonsky, "Hurricane Katrina—Our Experiences," *EMSNetwork News*, 6 September 2005, http://www.emsnetwork.org/cgi-bin/artman/exec/view.cgi?archive=56&num=18427.

Brugge, Doug., Benally, Timothy, and Yazzie-Lewis, Esther (eds), *The Navajo People and Uranium Mining*, Albuquerque: University of New Mexico Press, 2006.

Buck-Morss, Susan, *Thinking Past Terror: Islamism and Critical Theory on the Left*, London: Verso, 2003.

Burg, Avraham, *The Holocaust Is Over: We Must Rise From Its Ashes*, New York: Palgrave Macmillan, 2008.

Bustan Qaraaqa, "Why Permaculture?," http://www.bustanqaraaqa.org/al2/web/page/display/id/8.html (accessed 30 November 2009).

Carlton, David, and Carlo Schaerf (eds), *International Terrorism and World Security*, New York: Wiley, 1975.

Charny, Israel, *Fighting Suicide Bombing: A Worldwide Campaign for Life*, Westport: Praeger Security International, 2007.

Chomsky, Noam, "Terrorism and American Ideology," in *Blaming the Victims: Spurious Scholarship and the Palestinian Question*, Edward Said and Christopher Hitchens (eds), London: Verso, 1988, pp. 97–147.

Churchill, Ward, and Vander Wall, Jim, *The COINTELPRO Papers: Documents from the FBI's Secret Wars Against Dissent in the United States*, Boston: South End Press, 1990.

Clarno, Andy, "A Tale of Two Walled Cities: Neo-liberalization and Enclosure in Johannesburg and Jerusalem," *Political Power and Social Theory*, 19 (2008), pp. 159–205.

Clutterbuck, Richard, *Living With Terrorism*, London: Faber & Faber, 1975.

Coalition of Women for Peace, *Crossing the Line: The Tel Aviv-Jerusalem Fast Train*, Tel Aviv: Who Profits from the Occupation, 2010, http://www.whoprofits.org/articlefiles/WP-A1-Train.pdf (accessed 6 January 2011).

Cohen, Roger, "A Mideast Truce," *New York Times*, 16 November 2009.

Cohen, Stanley, *States of Denial: Knowing About Atrocities and Suffering*, Malden: Blackwell, 2001.

Collins, John, "Terrorism," in Collins, John and Glover, Ross (eds), *Collateral Language: A User's Guide to America's New War*, New York: New York University Press, 2002, pp. 155–173.

——— *Occupied By Memory: The Intifada Generation and the Palestinian State of Emergency*, New York: New York University Press, 2004.

——— "Looking towards Palestine: Photographic projects in Madrid," *Electronic Intifada*, 16 February 2005, http://electronicintifada.net/v2/article3622.shtml.

———— "From Portbou to Palestine, and Back," *Social Text*, 89 (2007), pp. 67–85.

———— "Dromocratic Palestine," *Middle East Report*, 248 (2008), pp. 8–13.

-———— "Confinement Under an Open Sky: Following the Speed Trap from Guernica to Gaza and Beyond," *Globalizations*, 5, 4 (2008), pp. 555–569.

Conway, Janet, "Indigenizing the global at the World Social Forum," *Alternatives International*, 13 March 2009, http://www.alterinter.org/article3069.html.

Coren, Ora, "Israel Aerospace Industries moving production to Mississippi," *Haaretz*, 18 November 2009, http://www.haaretz.com/hasen/spages/1128760. html (accessed 18 November 2009).

Coulthard, Glen, "Place against Empire: Understanding Indigenous Anti-Colonialism," *Affinities: A Journal of Radical Theory, Culture, and Action*, 4, 2 (2010), pp. 79–83.

Cowan, Greg, "Nomadic Resistance: Tent Embassies and Collapsible Architecture," *The Koori History Website*, http://kooriweb.org/foley/images/history/1970s/emb72/embarchit.htm (accessed 29 May 2008).

Creveld, Martin van, *Defending Israel: A Controversial Plan Toward Peace*, New York: St. Martin's Press, 2004.

Daniel, John, Southall, Roger, and Lutchmann, Jessica (eds), *State of the Nation: South Africa, 2004–2005*, Cape Town: HSRC Press, 2005.

Davis, Mike, *Planet of Slums*, London: Verso, 2006.

Deleuze, Gilles, "What is a *dispositif?*," in Timothy J. Armstrong (ed. and transl.), *Michel Foucault, Philosopher*, New York: Routledge, 2003, pp. 159–168.

Der Derian, James, "The (S)pace of International Relations: Simulation, Surveillance and Speed," *International Studies Quarterly*, 34 (1990), pp. 295–310.

———— "The Conceptual Cosmology of Paul Virilio," *Theory, Culture & Society*, 16, 5–6, 1999, pp. 215–227.

———— *Virtuous War: Mapping the Military-Industrial-Media-Entertainment Network*, Boulder: Westview Press, 2001.

Devji, Faisal, *Landscapes of the Jihad: Militancy, Morality, Modernity*, London: Hurst, 2005.

Donohue, K.G., *Freedom From Want: American Liberalism and the Idea of the Consumer*, Baltimore: The Johns Hopkins University Press, 2003.

Eichstaedt, Peter, *If You Poison Us: Uranium and Native Americans*, Santa Fe: Red Crane Books, 1994.

Egan, R. Danielle Egan, "Anthrax," in Collins, John and Glover, Ross (eds), *Collateral Language: A User's Guide to America's New War*, New York: New York University Press, 2002, pp. 15–26.

El-Haddad, Leila, "Safety is a State of Mind," *Gaza Mom: The Writings of a Mother From Gaza*, 31 December 2008, http://www.gazamom.com/2008/12/ (accessed 5 December 2009).

BIBLIOGRAPHY

Elkins, Caroline, and Pederson, Susan (eds), *Settler Colonialism in the Twentieth Century*, New York: Routledge, 2005.

Escobar, Arturo, "Beyond the Third World: Imperial Globality, Global Coloniality and Anti-Globalisation Social Movements," *Third World Quarterly*, 25, 1 (2004), pp. 207–230.

Fabian, Johannes, *Time and the Other: How Anthropology Makes Its Object*, New York: Columbia University Press, 1983.

Feldman, Allen, *Formations of Violence*, Chicago: University of Chicago Press, 1991.

———— "Strange Fruit: the South African Truth Commission and the Demonic Economies of Violence," *Social Analysis*, 46, 3 (2002), pp. 234–265.

Feldman, Yotam, "Dr. Naveh, or, how I learned to stop worrying and walk through walls," *Haaretz*, 25 October 2007, http://www.haaretz.com/weekend/magazine/dr-naveh-or-how-i-learned-to-stop-worrying-and-walk-through-walls-1.231912 (accessed 6 January 2011).

Finkelstein, Norman, "History's Verdict: The Cherokee Case," *Journal of Palestine Studies*, 24, 4 (1995), pp. 32–45.

———— *The Holocaust Industry: Reflection on the Exploitation of Jewish Suffering*, London: Verso, 2000.

Fixico, Donald, *Termination and Relocation: Federal Indian Policy 1945–1960*, Albuquerque: University of New Mexico Press, 1986.

Flapan, Simha, *The Birth of Israel: Myths and Realities*, New York: Pantheon, 1987.

Foley, Gary, "Black Power in Redfern 1968–1972," *The Koori History Website*. http://kooriweb.org/foley/essays/essay_1.html (accessed 29 May 2008).

Foucault, Michel, *The Archaeology of Knowledge* (transl. by A.M. Sheridan Smith), New York: Pantheon, 1972.

———— *"Society Must Be Defended": Lectures at the College de France, 1975–76*, Edited by M. Bertani and A. Fontana. Translated by D. Macey. New York: Picador, 2003.

Fox, Juliana Birnbaum, "Indigenous Science," *Cultural Survival Quarterly*, 33, 1 (Spring 2009), http://www.culturalsurvival.org/publications/cultural-survival-quarterly/australia/indigenous-science.

Galloway, Alexander, and Eugene Thacker, *The Exploit: A Theory of Networks*, Minneapolis: University of Minnesota Press, 2007.

Ghanim, Honaida, "Thanatopolitics: The Case of the Colonial Occupation of Palestine," in Ronit Lentin (ed.), *Thinking Palestine*, London: Zed Books, 2008, pp. 65–81.

Gilloch, Graeme, *Walter Benjamin: Critical Constellations*, Cambridge: Polity Press, 2002.

Glover, Ross, "The War On _____," in Collins, John and Glover, Ross (eds), *Collateral Language: A User's Guide to America's New War*, New York: New York University Press, 2002, pp. 207–222.

Goldberg, David Theo, "Racial Palestinianization," in Ronit Lentin (ed.), *Thinking Palestine*, London: Zed Books, 2008.

Gooding, Susan Staiger, "Narrating Law and Environmental Body Politics (In Times of War) in 'Indigenous America/America'," *Law & Society Review*, 39, 3 (2005).

Gregory, Derek, *The Colonial Present: Afghanistan, Palestine, Iraq*, Malden: Blackwell, 2004.

Guelke, Adrian, *Rethinking the Rise and Fall of Apartheid: South Africa and World Politics*, New York: Palgrave Macmillan, 2005.

Gunn, Janet Varner, *Second Life: A West Bank Memoir*, Minneapolis: University of Minnesota Press, 1995.

Hage, Ghassan, *Against Paranoid Nationalism: Searching for Hope in a Shrinking Society*, London: Pluto Press, 2003.

———— "'Comes a Time We Are All Enthusiasm': Understanding Palestinian Suicide Bombers in Times of Exighophobia," *Public Culture*, 15, 1 (2003), pp. 65–89.

Halawani, Rula, "Rula Halawani: Intimacy," *Nafas Art Magazine*, October 2006, http://universes-in-universe.org/nafas/articles/2006/rula_halawani.

Hall, Anthony J., *The American Empire and the Fourth World*, Montreal: McGill-Queen's University Press, 2003.

Hall, Stuart et al. (eds), *Policing the Crisis: Mugging, the State, and Law and Order*, London: Macmillan, 1978.

Halper, Jeff, "The 94 Percent Solution: A Matrix of Control," *Middle East Report*, 216 (2000), pp. 14–19.

Hardt, Michael, and Antonio Negri, *Empire*, Cambridge: Harvard University Press, 2000.

Harel, Amos, "Cast Lead expose: What did the IDF think would happen in Gaza?," *Haaretz*, 2 April 2009, http://www.haaretz.com/hasen/spages/1074218. html (accessed 4 November 2009).

Harlow, Barbara, "Remember the Solidarity Here and Everywhere," *Middle East Report*, 229 (Winter 2003).

Harris, Cole, "How Did Colonialism Dispossess? Comments from an Edge of Empire," *Annals of the Association of American Geographers*, 94, 1 (2004), pp. 165–182.

Harvey, David, *The Condition of Postmodernity*, Cambridge: Blackwell, 1989.

———— *Spaces of Global Capitalism: Towards a Theory of Uneven Geographical Development*, London: Verso, 2006.

Hassel, Conrad V., "Terror: The Crime of the Privileged—An Examination and Prognosis," *Terrorism: An International Journal*, 1, 1 (1977), pp. 1–16.

Herman, Edward, *The Real Terror Network: Terrorism in Fact and Propaganda*, Boston: South End Press, 1998.

"The Highway of Zinc," *Weekly Mail and Guardian*, 30 September 1994.

Holloway, David, *Cultures of the War on Terror: Empire, Ideology, and the Remaking of 9/11*, Montreal: McGill/Queen's University Press, 2008.

Honoré, Carl, *In Praise of Slowness: How a Worldwide Movement is Challenging the Cult of Speed*, San Francisco: HarperCollins, 2004.

Human Rights Watch Report, "Precisely Wrong: Gaza Civilians Killed by Israeli Drone-Launched Missiles," New York: Human Rights Watch, 2009, http://www.hrw.org/sites/default/files/reports/iopt0609web_0.pdf (accessed 1 December 2009).

——— "Separate and Unequal: Israel's Discriminatory Treatment of Palestinians in the Occupied Palestinian Territories," New York: Human Rights Watch, 2010, http://www.hrw.org/en/reports/2010/12/19/separate-and-unequal-0 (accessed 21 December 2010).

Isserman, Maurice, and Kazin, Michael, *America Divided: The Civil War of the 1960s*, 3rd edn., New York: Oxford University Press, 2007.

Jarecki, Eugene (dir.), *Why We Fight*, Culver City: Sony Pictures Home Entertainment, 2006.

Jenkins, Brian M, *International Terrorism: A New Kind of Warfare*, Santa Monica: RAND Corporation, 1974.

Johnson, Chalmers, *The Sorrows of Empire: Militarism, Secrecy, and the End of the Republic*, New York: Metropolitan Books, 2004.

Kanaaneh, Rhoda A., *Birthing the Nation: Strategies of Palestinian Women in Israel*, Berkeley: University of California Press, 2002.

Kanafani, Ghassan, *Men in the Sun and Other Palestinian Stories* (transl. by Hilary Kilpatrick), Boulder: Lynne Rienner, 1999.

——— *Palestine's Children: Returning to Haifa and Other Stories* (transl. by Barbara Harlow and Karen Riley), Boulder: Lynne Rienner, 2000.

Karavan, Dani, "The Memorial in Karavan's Own Words," *Walter Benjamin in Portbou*, http://walterbenjaminportbou.cat/en/content/el-memorial-segons-karavan (accessed 11 January 2011).

Karr, Timothy, "One US Corporation's Role in Egypt's Brutal Crackdown," *Huffington Post*, 28 January 2011, http://www.huffingtonpost.com/timothy-karr/one-us-corporations-role-_b_815281.html?ref=fb&src=sp.

Katz, Cindi, and Smith, Neil, "L.A. Intifada: Interview with Mike Davis," *Social Text*, 33 (1992), pp. 19–33.

Kellner, Douglas, "Spectacles of Terror and Media Manipulation: A Critique of Jihadist and Bush Media Politics," *Logos*, 2, 1 (2003), pp. 86–103.

Kelly, John D., and Kaplan, Martha, *Represented Communities: Fiji and World Decolonization*, Chicago: University of Chicago Press, 2001.

Kershner, Isabel, "A Test of Wills Over a Patch of Desert," *New York Times*, 25 August, 2010, http://www.nytimes.com/2010/08/26/world/middleeast/26israel.html (accessed 15 January 2011).

Kestler D'Amours, Jillian, "Plea deal 'only option' for political prisoner Ameer Makhoul," *Electronic Intifada*, 5 November 2010, http://electronicintifada.net/v2/article11611.shtml.

Khalidi, Rashid, "Palestinian Peasant Resistance to Zionism before World War I.," in *Blaming the Victims: Spurious Scholarship and the Palestinian Question*, Said, Edward and Hitchens, Christopher (eds), London: Verso, 1988, pp. 207–234.

Khalidi, Walid, *Before Their Diaspora: A Photographic History of the Palestinians, 1876–1948*, Washington: Institute for Palestine Studies, 1984.

——— (ed.) *All That Remains: The Palestinian Villages Occupied and Depopulated by Israel in 1948*, Washington: Institute for Palestine Studies, 2006.

Khalili, Laleh, *Heroes and Martyrs of Palestine: The Politics of National Commemoration*, Cambridge: Cambridge University Press, 2007.

Kimmerling, Baruch, *Politicide: Ariel Sharon's War Against the Palestinians*, London: Verso, 2003.

King, Jr., M.L., "The World House," *The World House Project*, http://www.theworldhouse.org/whessay.html.

King-Irani, Laurie, "International Human Rights: One day out of 365 is not enough," *Electronic Intifada*, 9 December 2004, http://electronicintifada.net/v2/article3422.shtml (accessed 12 December 2009).

Klare, Michael, *Resource Wars: The New Landscape of Global Conflict*, New York: Henry Holt, 2002.

Klein, Naomi, "How War Was Turned into a Brand," *The Guardian*, 16 June 2007.

Korn, Alina, "The Ghettoization of the Palestinians," in *Thinking Palestine*, Ronit Lentin (ed.), London: Zed Books, 2008, pp. 116–130.

Krautwurst, Udo, "What is Settler Colonialism? An Anthropological Meditation on Frantz Fanon's 'Concerning Violence'," *History and Anthropology*, 14, 1 (2003).

Kroker, Arthur, "The Mohawk Refusal," *CTheory.net*, 25 October 1995, http://www.ctheory.net/articles.aspx?id=153.

LaDuke, Winona, "Uranium Mining, Native Resistance, and the Greener Path," *Orion*, January/February 2009.

BIBLIOGRAPHY

Laor, Yitzhak, *The Myths of Liberal Zionism*, London: Verso, 2009.

Laqueur, Walter, *The Terrorism Reader*, Philadelphia: Temple University Press, 1978.

Lentin, Ronit (ed.), *Thinking Palestine*, London: Zed Books, 2008.

Li, Darryl, "The Gaza Strip as Laboratory: Notes in the Wake of Disengagement," *Journal of Palestine Studies*, 35, 2 (2006), pp. 38–55.

Linebaugh, Peter, and Marcus Rediker, *The Many-Headed Hydra: Sailors, Slaves, Commoners, and the Hidden History of the Revolutionary Atlantic*, Boston: Beacon Press, 2000.

Lockman, Zachary, and Beinin, Joel (eds), *Intifada: The Palestinian Uprising Against Israeli Occupation*, Boston: South End Press, 1989.

Lynch, Marc, *Voices of the New Arab Public: Iraq, al-Jazeera, and Middle East Politics Today*, New York: Columbia University Press, 2006.

Maathai, Wangari, "Nobel Lecture," Oslo, 10 December 2004, http://nobelprize. org/nobel_prizes/peace/laureates/2004/maathai-lecture-text.html (accessed 7 December 2009).

Macintyre, Donald, "Palestinians 'terrorised' by sonic boom flights," *The Independent*, 3 November 2005.

Makdisi, Saree, *Palestine Inside Out: An Everyday Occupation*, New York: Norton, 2008.

Mandel, Robert, *Armies Without States: The Privatization of Security*, Boulder: Lynne Rienner, 2002.

Mandelker, Barry Steven, "Indigenous People and Cultural Appropriation: Intellectual Property Problems and Solutions," *Canadian Intellectual Property Review*, 16 (2000).

Marcus, George, "Ethnography in/of the World System: The Emergence of Multi-Sited Ethnography," *Annual Review of Anthropology*, 24 (1995), pp. 95–117.

Martin, Randy, "War, by All Means," *Social Text*, 91 (2007), pp. 13–22.

Massad, Joseph, "The Persistence of the Palestinian Question," *Cultural Critique*, 59 (2005), pp. 1–23.

——— "The 'Post-Colonial' Colony: Time, Space, and Bodies in Palestine/Israel," in Fawzia Afzal-Khan and Kalpana Seshadri-Crooks (eds), *The Pre-Occupation of Postcolonial Studies*, Durham: Duke University Press, 2000, pp. 311–346.

Mbembe, Achille, "Necropolitics," *Public Culture*, 15, 1 (2003), pp. 11–40.

McMichael, Philip, *Development and Social Change: A Global Perspective*, 3rd edn., Thousand Oaks: Pine Forge Press, 2004.

McNeill, William, *The Pursuit of Power: Technology, Armed Force and Society Since A.D. 1000*, Chicago: University of Chicago Press, 1982.

BIBLIOGRAPHY

Mearsheimer, John J., and Walt, Stephen M., *The Israel Lobby and US Foreign Policy*, New York: Farrar, Straus & Giroux, 2007.

Mcdovoi, Leerom, "Global Society Must Be Defended: Biopolitics Without Borders," *Social Text*, 91 (2007), pp. 53–79.

Melman, Yossi, "Brazil to buy $350 million worth of drones from Israel," *Haaretz*, 11 November 2009, http://www.haaretz.com/hasen/spages/1127471.html (accessed 24 November 2009).

Morris, Benny, *The Birth of the Palestinian Refugee Problem, 1947–1949*, Cambridge: Cambridge University Press, 1987.

Myre, Greg, "Israel Briefly Reopens a Gaza Crossing to Send in Food," *New York Times*, 21 March 2006.

Nassar, Jamal R., and Heacock, Roger (eds), *Intifada: Palestine at the Crossroads*, New York: Birzeit University and Praeger Publishers, 1991.

Nelkin, Dorothy, "Native Americans and Nuclear Power," *Science, Technology & Human Values*, 6, 35 (1981), pp. 2–13.

Nevins, Joseph, *Operation Gatekeeper and Beyond: The War on 'Illegals' and the Remaking of the US-Mexico Boundary*, 2nd edn., New York: Routledge, 2010.

Nitzan, Jonathan, and Bichler, Shimshon, *The Global Political Economy of Israel*, London: Pluto Press, 2002.

Nyers, Peter, *Rethinking Refugees: Beyond States of Emergency*, New York: Routledge, 2006.

Obenzinger, Hilton, "Naturalizing Cultural Pluralism, Americanizing Zionism: The Settler Colonial Basis to Early-Twentieth-Century Progressive Thought," *South Atlantic Quarterly*, 107, 4 (2008), pp. 651–669.

Ouroussoff, Nicolai, "A Line in the Sand," *New York Times*, 1 January 2006.

"Palestinian cave-dweller fights Israeli eviction," *Haaretz*, 12 November 2009, http://www.haaretz.com/hasen/spages/1127461.html (accessed 19 November 2009).

"Palestinian Strategic Options: An Attempt at Analysis to Inform Action," *Journal of Palestine Studies*, 35, 1 (2005), pp. 91–102.

Pappe, Ilan, *A History of Modern Palestine*, 2nd edn., Cambridge: Cambridge University Press, 2004.

———— *The Ethnic Cleansing of Palestine*, Oxford: Oneworld, 2006.

———— "The *Mukhabarat* State of Israel," in Lentin, Ronit (ed.), *Thinking Palestine*, London: Zed Books, 2008, pp. 148–169.

Parmenter, Barbara McKean, *Giving Voice to Stones: Place and Identity in Palestinian Literature*, Austin: University of Texas Press, 1994.

Peretz, Martin, "Israel, the United States, and Evil," *The New Republic*, 14 September 2001.

Peteet, Julie, *Landscape of Hope and Despair: Palestinian Refugee Camps*, Philadelphia: University of Pennsylvania Press, 2005.

Piterberg, Gabriel, *The Returns of Zionism: Myth, Politics, and Scholarship in Israel*, London: Verso, 2008.

Polakow-Suransky, Sasha, *The Unspoken Alliance: Israel's Secret Relationship with Apartheid South Africa*, New York: Pantheon, 2010.

Public Committee Against Torture in Israel Report, "No Second Thoughts: The Changes in the Israeli Defense Forces: Combat Doctrine in Light of 'Operation Cast Lead'." Jerusalem: PCATI, 2009, http://www.stoptorture.org.il/files/no%20second%20thoughts_ENG_WEB.pdf (accessed 4 December, 2009).

Reeves, Jimmie L., and Campbell, Richard, *Cracked Coverage: Television News, the Anti-Cocaine Crusade, and the Reagan Legacy*, Durham: Duke University Press, 1994.

Reinhart, Tanya, *Israel/Palestine: How to End the War of 1948*, 2nd edn., New York: Seven Stories, 2004.

Robinson, Shira, "Occupied Citizens in a Liberal State: Palestinians Under Military Rule and the Colonial Formation of Israeli Society, 1948–1966," PhD dissertation, Stanford University, 2005.

Rodinson, Maxime, *Israel: A Colonial-Settler State?* (transl. by David Thorstad), New York: Monad Press, 1973.

Ron, James, *Frontiers and Ghettos: State Violence in Serbia and Israel*, Berkeley: University of California Press, 2003.

Ross, Oakland, "The caveman's day in court," *The Star*, 12 April 2009, http://www.thestar.com/comment/columnists/article/617187 (accessed 1 December 2009).

Roy, Olivier, *Globalized Islam: The Search for a New Ummah*, London: Hurst, 2004.

Roy, Sara, *The Gaza Strip: The Political Economy of De-Development*, Washington: Institute for Palestine Studies, 1995.

Russell, Charles A., and Bowman H. Miller, "Profile of a Terrorist," *Terrorism: An International Journal*, 1, 1 (1977), pp. 17–34.

Said, Edward, *Orientalism*, New York: Vintage, 1978.

———— *The World, the Text and the Critic*, Cambridge: Harvard University Press, 1983.

———— "The Essential Terrorist," in Edward Said and Christopher Hitchens (eds), *Blaming the Victims: Spurious Scholarship and the Palestinian Question*, pp. 149–158, London: Verso, 1988.

———— *The Question of Palestine*, New York: Vintage, 1992.

———— *Culture and Imperialism*, New York: Alfred A. Knopf, 1993.

—— "The Acre and the Goat," in *The Politics of Dispossession: The Struggle for Palestinian Self-Determination, 1969–1994*, New York: Pantheon, 1994, pp. 33–42.

—— "In the Shadow of the West," in Gauri Viswanathan (ed.), *Power, Politics, and Culture: Interviews With Edward W. Said*, New York: Pantheon, 2001.

—— "Dignity, Solidarity and the Penal Colony," *Counterpunch*, 25 September 2003.

—— "The Meaning of Rachel Corrie: Of dignity and solidarity," in Josie Sandercock et al. (eds), *Peace Under Fire: Israel/Palestine and the International Solidarity Movement*, London: Verso, 2004.

Sand, Shlomo, *The Invention of the Jewish People*, London: Verso, 2009.

Sanders, Edmund, and Batsheva Sobelman, "Israeli firms see a global market for their anti-terrorism know-how," *Los Angeles Times*, 27 November 2010, http://www.latimes.com/news/nationworld/world/la-fg-israel-homeland-security-20101128,0,823166,print.story.

Santos, Boaventura de Sousa, "Collective Suicide?" *Bad Subjects*, 63 (2003), http://bad.eserver.org/issues/2003/63/santos.html (accessed 8 December 2009).

—— *The Rise of the Global Left: The World Social Forum and Beyond*, London: Zed Books, 2006.

Sayigh, Rosemary, *Palestinians: From Peasants to Revolutionaries*, London: Zed Books, 1979.

Sayigh, Yezid, *Armed Struggle and the Search for State: The Palestinian National Movement, 1949–1993*, New York: Oxford University Press, 1997.

Scahill, Jeremy, *Blackwater: The Rise of the World's Most Powerful Mercenary Army*, New York: Nation Books, 2007.

Schechter, Danny, *Media Wars: News at a Time of Terror*, Lanham: Rowman & Littlefield, 2003.

Schell, Jonathan, *The Unconquerable World: Power, Nonviolence, and the Will of the People*, New York: Henry Holt, 2003.

Scheuerman, William E., *Liberal Democracy and the Social Acceleration of Time*, Baltimore and London: The Johns Hopkins University Press, 2004.

Seib, Philip (ed.), *New Media and the New Middle East*, New York: Palgrave Macmillan, 2007.

Seremetakis, C. Nadia, *The Last Word: Women, Death, and Divination in Inner Mani*, Chicago and London: University of Chicago Press, 1991.

Shafir, Gershon, *Land, Labor, and the Origins of the Israeli-Palestinian Conflict, 1882–1914*, Berkeley: University of California Press, 1996.

Shapiro, Michael J., *Violent Cartographies: Mapping Cultures of War*, Minneapolis: University of Minnesota Press, 1997.

Shavit, Ari, "Survival of the Fittest? An Interview with Benny Morris," *Logos*, 3, 1 (2004).

Shehadeh, Raja, *Palestinian Walks: Forays Into a Vanishing Landscape*, New York: Scribner, 2007.

Shlaim, Avi, *Collusion Across the Jordan: King Abdullah, the Zionist Movement, and the Partition of Palestine*, New York: Columbia University Press, 1988.

Shohat, Ella, "Rethinking Jews and Muslims: Quincentennial Reflections," *Middle East Report* 178 (1992), pp. 25–29.

Singer, P.W., *Corporate Warriors: The Rise of the Privatized Military Industry*, Ithaca: Cornell University Press, 2008.

Smith, Andrea, *Conquest: Sexual Violence and Native American Genocide*, Boston: South End Press, 2005.

Sorkin, Michael (ed.), *Against the Wall: Israel's Barrier to Peace*, New York and London: New Press, 2005.

Steer, G.L., *The Tree of Gernika: A Field Study of Modern War*, London: Faber & Faber, 2009 [1938].

Stohlman, Nancy, and Laurieann Aladin (eds), *Live From Palestine. International and Palestinian Direct Action Against the Israeli Occupation*, Boston: South End Press, 2003.

Suisman, Doug et al., *The Arc: A Formal Structure for a Palestinian State*, Santa Monica: RAND Corporation, 2005.

Suspect Detection Systems, "Technology," http://www.suspectdetection.com/tech.html (accessed 30 November 2009).

Swedenburg, Ted, *Memories of Revolt: The 1936–1939 Rebellion and the Palestinian National Past*, Minneapolis: University of Minnesota Press, 1995.

Tamari, Salim, "Building Other People's Homes: The Palestinian Peasant's Household and Work in Israel," *Journal of Palestine Studies*, 11, 1 (1981), pp. 31–66.

Taraki, Lisa, "The Development of Political Consciousness Among Palestinians in the Occupied Territories, 1967–1987," in Nassar, Jamal and Heacock, Roger (eds), *Intifada: Palestine at the Crossroads*, New York: Birzeit University and Praeger Publishers, 1991, pp. 53–71.

Teivainen, Teivo, "The World Social Forum and Global Democratisation: Learning from Porto Alegre," *Third World Quarterly*, 23, 4 (2002), pp. 621–632.

Tilley, Virginia, *The One-State Solution: A Breakthrough for Peace in the Israel-Palestine Deadlock*, Ann Arbor: University of Michigan Press, 2005.

"Top Secret America," *Washington Post*, June 2010, http://projects.washingtonpost.com/top-secret-america/ (accessed 2 October 2010)

Trudell, John, "Democracy," mothersworldmedia, 2003, http://www.youtube.com/watch?v=qRO8CjzFIh8 (accessed 3 July 2010).

———— Directed by Heather Rae, 2005.

———— *Lines From a Mined Mind: The Words of John Trudell*, Golden: Fulcrum, 2008.

Veracini, Lorenzo, "The Fourth Geneva Convention: Its Relevance for Settler Nations," *Arena Journal* 24 (2005), pp. 101–114.

———— *Israel and Settler Society*, London: Pluto Press, 2006.

———— "Settler Colonialism and Decolonisation," *Borderlands*, 6, 2 (2007), http://www.borderlands.net.au/vol6no2_2007/veracini_settler.htm.

Virilio, Paul, *Popular Defense & Ecological Struggles* (transl. by Mark Polizzotti), New York: Semiotext(e), 1990 [1978].

———— *Open Sky* (transl. by Julie Rose), London: Verso, 1997.

Virilio, Paul, and Sylvere Lotringer, *Pure War* (transl. by Mark Polizzotti), New York: Semiotext(e), 1997 [1983].

Virilio, Paul, "The Suicidal State," in James Der Derian (ed.), *The Virilio Reader*, Malden: Blackwell, 1998, pp. 29–45.

———— *Polar Inertia* (transl. by Patrick Camiller), London: Sage, 2000 [1990].

———— *Ground Zero* (transl. by Chris Turner), London: Verso, 2002.

Virilio, Paul, and Lotringer, Sylvere, *Crepuscular Dawn* (transl. by Mike Taormina), Los Angeles & New York: Semiotext(e), 2002.

Virilio, Paul, *City of Panic* (transl. by Julie Rose), Oxford and New York: Berg, 2005.

———— *Speed and Politics* (transl. by Mark Polizzotti), Los Angeles: Semiotext(e), 2006.

Warschawski, Michael, *Toward an Open Tomb: The Crisis of Israeli Society* (transl. by Peter Drucker), New York: Monthly Review Press, 2004.

Weir, Allison, "The LA Times" notion of 'relative calm'," *Electronic Intifada*, 25 February 2005, http://electronicintifada.net/v2/article3638.shtml (accessed 19 October 2009).

Weizman, Eyal, "The Politics of Verticality," *open Democracy*, 23 April 2002, http://www.opendemocracy.net/conflict-politicsverticality/article_801.jsp (accessed 9 October 2009).

———— *Hollow Land: Israel's Architecture of Occupation*, London: Verso, 2007.

———— "The Art of War," *Frieze* 99 (2006), http://www.frieze.com/feature_single.asp?f=1165 (accessed 5 December 2009).

Weyler, Rex, *Blood of the Land: The US Government and Corporate War Against the American Indian Movement*, New York: Vintage, 1984.

Wilkinson, Paul, *Political Terrorism*, New York: Macmillan, 1974.

Williams, Michael C., "Words, Images, Enemies: Securitization and International Politics," *International Studies Quarterly*, 47 (2003), pp. 511–531.

Williams, William A., *Empire As a Way of Life*, New York: Ig Publishing, 2007 [1980].

Wolfe, Patrick, "Settler Colonialism and the Elimination of the Native," *Journal of Genocide Research*, 8, 4 (2006), pp. 387–409.

Yiftachel, Oren, *Ethnocracy: Land and Identity Politics in Israel/Palestine*, Philadelphia: University of Pennsylvania Press, 2006.

———— "The horror show at al-Araqib village: from removal to approval," *Jews for Justice for Palestinians*, 2 August 2010, http://jfjfp.com/?p=16132 (accessed 15 January 2011).

Zerubavel, Yael, "The Death of Memory and the Memory of Death: Masada and the Holocaust as Historical Metaphors," *Representations*, 45 (1994), pp. 72–100.

INDEX